Family Maps
of
Auglaize County, Ohio
Deluxe Edition

With Homesteads, Roads, Waterways, Towns, Cemeteries, Railroads, and More

Family Maps
of
Auglaize County, Ohio
Deluxe Edition

With Homesteads, Roads, Waterways, Towns, Cemeteries, Railroads, and More

by Gregory A. Boyd, J.D.

Featuring **3** *Maps Per Township...*

Arphax Publishing Co.
www.arphax.com

Family Maps of Auglaize County, Ohio, Deluxe Edition: With Homesteads, Roads, Waterways, Towns, Cemeteries, Railroads, and More.
by Gregory A. Boyd, J.D.

ISBN 1-4203-1221-9

Printed in the United States of America

Published by Arphax Publishing Co., 2210 Research Park Blvd., Norman, Oklahoma, USA 73069
www.arphax.com

First Edition

ATTENTION HISTORICAL & GENEALOGICAL SOCIETIES, UNIVERSITIES, COLLEGES, CORPORATIONS, FAMILY REUNION COORDINATORS, AND PROFESSIONAL ORGANIZATIONS: Quantity discounts are available on bulk purchases of this book. For information, please contact Arphax Publishing Co., at the address listed above, or at (405) 366-6181, or visit our web-site at www.arphax.com and contact us through the "Bulk Sales" link.

—LEGAL—

This book is dedicated to my wonderful family:

Vicki, Jordan, & Amy Boyd

Contents

- Part I -

The Big Picture

- Part II -

Township Map Groups

(each Map Group contains a Patent Index, Patent Map, Road Map, & Historical Map)

Appendices

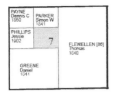

Preface

The quest for the discovery of my ancestors' origins, migrations, beliefs, and life-ways has brought me rewards that I could never have imagined. The Family Maps series of books is my first effort to share with historical and genealogical researchers, some of the tools that I have developed to achieve my research goals. I firmly believe that this effort will allow many people to reap the same sorts of treasures that I have.

Our Federal government's General Land Office of the Bureau of Land Management (the "GLO") has given genealogists and historians an incredible gift by virtue of its enormous database housed on its web-site at glorecords.blm.gov. Here, you can search for and find millions of parcels of land purchased by our ancestors in about thirty states.

This GLO web-site is one of the best FREE on-line tools available to family researchers. But, it is not for the faint of heart, nor is it for those unwilling or unable to to sift through and analyze the thousands of records that exist for most counties.

My immediate goal with this series is to spare you the hundreds of hours of work that it would take you to map the Land Patents for this county. Every Auglaize County homestead or land patent that I have gleaned from public GLO databases is mapped here. Consequently, I can usually show you in an instant, where your ancestor's land is located, as well as the names of nearby land-owners.

Originally, that was my primary goal. But after speaking to other genealogists, it became clear that there was much more that they wanted. Taking their advice set me back almost a full year, but I think you will agree it was worth the wait. Because now, you can learn so much more.

Now, this book answers these sorts of questions:

- Are there any variant spellings for surnames that I have missed in searching GLO records?
- Where is my family's traditional home-place?
- What cemeteries are near Grandma's house?
- My Granddad used to swim in such-and-such-Creek—where is that?
- How close is this little community to that one?
- Are there any other people with the same surname who bought land in the county?
- How about cousins and in-laws—did they buy land in the area?

And these are just for starters!

The rules for using the Family Maps books are simple, but the strategies for success are many. Some techniques are apparent on first use, but many are gained with time and experience. Please take the time to notice the roads, cemeteries, creek-names, family names, and unique first-names throughout the whole county. You cannot imagine what YOU might be the first to discover.

I hope to learn that many of you have answered age-old research questions within these pages or that you have discovered relationships previously not even considered. When these sorts of things happen to you, will you please let me hear about it? I would like nothing better. My contact information can always be found at www.arphax.com.

One more thing: please read the "How To Use This Book" chapter; it starts on the next page. This will give you the very best chance to find the treasures that lie within these pages.

My family and I wish you the very best of luck, both in life, and in your research.   Greg Boyd

How to Use This Book - A Graphical Summary

Part I
"The Big Picture"

Map A ‣ *Counties in the State*

Map B ‣ *Surrounding Counties*

Map C ‣ *Congressional Townships (Map Groups) in the County*

Map D ‣ *Cities & Towns in the County*

Map E ‣ *Cemeteries in the County*

Surnames in the County ‣ *Number of Land-Parcels for Each Surname*

Surname/Township Index ‣ *Directs you to Township Map Groups in Part II*

The <u>Surname/Township Index</u> can direct you to any number of **Township Map Groups**

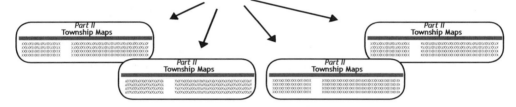

Part II
Township Map Groups
(1 for each Township in the County)

Each Township Map Group contains all four of of the following tools . . .

Land Patent Index ‣ *Every-name Index of Patents Mapped in this Township*

Land Patent Map ‣ *Map of Patents as listed in above Index*

Road Map ‣ *Map of Roads, City-centers, and Cemeteries in the Township*

Historical Map ‣ *Map of Railroads, Lakes, Rivers, Creeks, City-Centers, and Cemeteries*

Appendices

Appendix A ‣ *Congressional Authority enabling Patents within our Maps*

Appendix B ‣ *Section-Parts / Aliquot Parts (a comprehensive list)*

Appendix C ‣ *Multi-patentee Groups (Individuals within Buying Groups)*

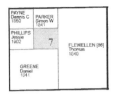

How to Use This Book

The two "Parts" of this Family Maps volume seek to answer two different types of questions. Part I deals with broad questions like: what counties surround Auglaize County, are there any ASHCRAFTs in Auglaize County, and if so, in which Townships or Maps can I find them? Ultimately, though, Part I should point you to a particular Township Map Group in Part II.

Part II concerns itself with details like: where exactly is this family's land, who else bought land in the area, and what roads and streams run through the land, or are located nearby. The Chart on the opposite page, and the remainder of this chapter attempt to convey to you the particulars of these two "parts", as well as how best to use them to achieve your research goals.

Part I
"The Big Picture"

Within Part I, you will find five "Big Picture" maps and two county-wide surname tools.

These include:

- Map A - Where Auglaize County lies within the state
- Map B - Counties that surround Auglaize County
- Map C - Congressional Townships of Auglaize County (+ Map Group Numbers)
- Map D - Cities & Towns of Auglaize County (with Index)
- Map E - Cemeteries of Auglaize County (with Index)
- Surnames in Auglaize County Patents (with Parcel-counts for each surname)
- Surname/Township Index (with Parcel-counts for each surname by Township)

The five "Big-Picture" Maps are fairly self-explanatory, yet should not be overlooked. This is particularly true of Maps "C", "D", and "E", all of which show Auglaize County and its Congressional Townships (and their assigned Map Group Numbers).

Let me briefly explain this concept of Map Group Numbers. These are a device completely of our own invention. They were created to help you quickly locate maps without having to remember the full legal name of the various Congressional Townships. It is simply easier to remember "Map Group 1" than a legal name like: "Township 9-North Range 6-West, 5th Principal Meridian." But the fact is that the TRUE legal name for these Townships IS terribly important. These are the designations that others will be familiar with and you will need to accurately record them in your notes. This is why both Map Group numbers AND legal descriptions of Townships are almost always displayed together.

Map "C" will be your first intoduction to "Map Group Numbers", and that is all it contains: legal Township descriptions and their assigned Map Group Numbers. Once you get further into your research, and more immersed in the details, you will likely want to refer back to Map "C" from time to time, in order to regain your bearings on just where in the county you are researching.

Remember, township boundaries are a completely artificial device, created to standardize land descriptions. But do not let them become a boundary in your mind when choosing which townships to research. Your relative's in-laws, children, cousins, siblings, and mamas and papas, might just as easily have lived in the township next to the one your grandfather lived in—rather than in the one where he actually lived. So Map "C" can be your guide to which other Townships/ Map Groups you likewise ought to analyze.

Of course, the same holds true for County lines; this is the purpose behind Map "B". It shows you surrounding counties that you may want to consider for further reserarch.

Map "D", the Cities and Towns map, is the first map with an index. Map "E" is the second (Cemeteries). Both, Maps "D" and "E" give you broad views of City (or Cemetery) locations in the County. But they go much further by pointing you toward pertinent Township Map Groups so you can locate the patents, roads, and waterways located near a particular city or cemetery.

Once you are familiar with these Family Maps volumes and the county you are researching, the "Surnames In Auglaize County" chapter (or its sister chapter in other volumes) is where you'll likely start your future research sessions. Here, you can quickly scan its few pages and see if anyone in the county possesses the surnames you are researching. The "Surnames in Auglaize County" list shows only two things: surnames and the number of parcels of land we have located for that surname in Auglaize County. But whether or not you immediately locate the surnames you are researching, please do not go any further without taking a few moments to scan ALL the surnames in these very few pages.

You cannot imagine how many lost ancestors are waiting to be found by someone willing to take just a little longer to scan the "Surnames In Auglaize County" list. Misspellings and typographical errors abound in most any index of this sort. Don't miss out on finding your Kinard that was written Rynard or Cox that was written Lox. If it looks funny or wrong, it very often is. And one of those little errors may well be your relative.

Now, armed with a surname and the knowledge that it has one or more entries in this book, you are ready for the "Surname/Township Index." Unlike the "Surnames In Auglaize County", which has only one line per Surname, the "Surname/Township Index" contains one line-item for each Township Map Group in which each surname is found. In other words, each line represents a different Township Map Group that you will need to review.

Specifically, each line of the Surname/Township

Index contains the following four columns of information:

1. Surname
2. Township Map Group Number (these Map Groups are found in Part II)
3. Parcels of Land (number of them with the given Surname within the Township)
4. Meridian/Township/Range (the legal description for this Township Map Group)

The key column here is that of the Township Map Group Number. While you should definitely record the Meridian, Township, and Range, you can do that later. Right now, you need to dig a little deeper. That Map Group Number tells you where in Part II that you need to start digging.

But before you leave the "Surname/Township Index", do the same thing that you did with the "Surnames in Auglaize County" list: take a moment to scan the pages of the Index and see if there are similarly spelled or misspelled surnames that deserve your attention. Here again, is an easy opportunity to discover grossly misspelled family names with very little effort. Now you are ready to turn to . . .

Part II
"Township Map Groups"

You will normally arrive here in Part II after being directed to do so by one or more "Map Group Numbers" in the Surname/Township Index of Part I.

Each Map Group represents a set of four tools dedicated to a single Congressional Township that is either wholly or partially within the county. If you are trying to learn all that you can about a particular family or their land, then these tools should usually be viewed in the order they are presented.

These four tools include:

1. a Land Patent Index
2. a Land Patent Map
3. a Road Map, and
4. an Historical Map

As I mentioned earlier, each grouping of this sort is assigned a Map Group Number. So, let's now move on to a discussion of the four tools that make up one of these Township Map Groups.

Land Patent Index

Each Township Map Group's Index begins with a title, something along these lines:

MAP GROUP 1: Index to Land Patents
Township 16-North Range 5-West (2nd PM)

The Index contains seven (7) columns. They are:

1. ID (a unique ID number for this Individual and a corresponding Parcel of land in this Township)
2. Individual in Patent (name)
3. Sec. (Section), and
4. Sec. Part (Section Part, or Aliquot Part)
5. Date Issued (Patent)
6. Other Counties (often means multiple counties were mentioned in GLO records, or the section lies within multiple counties).
7. For More Info . . . (points to other places within this index or elsewhere in the book where you can find more information)

While most of the seven columns are self-explanatory, I will take a few moments to explain the "Sec. Part." and "For More Info" columns.

The "Sec. Part" column refers to what surveryors and other land professionals refer to as an Aliquot Part. The origins and use of such a term mean little to a non-surveyor, and I have chosen to simply call these sub-sections of land what they are: a "Section Part". No matter what we call them, what we are referring to are things like a quarter-section or half-section or quarter-quarter-section. See Appendix "B" for most of the "Section Parts" you will come across (and many you will not) and what size land-parcel they represent.

The "For More Info" column of the Index may seem like a small appendage to each line, but please

recognize quickly that this is not so. And to understand the various items you might find here, you need to become familiar with the Legend that appears at the top of each Land Patent Index.

Here is a sample of the Legend . . .

LEGEND

"For More Info . . . " column

A = Authority (Legislative Act, See Appendix "A")

B = Block or Lot (location in Section unknown)

C = Cancelled Patent

F = Fractional Section

G = Group (Multi-Patentee Patent, see Appendix "C")

V = Overlaps another Parcel

R = Re-Issued (Parcel patented more than once)

Most parcels of land will have only one or two of these items in their "For More Info" columns, but when that is not the case, there is often some valuable information to be gained from further investigation. Below, I will explain what each of these items means to you you as a researcher.

A = Authority
(Legislative Act, See Appendix "A")
All Federal Land Patents were issued because some branch of our government (usually the U.S. Congress) passed a law making such a transfer of title possible. And therefore every patent within these pages will have an "A" item next to it in the index. The number after the "A" indicates which item in Appendix "A" holds the citation to the particular law which authorized the transfer of land to the public. As it stands, most of the Public Land data compiled and released by our government, and which serves as the basis for the patents mapped here, concerns itself with "Cash Sale" homesteads. So in some Counties, the law which authorized cash sales will be the primary, if not the only, entry in the Appendix.

B = Block or Lot (location in Section unknown)
A "B" designation in the Index is a tip-off that the EXACT location of the patent within the map is not apparent from the legal description. This Patent will nonetheless be noted within the proper

Section along with any other Lots purchased in the Section. Given the scope of this project (many states and many Counties are being mapped), trying to locate all relevant plats for Lots (if they even exist) and accurately mapping them would have taken one person several lifetimes. But since our primary goal from the onset has been to establish relationships between neighbors and families, very little is lost to this goal since we can still observe who all lived in which Section.

C = Cancelled Patent

A Cancelled Patent is just that: cancelled. Whether the original Patentee forfeited his or her patent due to fraud, a technicality, non-payment, or whatever, the fact remains that it is significant to know who received patents for what parcels and when. A cancellation may be evidence that the Patentee never physically re-located to the land, but does not in itself prove that point. Further evidence would be required to prove that. See also, Re-issued Patents, below.

F = Fractional Section

A Fractional Section is one that contains less than 640 acres, almost always because of a body of water. The exact size and shape of land-parcels contained in such sections may not be ascertainable, but we map them nonetheless. Just keep in mind that we are not mapping an actual parcel to scale in such instances. Another point to consider is that we have located some fractional sections that are not so designated by the Bureau of Land Management in their data. This means that not all fractional sections have been so identified in our indexes.

G = Group
(Multi-Patentee Patent, see Appendix "C")

A "G" designation means that the Patent was issued to a GROUP of people (Multi-patentees). The "G" will always be followed by a number. Some such groups were quite large and it was impractical if not impossible to display each individual in our maps without unduly affecting readability. EACH person in the group is named in the Index, but they won't all be found on the Map. You will find the name of the first person in such a Group on the map with the Group number next to it, enclosed in [square brackets].

To find all the members of the Group you can either scan the Index for all people with the same Group Number or you can simply refer to Appendix "C" where all members of the Group are listed next to their number.

O = Overlaps another Parcel

An Overlap is one where PART of a parcel of land gets issued on more than one patent. For genealogical purposes, both transfers of title are important and both Patentees are mapped. If the ENTIRE parcel of land is re-issued, that is what we call it, a Re-Issued Patent (see below). The number after the "O" indicates the ID for the overlapping Patent(s) contained within the same Index. Like Re-Issued and Cancelled Patents, Overlaps may cause a map-reader to be confused at first, but for genealogical purposes, all of these parties' relationships to the underlying land is important, and therefore, we map them.

R = Re-Issued (Parcel patented more than once)

The label, "Re-issued Patent" describes Patents which were issued more than once for land with the EXACT SAME LEGAL DESCRIPTION. Whether the original patent was cancelled or not, there were a good many parcels which were patented more than once. The number after the "R" indicates the ID for the other Patent contained within the same Index that was for the same land. A quick glance at the map itself within the relevant Section will be the quickest way to find the other Patentee to whom the Parcel was transferred. They should both be mapped in the same general area.

I have gone to some length describing all sorts of anomalies either in the underlying data or in their representation on the maps and indexes in this book. Most of this will bore the most ardent reseracher, but I do this with all due respect to those researchers who will inevitably (and rightfully) ask: "Why isn't so-and-so's name on the exact spot that the index says it should be?"

In most cases it will be due to the existence of a Multi-Patentee Patent, a Re-issued Patent, a Cancelled Patent, or Overlapping Parcels named in separate Patents. I don't pretend that this discussion will answer every question along these lines, but I hope it will at least convince you of the complexity of the subject.

Not to despair, this book's companion web-site will offer a way to further explain "odd-ball" or errant data. Each book (County) will have its own web-page or pages to discuss such situations. You can go to www.arphax.com to find the relevant web-page for Auglaize County.

Land Patent Map

On the first two-page spread following each Township's Index to Land Patents, you'll find the corresponding Land Patent Map. And here lies the real heart of our work. For the first time anywhere, researchers will be able to observe and analyze, on a grand scale, most of the original land-owners for an area AND see them mapped in proximity to each one another.

We encourage you to make vigorous use of the accompanying Index described above, but then later, to abandon it, and just stare at these maps for a while. This is a great way to catch misspellings or to find collateral kin you'd not known were in the area.

Each Land Patent Map represents one Congressional Township containing approximately 36-square miles. Each of these square miles is labeled by an accompanying Section Number (1 through 36, in most cases). Keep in mind, that this book concerns itself solely with Auglaize County's patents. Townships which creep into one or more other counties will not be shown in their entirety in any one book. You will need to consult other books, as they become available, in order to view other countys' patents, cities, cemeteries, etc.

But getting back to Auglaize County: each Land Patent Map contains a Statistical Chart that looks like the following:

Township Statistics

Parcels Mapped	:	173
Number of Patents	:	163
Number of Individuals	:	152
Patentees Identified	:	151
Number of Surnames	:	137
Multi-Patentee Parcels	:	4
Oldest Patent Date	:	11/27/1820
Most Recent Patent	:	9/28/1917
Block/Lot Parcels	:	0
Parcels Re-Issued	:	3
Parcels that Overlap	:	8
Cities and Towns	:	6
Cemeteries	:	6

This information may be of more use to a social statistician or historian than a genealogist, but I think all three will find it interesting.

Most of the statistics are self-explanatory, and what is not, was described in the above discussion of the Index's Legend, but I do want to mention a few of them that may affect your understanding of the Land Patent Maps.

First of all, Patents often contain more than one Parcel of land, so it is common for there to be more Parcels than Patents. Also, the Number of Individuals will more often than not, not match the number of Patentees. A Patentee is literally the person or PERSONS named in a patent. So, a Patent may have a multi-person Patentee or a single-person patentee. Nonetheless, we account for all these individuals in our indexes.

On the lower-righthand side of the Patent Map is a Legend which describes various features in the map, including Section Boundaries, Patent (land) Boundaries, Lots (numbered), and Multi-Patentee Group Numbers. You'll also find a "Helpful Hints" Box that will assist you.

One important note: though the vast majority of Patents mapped in this series will prove to be reasonably accurate representations of their actual locations, we cannot claim this for patents lying along state and county lines, or waterways, or that have been platted (lots). Shifting boundaries and sparse legal descriptions in the GLO data make this a reality that we have nonetheless tried to overcome by estimating these patents' locations the best that we can.

Road Map

On the two-page spread following each Patent Map you will find a Road Map covering the exact same area (the same Congressional Township).

For me, fully exploring the past means that every once in a while I must leave the library and travel to the actual locations where my ancestors once walked and worked the land. Our Township Road Maps are a great place to begin such a quest.

Keep in mind that the scaling and proportion of these maps was chosen in order to squeeze hundreds of people-names, road-names, and place-names into tinier spaces than you would traditionally see. These are not professional road-maps, and like any secondary genealogical source, should be looked upon as an entry-way to original sources— in this case, original patents and applications, professionally produced maps and surveys, etc.

Both our Road Maps and Historical Maps contain cemeteries and city-centers, along with a listing of these on the left-hand side of the map. I should note that I am showing you city center-points, rather than city-limit boundaries, because in many instances, this will represent a place where settlement began. This may be a good time to mention that many cemeteries are located on private property, Always check with a local historical or genealogical society to see if a particular cemetery is publicly accessible (if it is not obviously so). As a final point, look for your surnames among the road-names. You will often be surprised by what you find.

Historical Map

The third and final map in each Map Group is our attempt to display what each Township might have looked like before the advent of modern roads. In frontier times, people were usually more determined to settle near rivers and creeks than they were near roads, which were often few and far between. As was the case with the Road Map, we've included the same cemeteries and city-centers. We've also included railroads, many of which came along before most roads.

While some may claim "Historical Map" to be a bit of a misnomer for this tool, we settled for this label simply because it was almost as accurate as saying "Railroads, Lakes, Rivers, Cities, and Cemeteries," and it is much easier to remember.

In Closing . . .

By way of example, here is A Really Good Way to Use a Township Map Group. First, find the person you are researching in the Township's Index to Land Patents, which will direct you to the proper Section and parcel on the Patent Map. But before leaving the Index, scan all the patents within it, looking for other names of interest. Now, turn to the Patent Map and locate your parcels of land. Pay special attention to the names of patent-holders who own land surrounding your person of interest. Next, turn the page and look at the same Section(s) on the Road Map. Note which roads are closest to your parcels and also the names of nearby towns and cemeteries. Using other resources, you may be able to learn of kin who have been buried here, plus, you may choose to visit these cemeteries the next time you are in the area.

Finally, turn to the Historical Map. Look once more at the same Sections where you found your research subject's land. Note the nearby streams, creeks, and other geographical features. You may be surprised to find family names were used to name them, or you may see a name you haven't heard mentioned in years and years—and a new research possibility is born.

Many more techniques for using these Family Maps volumes will no doubt be discovered. If from time to time, you will navigate to Auglaize County's web-page at www.arphax.com (use the "Research" link), you can learn new tricks as they become known (or you can share ones you have employed). But for now, you are ready to get started. So, go, and good luck.

– Part I –

The Big Picture

Map A - Where Auglaize County, Ohio Lies Within the State

--- Legend ---

State Boundary

County Boundaries

Auglaize County, Ohio

--- Helpful Hints ---

1 We start with Map "A" which simply shows us where within the State this county lies.

2 Map "B" zooms in further to help us more easily identify surrounding Counties.

3 Map "C" zooms in even further to reveal the Congressional Townships that either lie within or intersect Auglaize County.

Map B - Auglaize County, Ohio and Surrounding Counties

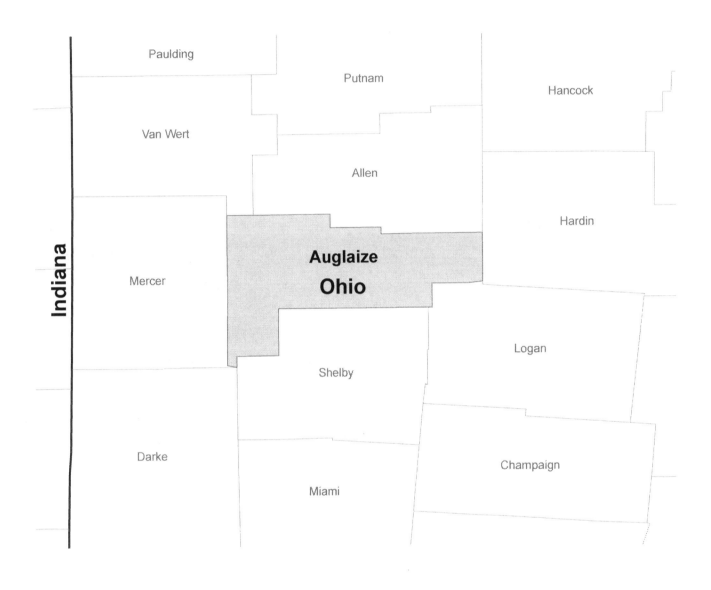

——— Legend ———

State Boundaries (when applicable)

——— County Boundary

——— Helpful Hints ———

1 Many Patent-holders and their families settled across county lines. It is always a good idea to check nearby counties for your families.

2 Refer to Map "A" to see a broader view of where this County lies within the State, and Map "C" to see which Congressional Townships lie within Auglaize County.

Map C - Congressional Townships of Auglaize County, Ohio

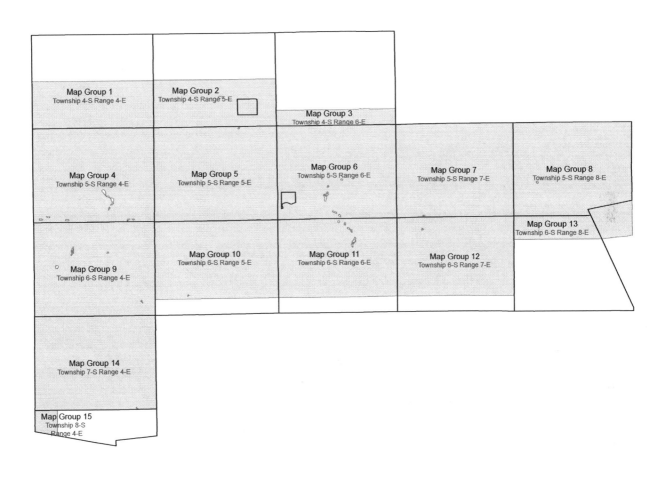

——— Legend ———

Auglaize County, Ohio

Congressional Townships

——— Helpful Hints ———

1 Many Patent-holders and their families settled across county lines. It is always a good idea to check nearby counties for your families (See Map "B").

2 Refer to Map "A" to see a broader view of where this county lies within the State, and Map "B" for a view of the counties surrounding Auglaize County.

Map D Index: Cities & Towns of Auglaize County, Ohio

The following represents the Cities and Towns of Auglaize County, along with the corresponding Map Group in which each is found. Cities and Towns are displayed in both the Road and Historical maps in the Group.

City/Town	Map Group No.
Bay (historical)	5
Breezewood	9
Buckland	5
Bulkhead	9
Cridersville	3
Egypt	14
Fryburg	11
Geyer	12
Glynwood	5
Green Acres	3
Gutman	12
Harmons Landing	9
Holden	8
Kossuth	1
Lock Two	14
Minster	14
Moulton	5
New Bremen	14
New Hampshire	13
New Knoxville	10
Pusheta Town (historical)	5
Rineharts (historical)	7
Saint Johns	12
Saint Marys	9
Sandy Beach	9
Santa Fe	12
Sherwood Forest (subdivision)	6
Slater	12
South Shore Acres	9
Southmoor Shores	9
Uniopolis	7
Villa Nova	9
Wapakoneta	6
Waynesfield	8

Map D - Cities & Towns of Auglaize County, Ohio

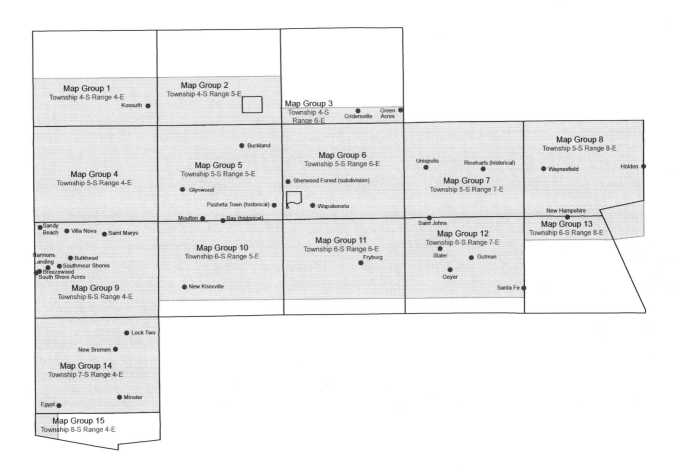

— Legend —

Auglaize County, Ohio

Congressional Townships

— Helpful Hints —

1 Cities and towns are marked only at their center-points as published by the USGS and/or NationalAtlas.gov. This often enables us to more closely approximate where these might have existed when first settled.

2 To see more specifically where these Cities & Towns are located within the county, refer to both the Road and Historical maps in the Map-Group referred to above. See also, the Map "D" Index on the opposite page.

Map E Index: Cemeteries of Auglaize County, Ohio

The following represents many of the Cemeteries of Auglaize County, along with the corresponding Township Map Group in which each is found. Cemeteries are displayed in both the Road and Historical maps in the Map Groups referred to below.

Cemetery	Map Group No.		Cemetery	Map Group No.
Arnett Cem.	10		Vaughan Cem.	7
Benner Cem.	9		Walnut Hill Cem.	8
Berry Cem.	8		Wesley Chapel Cem.	7
Bethel Cem.	6		Wheeler Cem.	6
Buckland Cem.	5		Willow Branch Cem.	8
Burk Cem.	10		Willow Grove Cem.	14
Calvary Cem.	4		Wisely Cem.	10
Concord Cem.	8		Zion Cem.	2
Conner-Kaiser Cem.	6		Zion Cem.	5
Craft Cem.	6			
Crow Cem.	5			
Elm Grove Cem.	9			
Evergreen Cem.	6			
Fairmount Cem.	7			
Fort Amanda Cem.	2			
German Cem.	14			
Gethsemane Cem.	9			
Geyer Cem.	12			
Greenlawn Cem.	6			
Haruff Cem.	11			
Helminger Cem.	12			
Hittepole Cem.	10			
Hopewell Cem.	8			
Horn Cem.	8			
Jacob Baker Cem.	5			
Julion Cem.	5			
Keller Cem.	11			
Kossuth Cem.	1			
Lockhart Cem.	7			
Lutheran Cem.	9			
Mars Hill Cem.	8			
Mount Lookout Cem.	7			
Mount Tabor Cem.	12			
Mount Union Cem.	1			
New Salem Cem.	1			
Old Catholic Cem.	9			
Old Saint Johns Cem.	11			
Old Saint Josephs Cem.	6			
Old Saint Marys Cem.	9			
Olive Branch Cem.	10			
Pilger Ruhe Cem.	10			
Plank Road Cem.	14			
Pratt Cem.	4			
Protestant Evangelical Cem.	10			
Reinhart Cem.	6			
Robbins Cem.	1			
Rupert Cem.	11			
Saint Augustines Cem.	14			
Saint Johns Cem.	7			
Saint Johns Cem.	11			
Saint Johns Cem.	11			
Saint Joseph Cem.	6			
Saint Josephs Cem.	14			
Saint Thomas Cem.	5			
Schemmel Cem.	11			
Scott Cem.	11			
Stevely Cem.	6			
Stiles Cem.	7			
Tam Cem.	6			

Map E - Cemeteries of Auglaize County, Ohio

New Salem Cem. · Mount Union Cem. Robbins Cem. Kossuth Cem. **Map Group 1** Township 4-S Range 4-E	Zion Cem. Fort Amanda Cem. **Map Group 2** Township 4-S Range 5-E	**Map Group 3** Township 4-S Range 6-E	

Calvary Cem. Pratt Cem. **Map Group 4** Township 5-S Range 4-E	Jacob Baker Cem. Buckland Cem. **Map Group 5** Township 5-S Range 5-E Saint Thomas Cem. Crow Cem. Zion Cem. Julion Cem.	Wheeler Cem. Bethel Cem. Stevely Cem. Craft Cem. Conner-Kaiser Cem. **Map Group 6** Township 5-S Range 6-E Tam Cem. Evergreen Cem. Reinhart Old Saint Josephs Cem. Cem. Greenlawn Cem. Saint Joseph Cem.	Stiles Cem. Vaughan Cem. Fairmount Cem. Mount Lookout Cem. **Map Group 7** Township 5-S Range 7-E Wesley Chapel Cem. Lockhart Cem. Saint Johns Cem.

Horn Cem. Mars Hill Cem. Hopewell Cem. Berry Cem. Concord Cem. Willow Branch Cem. **Map Group 8** Township 5-S Range 8-E Walnut Hill Cem.			

Benner Cem. Old Catholic Cem. Old Saint Marys Cem. Lutheran Cem. Gethsemane Cem. Elm Grove Cem. **Map Group 9** Township 6-S Range 4-E	**Map Group 10** Township 6-S Range 5-E Burk Cem. Arnett Cem. Wisely Cem. Pilger Ruhe Cem. Hittepole Cem. Olive Branch Cem. Protestant Evangelical Cem.	Haruff Cem. Keller Cem. Old Saint Saint Johns Cem. Johns Cem. Saint Johns Cem. Schemmel Cem. Rupert Cem. Scott Cem. **Map Group 11** Township 6-S Range 6-E	**Map Group 12** Township 6-S Range 7-E Mount Tabor Cem. Geyer Cem. Helminger Cem.

	Map Group 13 Township 6-S Range 8-E

Willow Grove Cem. German Cem. Plank Road Cem. **Map Group 14** Township 7-S Range 4-E Saint Josephs Cem. Saint Augustines Cem. **Map Group 15** Township 8-S Range 4-E

— Legend —

Auglaize County, Ohio

Congressional Townships

— Helpful Hints —

1 Cemeteries are marked at locations as published by the USGS and/or NationalAtlas.gov.

2 To see more specifically where these Cemeteries are located, refer to the Road & Historical maps in the Map-Group referred to above. See also, the Map "E" Index on the opposite page to make sure you don't miss any of the Cemeteries located within this Congressional township.

Surnames in Auglaize County, Ohio Patents

The following list represents the surnames that we have located in Auglaize County, Ohio Patents and the number of parcels that we have mapped for each one. Here is a quick way to determine the existence (or not) of Patents to be found in the subsequent indexes and maps of this volume.

Surname	# of Land Parcels	Surname	# of Land Parcels	Surname	# of Land Parcels	Surname	# of Land Parcels
ABBEY	2	BECHDOLT	1	BOWER	1	CASE	1
ABERNATHY	1	BECHTEL	1	BOWERS	2	CASPER	2
ADAIR	1	BECKEMAN	1	BOWMAN	1	CASTEEL	1
ADELMEYER	2	BECKMAN	1	BOYLES	1	CASTLE	1
ADGATE	1	BEDINGHOUSE	1	BRACKNEY	3	CATRON	2
AFFOLTIR	1	BEEM	1	BRACKSEACK	1	CATROW	3
ALBAS	2	BEER	2	BRAMBLET	1	CAVINDER	1
ALBR	1	BEERY	2	BRAMMELAGE	1	CECIL	7
ALBRANT	1	BEIDLEMAN	2	BRANHAM	1	CHAMBERLIN	8
ALEXANDER	1	BEIENSDORFER	1	BRANNAN	1	CHAMBERS	2
ALLEN	8	BELKNAP	2	BRANNUM	1	CHANEY	5
ANTHONY	2	BELNAP	1	BREES	2	CHATTERTON	1
APGAR	1	BENHERT	1	BREHANT	1	CHILDERS	1
APPLE	3	BENNER	8	BRENTLINGER	1	CIRCLE	1
ARIMAN	1	BERNER	2	BRESAR	1	CIRKLE	1
ARMSTRONG	7	BERRY	8	BREWSTER	1	CLARK	1
ARNET	3	BERRYMAN	1	BRIGHT	1	CLAUSON	1
ARNOLD	1	BESSE	1	BRINTLINGER	1	CLAWSON	2
ARNS	1	BETHERS	1	BRITLER	1	CLAYTON	2
ARTENBRACK	1	BICK	1	BROADWELL	3	CLEVELAND	1
ARTHUR	6	BIER	1	BROBST	1	CLEVERSTEIN	1
ASPINALL	2	BIGGS	2	BROCK	5	CLINE	1
AUBELIN	2	BILGA	2	BRODERICK	2	CLOSSON	1
AUFDERHAR	1	BILLGER	4	BROWN	8	COATS	1
AUFDERHARK	1	BILTER	1	BROWNELL	1	COCHRAN	1
AUFFORTH	1	BINK	2	BRUGGEMAN	2	COCHRUN	1
AUGHENBAUGH	1	BINKLEY	1	BRUMFIELD	1	CODDINGTON	1
AUGHENBOUGH	2	BISHOP	1	BRUNE	2	COLE	2
AUGKINBAUGH	3	BITLER	7	BRUNS	1	COLEMAN	12
AYERS	3	BLACK	11	BUB	1	COLGAN	2
AYRES	6	BLAKELY	1	BUCHANNAN	2	COLLIER	4
BABCOCK	2	BLAKKA	1	BUCK	2	COLLINS	4
BACH	1	BLANCK	1	BUCKHART	1	COLLISTER	1
BACK	1	BLAND	2	BUFENBARGER	3	CONGER	3
BADGLEY	2	BLEAKLY	1	BUFFENBARGER	10	CONKEL	1
BAILEY	6	BLISS	3	BUFFINBARGER	4	CONNELLY	1
BAILY	5	BLUEST	1	BULMAHNN	1	CONNER	2
BAKEMAN	1	BOARDMAN	2	BULMAHUN	1	CONOVER	4
BAKER	9	BOB	2	BUNN	1	CONRAD	2
BALL	1	BOBB	3	BURGET	2	COOK	1
BALLARD	5	BOBP	1	BURK	2	COOPER	1
BALTZELL	2	BODENBENDER	1	BURKET	1	COPELAND	15
BARBER	2	BODKIN	1	BURTON	1	COPSEY	2
BARGMANN	1	BOGGESS	2	BUSH	5	CORDER	6
BARHORST	1	BOLANDER	1	BUSSE	1	CORNELL	1
BARLETT	1	BOLKINS	1	BUTTERWORTH	2	CORSON	4
BARNAR	2	BOND	1	BYENBROOK	2	COTTERL	1
BARNES	3	BONER	1	CALBE	1	COTTERLIN	1
BARNETT	10	BONSER	1	CALDWELL	3	COUNSELLOR	1
BARNEY	1	BOOCKER	1	CALL	1	COVER	2
BARR	2	BOOKER	1	CALLISON	1	COVERSTONE	1
BARRINGTON	7	BORDEN	3	CAMMON	1	COVERT	1
BASIL	3	BORT	1	CAMPBELL	10	COWAN	1
BASINK	1	BORTON	10	CANON	2	COX	2
BASS	1	BOSCHE	34	CAREY	4	COY	1
BATCHELER	1	BOTHE	4	CARL	1	CRABB	1
BATES	4	BOTHIN	1	CARMEAN	2	CRAFT	3
BAUGHMAN	4	BOTKIN	5	CARMONY	2	CRAMER	6
BAYLIFF	4	BOTKINS	1	CARPER	1	CRAWEL	1
BEAR	1	BOWDENTISSEL	1	CARSWELL	2	CRAWFORD	4
BEARD	1	BOWDLE	7	CARTER	5	CREIGHTON	2
BECHDOLETT	1	BOWEN	1	CARY	3	CREMEEN	1

Surname	# of Land Parcels	Surname	# of Land Parcels	Surname	# of Land Parcels	Surname	# of Land Parcels
CRETCHER	13	ELROD	1	GARDINER	3	HAWTHORNE	1
CRISTY	1	ELSAS	2	GARMIRE	2	HAY	2
CROFT	2	ELSHOF	1	GARRETSONE	1	HAYS	1
CROSIER	2	ELSWORTH	3	GAST	2	HAYWOOD	1
CROSS	1	EMERICK	1	GAULHOUST	1	HEADEPOHL	1
CROWDER	1	EMMERT	1	GAUSEPOHL	2	HEATH	1
CROWEL	1	ENNEKING	4	GAVER	1	HEBENSTREIT	1
CROZIER	2	EPART	1	GEARHEART	5	HEIDOCKER	1
CULP	1	ESCHMEIRE	2	GEHVERS	1	HEIGHTON	1
CUMMINGS	3	ESPY	4	GEIER	2	HEIL	1
CUMMINS	1	EVERSOLE	6	GEISLER	2	HEINE	1
CUNNINGHAM	4	EWEN	2	GEYER	1	HELFENSTEIN	11
CURL	1	FAIK	1	GHORMLEY	1	HELINLINGER	1
CURTIS	1	FAIRFIELD	4	GIBESON	1	HELM	3
DARLINGHAUS	1	FALER	1	GILBERT	1	HELMINGES	1
DARR	1	FALES	1	GILROY	2	HELMLENGER	2
DARSTON	1	FARIS	1	GLASER	1	HELMSING	1
DAVIDSON	2	FARNSLER	3	GODDARD	2	HEMMERT	1
DAVIS	8	FELDMAN	2	GOLDING	1	HENDERSHOT	1
DAVISON	5	FELDMANN	2	GOODENOW	1	HENRICH	1
DAVISSON	1	FERRAL	1	GOODSEL	1	HENRY	6
DAWSON	9	FERREL	1	GORDAN	1	HERBST	2
DAY	2	FETTERS	1	GORDON	5	HERGENROTHER	1
DEALONG	1	FIELD	1	GRABLE	1	HERMAN	2
DEEMS	2	FINDLY	1	GRAHAM	4	HERMES	1
DEIHL	1	FINLAW	1	GRANER	1	HEROFF	3
DEKLAR	1	FISHER	3	GRANT	2	HERTIG	1
DELANY	2	FISHPAW	1	GRAY	5	HERZING	5
DELONG	5	FLADERIOHAN	1	GREBER	2	HESTER	1
DENISTON	2	FLEDDERIOHAN	3	GREEN	7	HEUSCH	1
DENNEY	7	FLEDDERJOHAN	1	GREESHOPF	1	HEYSLER	2
DENNY	1	FLEDDERJOHN	1	GREGORY	1	HIGHER	1
DENTON	1	FLEGAL	1	GREIDER	4	HILLMANN	1
DEPRES	1	FLEGEL	1	GRINKEMEYER	1	HINDEL	1
DICK	1	FLEMMING	2	GRIZER	2	HINDERS	1
DICKMAN	1	FLOHR	1	GRONER	1	HINKLE	5
DIEAHL	1	FLOWERS	2	GROSS	4	HIPPLE	1
DIEGEL	2	FOLKAMPF	1	GUDORF	1	HITEMAN	1
DIXON	1	FONKMAN	1	GUTHRIE	2	HITTEL	6
DOENYES	1	FONTS	1	GUTRIDGE	2	HOBERG	1
DOHMANN	1	FOREMAN	3	GUYER	1	HODGES	1
DONNEBERG	1	FORIS	1	HAGY	1	HOFFMAN	3
DONNEL	2	FORNEY	3	HAHN	2	HOGE	1
DOSTON	1	FORNHOLT	1	HAINES	3	HOHNE	1
DOTY	1	FORSYTHE	1	HALL	4	HOLBROOK	3
DOUGHERTY	1	FOSTER	2	HALLER	4	HOLDRIDGE	3
DOUNAN	1	FOULKE	1	HAMER	1	HOLLA	1
DOUTE	3	FOWLER	1	HAMILTON	4	HOLLINGSWORTH	1
DOUTEE	3	FRAME	1	HAMMELL	2	HOLLY	5
DOUTEY	1	FRANKLIN	2	HANEY	1	HOLSINGER	1
DOUTY	1	FRANKS	3	HANKINS	1	HOLTFOCHT	2
DOWTY	1	FRANTS	1	HANKS	2	HOLTZMAN	1
DREES	2	FRAZIER	2	HANSER	1	HOOK	1
DREESE	1	FREAS	1	HANSFELD	2	HOOPES	2
DRESHU	1	FREDERICKS	1	HARBERT	1	HOOVER	1
DUMBROFF	2	FREEMAN	1	HARDEN	2	HORMEL	1
DUNGAN	1	FREISNER	1	HARDENBROOK	1	HORN	1
DUNLAP	2	FRELING	1	HARMEL	1	HORSIMER	1
DURSTEN	2	FRENCH	8	HARROD	20	HORTAS	1
DYE	1	FREYMAN	1	HARSHBARGER	2	HOSNIRE	1
EARL	1	FRIEDLINE	1	HARSHMAN	1	HOTTES	1
EBERD	1	FRISCHE	3	HART	1	HOUCK	1
EDGE	4	FRY	1	HARTLEY	2	HOUSE	2
EDMISTON	4	FULLENKAMP	1	HARVEY	10	HOUSTON	2
ELLEMAN	1	FULLER	3	HASKILL	8	HOVER	9
ELLERMAN	5	FULTON	1	HATCHER	1	HOWELL	13
ELLERMANN	4	FURNOW	1	HATFIELD	1	HUDSON	6
ELLIOTT	19	FURROW	1	HATHAWAY	2	HUFFMAN	1
ELLIS	1	GANT	1	HAUKINSON	1	HUGEMAN	1
ELLISON	1	GARBERRY	1	HAWTHORN	2	HUKRIDE	1

Surname	# of Land Parcels	Surname	# of Land Parcels	Surname	# of Land Parcels	Surname	# of Land Parcels
HULL	2	KOTTERHEINRICH	1	MARZ	1	MOORE	10
HUNT	2	KRAMER	3	MASTERS	1	MOORMAN	1
HUNTER	1	KRANER	2	MATHENY	1	MOORMANN	1
HURLEY	6	KRUSI	3	MATHER	1	MORECRAFT	11
HURTLE	1	KUCK	1	MATHERS	2	MOREY	1
HUTCHEN	1	KUHN	1	MCARTHUR	1	MORGAN	2
HUTSON	1	KUNNEG	1	MCCAHON	1	MORRIS	19
HUTZLER	1	KUNNING	1	MCCAIN	1	MORROW	3
ICE	2	KUPER	1	MCCARTNEY	2	MORTON	1
INGLERIGHT	1	LAMB	2	MCCLEAN	2	MOSLER	1
INSKEEP	4	LANDCOMMER	1	MCCLELLAN	2	MOUNTS	1
JACKSON	3	LANDIS	1	MCCONNEL	1	MOURER	1
JACOBS	2	LANE	3	MCCONNELL	3	MULLER	3
JAY	1	LANKOM	1	MCCORCLE	4	MUNDAY	2
JEFFERY	3	LAREW	1	MCCORMICK	1	MURKER	1
JEFFREY	2	LAUER	1	MCCOY	6	MURRAY	5
JEFFRIES	3	LAUGER	1	MCCULLOUGH	3	MURRY	6
JENKINS	1	LAURY	1	MCDONALD	3	MUSSELMAN	1
JETT	1	LAYTON	1	MCFARLAND	3	MUSSER	1
JIAMS	1	LEATHERMAN	5	MCGEEHAN	2	MYERS	4
JOHNS	5	LEATHERS	3	MCGRADY	1	NAGLE	4
JOHNSTON	3	LEBEL	3	MCINTIRE	1	NASON	1
JONES	8	LEMASTERS	2	MCKEE	2	NAUMBURGER	1
JORDAN	2	LEMKOHL	2	MCKINNEY	1	NEAL	1
JOY	2	LENNENEVER	1	MCKNIGHT	3	NEEDLES	1
JUDY	1	LENOX	1	MCLAUGHLIN	4	NEESE	8
JULIAN	1	LEPPERT	1	MCMILLIN	2	NEITER	1
JULIEN	1	LEVERING	1	MCNABB	1	NELSON	1
JUSTICE	2	LEVINGSTON	1	MCNAMUR	1	NERR	1
KADIEBERT	1	LEWIS	3	MCNEIL	1	NEWMAN	1
KAHLER	1	LIBLING	2	MCPHERON	1	NICHOLS	1
KALLMEIER	2	LIGHTFOOT	1	MCVEIGH	1	NICKELL	1
KATTERHEINRICH	2	LINDER	1	MCVICKER	1	NIEHING	1
KATTERHENRICH	1	LINDLEY	1	MEAD	1	NIEMAN	1
KATTMAN	2	LINING	2	MEANS	3	NIETERT	1
KEAM	1	LINTCH	4	MECKSTOTT	1	NIEWATZ	1
KEENER	1	LISLE	2	MECKSTROTT	1	NIPGEN	3
KEEVER	1	LLOYD	2	MEDBERY	1	NIPPGEN	1
KELLER	4	LOCKART	1	MEDEARIS	2	NOBLE	10
KEMPER	4	LOCKET	1	MEFFERD	1	NOGGLE	1
KENEDY	1	LONG	1	MELCHER	1	NOKEL	1
KENEFAK	1	LONGWITH	2	MELLINGER	3	NOLAN	1
KENINGER	1	LONGWORTH	5	MESLOH	1	NOLL	1
KENT	8	LOONEY	1	MESSER	1	NOROT	1
KENTNER	3	LOWREY	1	METSKER	1	NORRIS	1
KERNS	3	LOWRY	1	MEYER	2	NORTH	2
KERR	2	LUCAS	5	MEYERS	1	NORTON	1
KIESEKAMP	2	LUERS	1	MICHAEL	3	NURMEIER	1
KINDLE	2	LURES	1	MIDDLEBECKE	1	NUSMEIER	1
KING	5	LUSK	10	MILES	1	NUSMEIRE	1
KINNING	1	LUTTERBECK	2	MILLER	42	NYE	1
KINTNER	1	LUTTERBIEN	1	MILLIGAN	1	OAKLEY	1
KIRKBRIDE	2	LUTTRELL	1	MINK	1	OAR	1
KIRKPATRICK	3	LYONS	1	MIRING	1	OLIPHANT	1
KISER	2	MACER	2	MITCHELL	1	OLMAN	1
KITE	1	MACKLIN	2	MITTENDORF	1	ONERLA	1
KLATTA	1	MADDEN	6	MITZ	1	OPDYCKE	4
KLINE	3	MAENS	2	MIX	5	OPDYKE	2
KLIPFEL	3	MAHEN	2	MOEKER	1	ORTH	1
KLOAS	1	MAHIN	7	MOFFETT	2	ORTMAN	1
KLOPF	2	MAJOR	1	MOFFITT	1	ORTON	1
KLUE	1	MAJORS	3	MOHR	3	OSBORN	1
KLUIS	1	MALAIM	1	MOHRMAN	4	OSBORNE	2
KNARR	1	MALCOS	1	MOJER	1	OSTERLOH	4
KNECHT	3	MANNING	3	MOKKARHIDER	1	OVERHALSER	1
KNUPKE	1	MARKS	2	MONEYSMITH	2	OVERLAY	1
KOCH	2	MARQUIS	2	MONGER	1	OVERLEY	1
KOFMAN	1	MARSHALL	8	MONROE	1	OXLY	2
KOKENGE	1	MARTIN	3	MONTER	2	PAIRO	1
KOOK	1	MARTZ	1	MOORCRAFT	1	PARLETT	1

Surname	# of Land Parcels	Surname	# of Land Parcels	Surname	# of Land Parcels	Surname	# of Land Parcels
PARNELL	1	ROUCH	1	SNYDER	2	THORN	2
PATRICK	1	RUMAN	1	SOLLMAN	3	THROCKMORTON	1
PATTERSON	5	RUNKLE	2	SOLMON	1	TINDALL	1
PATTON	2	RUNYAN	1	SOURMANN	2	TINGLE	1
PAUL	1	RUNYON	1	SPALDING	1	TIPPIE	4
PEACHE	1	RUSSEL	3	SPEES	6	TOBIAS	9
PENCE	4	RUSSELL	2	SPRAY	4	TODD	1
PENESON	1	RYAN	3	SPREHEE	1	TOLMAN	3
PENING	1	RYASON	2	SPROUL	3	TOMAN	1
PENNY	1	SACKETT	1	SPURRIER	3	TOMON	1
PETERS	1	SAMMETINGER	1	STALLO	9	TONG	1
PETTIT	4	SAMSON	3	STARKEY	1	TONGAMAN	2
PETTY	1	SATTERTHWAIT	1	STARRET	1	TREBEIN	2
PFAFF	1	SAUM	2	STARRETT	1	TRESHER	1
PHENEGAR	1	SAVIN	1	STATLER	5	TRINT	1
PHILLIPS	4	SAWYER	4	STAUTHITE	2	TROYER	1
PICKEREL	1	SCHAMMEL	1	STEBLETON	1	TRUMBO	1
PIERCE	3	SCHARDELMANN	1	STEEN	2	TUCKER	3
PITMAN	1	SCHAUL	1	STEINEMAN	1	TUNEMANN	1
PLACE	1	SCHEMMEL	3	STEINEMANN	1	TUPP	1
POLMANN	1	SCHLICHTIG	1	STEINMANN	1	TURNER	3
POOL	2	SCHLOSSER	2	STELTZER	2	TYRRELL	1
PORTER	2	SCHOOLER	5	STEVENS	3	UPTON	2
POST	1	SCHOULTE	1	STEWART	1	VAN ANTWERP	2
POWELL	4	SCHRER	3	STILES	4	VAN BLARACOM	4
PRATT	5	SCHROEDER	5	STILL	1	VAN BLARICOM	1
PRICTCHARD	1	SCHULZE	1	STILLNAG	1	VAN GUNDY	1
PRIMMER	1	SCHURE	1	STINE	1	VAN HORNE	23
PRITCHARD	1	SCHWEINEFUSZ	1	STOCKDALE	2	VAN NORTWICK	1
PURCELL	1	SCHWENKE	1	STOCKER	1	VAN NUYS	1
QURTMAN	1	SCOTT	7	STODDARD	33	VANARSDAL	2
RAIN	1	SEAMAR	2	STOKER	4	VANCE	1
RAMSEY	1	SEITER	4	STONEROCK	2	VANDERVEER	4
RASH	1	SEIVERT	1	STORCK	2	VANFLEET	2
RATHBURN	1	SELVY	1	STORTS	2	VANNUYS	1
REABURN	1	SERGES	1	STOUT	3	VAUGHAN	3
REAMES	2	SESSIONS	1	STRASBURG	3	VEHORN	1
REED	5	SHAEFFER	2	STRAWSBURG	2	VENNEMANN	3
REES	1	SHAFER	1	STRICKER	1	VERTH	1
REKEL	1	SHAFFER	4	STRICKLE	1	VICKER	1
RHODES	1	SHARER	1	STRICKLER	1	VINSON	2
RICE	1	SHAUL	3	STROH	3	VINTER	1
RICHARDSON	11	SHAW	4	STUBBE	1	VOEGE	1
RIDLEY	2	SHEETS	2	STUBBS	1	VOLL	1
RIEMAN	1	SHELBY	2	STUDEBAKER	1	VOORHIS	3
RILEY	1	SHELMITTER	2	STUKEY	1	WAGGONER	2
RINEHART	4	SHEPHERD	2	STURGEON	1	WAITE	3
RINGER	4	SHEPPER	1	SULLIVAN	4	WALCK	1
RISBARGER	1	SHERIDEN	1	SUNDERLAND	4	WALKE	1
RITCHEY	1	SHERMER	3	SURMANN	1	WALKER	3
RITTER	2	SHIGLEY	1	SUTER	1	WALLACE	1
ROACH	1	SHINN	1	SUTTON	2	WALTER	3
ROBERTS	3	SHIRDEN	1	SWEARINGEN	2	WALTON	1
ROBINS	2	SHOCKEY	2	SWICKARD	3	WARLING	1
ROBINSON	7	SHREDER	2	SWINEHART	3	WATERS	2
ROCK	4	SHULENBARG	1	SWISHER	1	WATKIN	1
RODEKORTH	1	SHULL	1	TABA	1	WATSON	1
ROELLE	1	SIDES	1	TAFE	1	WATT	3
ROFLES	2	SIFORT	1	TAM	4	WATTON	1
ROGERS	2	SILLIN	1	TAMPLETON	2	WAYMIRE	2
ROHENKOHL	1	SIMES	1	TANGEMANN	1	WAYNER	2
ROLFES	2	SKILLINGS	2	TAUBEN	2	WEAVER	4
ROLLINS	1	SKILLMAN	2	TAYLOR	4	WEIMART	1
RONEY	4	SKINNER	16	TEMPLETON	2	WELDEHR	2
ROOF	4	SLATER	2	TERWILLEGER	2	WELDELN	1
ROOTS	1	SLOSS	1	TERWILLIGER	2	WELLER	2
ROSS	5	SMITH	28	THAYER	1	WELLMAN	6
ROSTORFER	1	SNAVELY	1	THERSTICKER	1	WELLMANN	1
ROTH	3	SNELLER	1	THIMANN	2	WELLS	4
ROTT	1	SNIDER	3	THOMAS	4	WELTY	1

Surname	# of Land Parcels
WERST	3
WESJOHN	1
WEST	2
WETSTONE	1
WETTERER	1
WHEATLAND	1
WHEELER	9
WHETSTONE	8
WICHER	1
WICHMANN	1
WICKMAN	1
WIEMEYER	1
WIENNER	1
WIERWILLE	1
WILCOX	2
WILDENBREW	1
WILDS	11
WILEY	2
WILHELM	1
WILKINS	8
WILLIAMS	29
WILSON	4
WIMERT	2
WINDELER	1
WINGET	1
WINTHORT	1
WISE	1
WISS	2
WITHAM	3
WOOD	3
WOODBURY	2
WOODRUFF	4
WORMANN	2
WRIGHT	4
WULF	1
WUPPENHARST	2
WYLAND	3
YOAKAM	1
YORK	1
YOSTING	1
YOUNG	5
YOUNKER	1
ZANGLEIN	2
ZEHNER	3
ZINK	1
ZINN	1

Surname/Township Index

This Index allows you to determine which Township Map Group(s) contain individuals with the following surnames. Each Map Group has a corresponding full-name index of all individuals who obtained patents for land within its Congressional township's borders. After each index you will find the Patent Map to which it refers, and just thereafter, you can view the township's Road Map and Historical Map, with the latter map displaying streams, railroads, and more.

So, once you find your Surname here, proceed to the Index at the beginning of the Map Group indicated below.

Surname	Map Group	Parcels of Land	Meridian/Township/Range		
ABBEY	**11**	2	1st PM	6-S	6-E
ABERNATHY	**8**	1	1st PM	5-S	8-E
ADAIR	**13**	1	1st PM	6-S	8-E
ADELMEYER	**14**	2	1st PM	7-S	4-E
ADGATE	**1**	1	1st PM	4-S	4-E
AFFOLTIR	**7**	1	1st PM	5-S	7-E
ALBAS	**14**	2	1st PM	7-S	4-E
ALBR	**11**	1	1st PM	6-S	6-E
ALBRANT	**11**	1	1st PM	6-S	6-E
ALEXANDER	**10**	1	1st PM	6-S	5-E
ALLEN	**7**	7	1st PM	5-S	7-E
" "	**14**	1	1st PM	7-S	4-E
ANTHONY	**3**	2	1st PM	4-S	6-E
APGAR	**4**	1	1st PM	5-S	4-E
APPLE	**12**	2	1st PM	6-S	7-E
" "	**5**	1	1st PM	5-S	5-E
ARIMAN	**14**	1	1st PM	7-S	4-E
ARMSTRONG	**6**	3	1st PM	5-S	6-E
" "	**9**	3	1st PM	6-S	4-E
" "	**4**	1	1st PM	5-S	4-E
ARNET	**10**	3	1st PM	6-S	5-E
ARNOLD	**8**	1	1st PM	5-S	8-E
ARNS	**14**	1	1st PM	7-S	4-E
ARTENBRACK	**11**	1	1st PM	6-S	6-E
ARTHUR	**6**	5	1st PM	5-S	6-E
" "	**12**	1	1st PM	6-S	7-E
ASPINALL	**10**	2	1st PM	6-S	5-E
AUBELIN	**14**	2	1st PM	7-S	4-E
AUFDERHAR	**10**	1	1st PM	6-S	5-E
AUFDERHARK	**10**	1	1st PM	6-S	5-E
AUFFORTH	**10**	1	1st PM	6-S	5-E
AUGHENBAUGH	**6**	1	1st PM	5-S	6-E
AUGHENBOUGH	**6**	2	1st PM	5-S	6-E
AUGKINBAUGH	**10**	3	1st PM	6-S	5-E
AYERS	**5**	3	1st PM	5-S	5-E
AYRES	**6**	6	1st PM	5-S	6-E
BABCOCK	**12**	2	1st PM	6-S	7-E
BACH	**11**	1	1st PM	6-S	6-E
BACK	**11**	1	1st PM	6-S	6-E
BADGLEY	**9**	2	1st PM	6-S	4-E
BAILEY	**7**	5	1st PM	5-S	7-E
" "	**12**	1	1st PM	6-S	7-E
BAILY	**12**	4	1st PM	6-S	7-E
" "	**7**	1	1st PM	5-S	7-E

Surname	Map Group	Parcels of Land	Meridian/Township/Range
BAKEMAN	**14**	1	1st PM 7-S 4-E
BAKER	**6**	5	1st PM 5-S 6-E
" "	**2**	2	1st PM 4-S 5-E
" "	**5**	2	1st PM 5-S 5-E
BALL	**12**	1	1st PM 6-S 7-E
BALLARD	**8**	5	1st PM 5-S 8-E
BALTZELL	**6**	1	1st PM 5-S 6-E
" "	**7**	1	1st PM 5-S 7-E
BARBER	**12**	2	1st PM 6-S 7-E
BARGMANN	**14**	1	1st PM 7-S 4-E
BARHORST	**14**	1	1st PM 7-S 4-E
BARLETT	**6**	1	1st PM 5-S 6-E
BARNAR	**14**	2	1st PM 7-S 4-E
BARNES	**5**	3	1st PM 5-S 5-E
BARNETT	**6**	7	1st PM 5-S 6-E
" "	**10**	3	1st PM 6-S 5-E
BARNEY	**5**	1	1st PM 5-S 5-E
BARR	**2**	2	1st PM 4-S 5-E
BARRINGTON	**9**	4	1st PM 6-S 4-E
" "	**5**	2	1st PM 5-S 5-E
" "	**10**	1	1st PM 6-S 5-E
BASIL	**7**	3	1st PM 5-S 7-E
BASINK	**9**	1	1st PM 6-S 4-E
BASS	**6**	1	1st PM 5-S 6-E
BATCHELER	**4**	1	1st PM 5-S 4-E
BATES	**10**	3	1st PM 6-S 5-E
" "	**8**	1	1st PM 5-S 8-E
BAUGHMAN	**12**	4	1st PM 6-S 7-E
BAYLIFF	**12**	3	1st PM 6-S 7-E
" "	**7**	1	1st PM 5-S 7-E
BEAR	**6**	1	1st PM 5-S 6-E
BEARD	**5**	1	1st PM 5-S 5-E
BECHDOLETT	**12**	1	1st PM 6-S 7-E
BECHDOLT	**12**	1	1st PM 6-S 7-E
BECHTEL	**11**	1	1st PM 6-S 6-E
BECKEMAN	**14**	1	1st PM 7-S 4-E
BECKMAN	**14**	1	1st PM 7-S 4-E
BEDINGHOUSE	**14**	1	1st PM 7-S 4-E
BEEM	**1**	1	1st PM 4-S 4-E
BEER	**12**	2	1st PM 6-S 7-E
BEERY	**12**	2	1st PM 6-S 7-E
BEIDLEMAN	**6**	2	1st PM 5-S 6-E
BEIENSDORFER	**11**	1	1st PM 6-S 6-E
BELKNAP	**3**	2	1st PM 4-S 6-E
BELNAP	**3**	1	1st PM 4-S 6-E
BENHERT	**14**	1	1st PM 7-S 4-E
BENNER	**9**	7	1st PM 6-S 4-E
" "	**14**	1	1st PM 7-S 4-E
BERNER	**14**	2	1st PM 7-S 4-E
BERRY	**8**	5	1st PM 5-S 8-E
" "	**9**	2	1st PM 6-S 4-E
" "	**7**	1	1st PM 5-S 7-E
BERRYMAN	**2**	1	1st PM 4-S 5-E
BESSE	**7**	1	1st PM 5-S 7-E
BETHERS	**7**	1	1st PM 5-S 7-E
BICK	**11**	1	1st PM 6-S 6-E
BIER	**12**	1	1st PM 6-S 7-E
BIGGS	**7**	1	1st PM 5-S 7-E
" "	**12**	1	1st PM 6-S 7-E
BILGA	**12**	2	1st PM 6-S 7-E

Surname	Map Group	Parcels of Land	Meridian/Township/Range
BILLGER	**12**	4	1st PM 6-S 7-E
BILTER	**12**	1	1st PM 6-S 7-E
BINK	**11**	2	1st PM 6-S 6-E
BINKLEY	**3**	1	1st PM 4-S 6-E
BISHOP	**12**	1	1st PM 6-S 7-E
BITLER	**7**	3	1st PM 5-S 7-E
" "	**12**	3	1st PM 6-S 7-E
" "	**6**	1	1st PM 5-S 6-E
BLACK	**8**	11	1st PM 5-S 8-E
BLAKELY	**10**	1	1st PM 6-S 5-E
BLAKKA	**14**	1	1st PM 7-S 4-E
BLANCK	**6**	1	1st PM 5-S 6-E
BLAND	**5**	2	1st PM 5-S 5-E
BLEAKLY	**10**	1	1st PM 6-S 5-E
BLISS	**2**	1	1st PM 4-S 5-E
" "	**4**	1	1st PM 5-S 4-E
" "	**9**	1	1st PM 6-S 4-E
BLUEST	**11**	1	1st PM 6-S 6-E
BOARDMAN	**10**	2	1st PM 6-S 5-E
BOB	**6**	1	1st PM 5-S 6-E
" "	**11**	1	1st PM 6-S 6-E
BOBB	**11**	3	1st PM 6-S 6-E
BOBP	**6**	1	1st PM 5-S 6-E
BODENBENDER	**12**	1	1st PM 6-S 7-E
BODKIN	**12**	1	1st PM 6-S 7-E
BOGGESS	**13**	2	1st PM 6-S 8-E
BOLANDER	**10**	1	1st PM 6-S 5-E
BOLKINS	**9**	1	1st PM 6-S 4-E
BOND	**8**	1	1st PM 5-S 8-E
BONER	**3**	1	1st PM 4-S 6-E
BONSER	**5**	1	1st PM 5-S 5-E
BOOCKER	**14**	1	1st PM 7-S 4-E
BOOKER	**6**	1	1st PM 5-S 6-E
BORDEN	**6**	3	1st PM 5-S 6-E
BORT	**14**	1	1st PM 7-S 4-E
BORTON	**6**	7	1st PM 5-S 6-E
" "	**5**	2	1st PM 5-S 5-E
" "	**9**	1	1st PM 6-S 4-E
BOSCHE	**9**	15	1st PM 6-S 4-E
" "	**4**	12	1st PM 5-S 4-E
" "	**14**	3	1st PM 7-S 4-E
" "	**5**	2	1st PM 5-S 5-E
" "	**10**	2	1st PM 6-S 5-E
BOTHE	**6**	4	1st PM 5-S 6-E
BOTHIN	**9**	1	1st PM 6-S 4-E
BOTKIN	**9**	5	1st PM 6-S 4-E
BOTKINS	**5**	1	1st PM 5-S 5-E
BOWDENTISSEL	**6**	1	1st PM 5-S 6-E
BOWDLE	**8**	7	1st PM 5-S 8-E
BOWEN	**14**	1	1st PM 7-S 4-E
BOWER	**2**	1	1st PM 4-S 5-E
BOWERS	**11**	2	1st PM 6-S 6-E
BOWMAN	**7**	1	1st PM 5-S 7-E
BOYLES	**4**	1	1st PM 5-S 4-E
BRACKNEY	**12**	2	1st PM 6-S 7-E
" "	**7**	1	1st PM 5-S 7-E
BRACKSEACK	**10**	1	1st PM 6-S 5-E
BRAMBLET	**10**	1	1st PM 6-S 5-E
BRAMMELAGE	**14**	1	1st PM 7-S 4-E
BRANHAM	**10**	1	1st PM 6-S 5-E

Surname	Map Group	Parcels of Land	Meridian/Township/Range
BRANNAN	**10**	1	1st PM 6-S 5-E
BRANNUM	**10**	1	1st PM 6-S 5-E
BREES	**5**	2	1st PM 5-S 5-E
BREHANT	**5**	1	1st PM 5-S 5-E
BRENTLINGER	**7**	1	1st PM 5-S 7-E
BRESAR	**11**	1	1st PM 6-S 6-E
BREWSTER	**14**	1	1st PM 7-S 4-E
BRIGHT	**4**	1	1st PM 5-S 4-E
BRINTLINGER	**7**	1	1st PM 5-S 7-E
BRITLER	**12**	1	1st PM 6-S 7-E
BROADWELL	**4**	3	1st PM 5-S 4-E
BROBST	**7**	1	1st PM 5-S 7-E
BROCK	**5**	3	1st PM 5-S 5-E
" "	**6**	1	1st PM 5-S 6-E
" "	**10**	1	1st PM 6-S 5-E
BRODERICK	**12**	2	1st PM 6-S 7-E
BROWN	**7**	2	1st PM 5-S 7-E
" "	**10**	2	1st PM 6-S 5-E
" "	**3**	1	1st PM 4-S 6-E
" "	**6**	1	1st PM 5-S 6-E
" "	**8**	1	1st PM 5-S 8-E
" "	**11**	1	1st PM 6-S 6-E
BROWNELL	**4**	1	1st PM 5-S 4-E
BRUGGEMAN	**14**	2	1st PM 7-S 4-E
BRUMFIELD	**3**	1	1st PM 4-S 6-E
BRUNE	**14**	2	1st PM 7-S 4-E
BRUNS	**14**	1	1st PM 7-S 4-E
BUB	**5**	1	1st PM 5-S 5-E
BUCHANNAN	**6**	2	1st PM 5-S 6-E
BUCK	**10**	2	1st PM 6-S 5-E
BUCKHART	**12**	1	1st PM 6-S 7-E
BUFENBARGER	**13**	2	1st PM 6-S 8-E
" "	**8**	1	1st PM 5-S 8-E
BUFFENBARGER	**8**	6	1st PM 5-S 8-E
" "	**13**	4	1st PM 6-S 8-E
BUFFINBARGER	**8**	3	1st PM 5-S 8-E
" "	**13**	1	1st PM 6-S 8-E
BULMAHNN	**14**	1	1st PM 7-S 4-E
BULMAHUN	**14**	1	1st PM 7-S 4-E
BUNN	**9**	1	1st PM 6-S 4-E
BURGET	**8**	2	1st PM 5-S 8-E
BURK	**6**	2	1st PM 5-S 6-E
BURKET	**11**	1	1st PM 6-S 6-E
BURTON	**9**	1	1st PM 6-S 4-E
BUSH	**11**	2	1st PM 6-S 6-E
" "	**12**	2	1st PM 6-S 7-E
" "	**4**	1	1st PM 5-S 4-E
BUSSE	**14**	1	1st PM 7-S 4-E
BUTTERWORTH	**6**	1	1st PM 5-S 6-E
" "	**11**	1	1st PM 6-S 6-E
BYENBROOK	**14**	2	1st PM 7-S 4-E
CALBE	**11**	1	1st PM 6-S 6-E
CALDWELL	**8**	1	1st PM 5-S 8-E
" "	**12**	1	1st PM 6-S 7-E
" "	**13**	1	1st PM 6-S 8-E
CALL	**8**	1	1st PM 5-S 8-E
CALLISON	**12**	1	1st PM 6-S 7-E
CAMMON	**14**	1	1st PM 7-S 4-E
CAMPBELL	**5**	3	1st PM 5-S 5-E
" "	**3**	2	1st PM 4-S 6-E

Surname	Map Group	Parcels of Land	Meridian/Township/Range		
CAMPBELL (Cont'd)	**8**	2	1st PM	5-S	8-E
" "	**10**	2	1st PM	6-S	5-E
" "	**12**	1	1st PM	6-S	7-E
CANON	**11**	2	1st PM	6-S	6-E
CAREY	**11**	2	1st PM	6-S	6-E
" "	**10**	1	1st PM	6-S	5-E
" "	**12**	1	1st PM	6-S	7-E
CARL	**5**	1	1st PM	5-S	5-E
CARMEAN	**1**	2	1st PM	4-S	4-E
CARMONY	**7**	2	1st PM	5-S	7-E
CARPER	**9**	1	1st PM	6-S	4-E
CARSWELL	**5**	2	1st PM	5-S	5-E
CARTER	**7**	4	1st PM	5-S	7-E
" "	**9**	1	1st PM	6-S	4-E
CARY	**5**	2	1st PM	5-S	5-E
" "	**6**	1	1st PM	5-S	6-E
CASE	**6**	1	1st PM	5-S	6-E
CASPER	**12**	2	1st PM	6-S	7-E
CASTEEL	**7**	1	1st PM	5-S	7-E
CASTLE	**11**	1	1st PM	6-S	6-E
CATRON	**6**	2	1st PM	5-S	6-E
CATROW	**6**	3	1st PM	5-S	6-E
CAVINDER	**8**	1	1st PM	5-S	8-E
CECIL	**10**	7	1st PM	6-S	5-E
CHAMBERLIN	**5**	4	1st PM	5-S	5-E
" "	**1**	2	1st PM	4-S	4-E
" "	**2**	2	1st PM	4-S	5-E
CHAMBERS	**12**	2	1st PM	6-S	7-E
CHANEY	**6**	3	1st PM	5-S	6-E
" "	**5**	2	1st PM	5-S	5-E
CHATTERTON	**10**	1	1st PM	6-S	5-E
CHILDERS	**11**	1	1st PM	6-S	6-E
CIRCLE	**2**	1	1st PM	4-S	5-E
CIRKLE	**2**	1	1st PM	4-S	5-E
CLARK	**3**	1	1st PM	4-S	6-E
CLAUSON	**5**	1	1st PM	5-S	5-E
CLAWSON	**5**	2	1st PM	5-S	5-E
CLAYTON	**6**	2	1st PM	5-S	6-E
CLEVELAND	**10**	1	1st PM	6-S	5-E
CLEVERSTEIN	**12**	1	1st PM	6-S	7-E
CLINE	**13**	1	1st PM	6-S	8-E
CLOSSON	**5**	1	1st PM	5-S	5-E
COATS	**8**	1	1st PM	5-S	8-E
COCHRAN	**2**	1	1st PM	4-S	5-E
COCHRUN	**1**	1	1st PM	4-S	4-E
CODDINGTON	**13**	1	1st PM	6-S	8-E
COLE	**10**	2	1st PM	6-S	5-E
COLEMAN	**7**	5	1st PM	5-S	7-E
" "	**12**	5	1st PM	6-S	7-E
" "	**8**	1	1st PM	5-S	8-E
" "	**15**	1	1st PM	8-S	4-E
COLGAN	**9**	1	1st PM	6-S	4-E
" "	**12**	1	1st PM	6-S	7-E
COLLIER	**12**	4	1st PM	6-S	7-E
COLLINS	**5**	2	1st PM	5-S	5-E
" "	**9**	2	1st PM	6-S	4-E
COLLISTER	**12**	1	1st PM	6-S	7-E
CONGER	**10**	3	1st PM	6-S	5-E
CONKEL	**3**	1	1st PM	4-S	6-E
CONNELLY	**13**	1	1st PM	6-S	8-E

Surname	Map Group	Parcels of Land	Meridian/Township/Range		
CONNER	7	1	1st PM	5-S	7-E
" "	12	1	1st PM	6-S	7-E
CONOVER	1	4	1st PM	4-S	4-E
CONRAD	6	2	1st PM	5-S	6-E
COOK	6	1	1st PM	5-S	6-E
COOPER	14	1	1st PM	7-S	4-E
COPELAND	12	13	1st PM	6-S	7-E
" "	7	2	1st PM	5-S	7-E
COPSEY	10	2	1st PM	6-S	5-E
CORDER	12	5	1st PM	6-S	7-E
" "	7	1	1st PM	5-S	7-E
CORNELL	14	1	1st PM	7-S	4-E
CORSON	8	2	1st PM	5-S	8-E
" "	13	2	1st PM	6-S	8-E
COTTERL	10	1	1st PM	6-S	5-E
COTTERLIN	14	1	1st PM	7-S	4-E
COUNSELLOR	12	1	1st PM	6-S	7-E
COVER	8	2	1st PM	5-S	8-E
COVERSTONE	10	1	1st PM	6-S	5-E
COVERT	4	1	1st PM	5-S	4-E
COWAN	3	1	1st PM	4-S	6-E
COX	8	2	1st PM	5-S	8-E
COY	12	1	1st PM	6-S	7-E
CRABB	7	1	1st PM	5-S	7-E
CRAFT	11	3	1st PM	6-S	6-E
CRAMER	8	6	1st PM	5-S	8-E
CRAWEL	12	1	1st PM	6-S	7-E
CRAWFORD	6	3	1st PM	5-S	6-E
" "	8	1	1st PM	5-S	8-E
CREIGHTON	4	2	1st PM	5-S	4-E
CREMEEN	5	1	1st PM	5-S	5-E
CRETCHER	7	11	1st PM	5-S	7-E
" "	3	2	1st PM	4-S	6-E
CRISTY	5	1	1st PM	5-S	5-E
CROFT	5	2	1st PM	5-S	5-E
CROSIER	2	2	1st PM	4-S	5-E
CROSS	9	1	1st PM	6-S	4-E
CROWDER	5	1	1st PM	5-S	5-E
CROWEL	12	1	1st PM	6-S	7-E
CROZIER	2	2	1st PM	4-S	5-E
CULP	2	1	1st PM	4-S	5-E
CUMMINGS	11	2	1st PM	6-S	6-E
" "	10	1	1st PM	6-S	5-E
CUMMINS	5	1	1st PM	5-S	5-E
CUNNINGHAM	6	3	1st PM	5-S	6-E
" "	12	1	1st PM	6-S	7-E
CURL	6	1	1st PM	5-S	6-E
CURTIS	10	1	1st PM	6-S	5-E
DARLINGHAUS	14	1	1st PM	7-S	4-E
DARR	6	1	1st PM	5-S	6-E
DARSTON	14	1	1st PM	7-S	4-E
DAVIDSON	8	2	1st PM	5-S	8-E
DAVIS	6	3	1st PM	5-S	6-E
" "	14	2	1st PM	7-S	4-E
" "	3	1	1st PM	4-S	6-E
" "	5	1	1st PM	5-S	5-E
" "	7	1	1st PM	5-S	7-E
DAVISON	12	4	1st PM	6-S	7-E
" "	8	1	1st PM	5-S	8-E
DAVISSON	8	1	1st PM	5-S	8-E

Surname	Map Group	Parcels of Land	Meridian/Township/Range
DAWSON	**8**	9	1st PM 5-S 8-E
DAY	**8**	2	1st PM 5-S 8-E
DEALONG	**3**	1	1st PM 4-S 6-E
DEEMS	**11**	2	1st PM 6-S 6-E
DEIHL	**6**	1	1st PM 5-S 6-E
DEKLAR	**6**	1	1st PM 5-S 6-E
DELANY	**11**	2	1st PM 6-S 6-E
DELONG	**3**	5	1st PM 4-S 6-E
DENISTON	**2**	2	1st PM 4-S 5-E
DENNEY	**4**	7	1st PM 5-S 4-E
DENNY	**4**	1	1st PM 5-S 4-E
DENTON	**13**	1	1st PM 6-S 8-E
DEPRES	**6**	1	1st PM 5-S 6-E
DICK	**11**	1	1st PM 6-S 6-E
DICKMAN	**14**	1	1st PM 7-S 4-E
DIEAHL	**6**	1	1st PM 5-S 6-E
DIEGEL	**10**	2	1st PM 6-S 5-E
DIXON	**8**	1	1st PM 5-S 8-E
DOENYES	**9**	1	1st PM 6-S 4-E
DOHMANN	**14**	1	1st PM 7-S 4-E
DONNEBERG	**14**	1	1st PM 7-S 4-E
DONNEL	**8**	2	1st PM 5-S 8-E
DOSTON	**14**	1	1st PM 7-S 4-E
DOTY	**4**	1	1st PM 5-S 4-E
DOUGHERTY	**3**	1	1st PM 4-S 6-E
DOUNAN	**13**	1	1st PM 6-S 8-E
DOUTE	**4**	2	1st PM 5-S 4-E
" "	**9**	1	1st PM 6-S 4-E
DOUTEE	**9**	3	1st PM 6-S 4-E
DOUTEY	**9**	1	1st PM 6-S 4-E
DOUTY	**9**	1	1st PM 6-S 4-E
DOWTY	**9**	1	1st PM 6-S 4-E
DREES	**14**	2	1st PM 7-S 4-E
DREESE	**15**	1	1st PM 8-S 4-E
DRESHU	**11**	1	1st PM 6-S 6-E
DUMBROFF	**5**	1	1st PM 5-S 5-E
" "	**6**	1	1st PM 5-S 6-E
DUNGAN	**4**	1	1st PM 5-S 4-E
DUNLAP	**12**	2	1st PM 6-S 7-E
DURSTEN	**14**	2	1st PM 7-S 4-E
DYE	**4**	1	1st PM 5-S 4-E
EARL	**13**	1	1st PM 6-S 8-E
EBERD	**14**	1	1st PM 7-S 4-E
EDGE	**7**	4	1st PM 5-S 7-E
EDMISTON	**6**	2	1st PM 5-S 6-E
" "	**7**	2	1st PM 5-S 7-E
ELLEMAN	**14**	1	1st PM 7-S 4-E
ELLERMAN	**14**	5	1st PM 7-S 4-E
ELLERMANN	**14**	4	1st PM 7-S 4-E
ELLIOTT	**11**	12	1st PM 6-S 6-E
" "	**5**	4	1st PM 5-S 5-E
" "	**4**	1	1st PM 5-S 4-E
" "	**6**	1	1st PM 5-S 6-E
" "	**10**	1	1st PM 6-S 5-E
ELLIS	**5**	1	1st PM 5-S 5-E
ELLISON	**12**	1	1st PM 6-S 7-E
ELROD	**12**	1	1st PM 6-S 7-E
ELSAS	**12**	2	1st PM 6-S 7-E
ELSHOF	**10**	1	1st PM 6-S 5-E
ELSWORTH	**8**	3	1st PM 5-S 8-E

Surname	Map Group	Parcels of Land	Meridian/Township/Range
EMERICK	**6**	1	1st PM 5-S 6-E
EMMERT	**6**	1	1st PM 5-S 6-E
ENNEKING	**14**	4	1st PM 7-S 4-E
EPART	**6**	1	1st PM 5-S 6-E
ESCHMEIRE	**10**	2	1st PM 6-S 5-E
ESPY	**4**	2	1st PM 5-S 4-E
" "	**6**	2	1st PM 5-S 6-E
EVERSOLE	**12**	6	1st PM 6-S 7-E
EWEN	**5**	2	1st PM 5-S 5-E
FAIK	**14**	1	1st PM 7-S 4-E
FAIRFIELD	**6**	3	1st PM 5-S 6-E
" "	**11**	1	1st PM 6-S 6-E
FALER	**12**	1	1st PM 6-S 7-E
FALES	**4**	1	1st PM 5-S 4-E
FARIS	**11**	1	1st PM 6-S 6-E
FARNSLER	**10**	3	1st PM 6-S 5-E
FELDMAN	**14**	2	1st PM 7-S 4-E
FELDMANN	**14**	2	1st PM 7-S 4-E
FERRAL	**8**	1	1st PM 5-S 8-E
FERREL	**14**	1	1st PM 7-S 4-E
FETTERS	**12**	1	1st PM 6-S 7-E
FIELD	**14**	1	1st PM 7-S 4-E
FINDLY	**1**	1	1st PM 4-S 4-E
FINLAW	**7**	1	1st PM 5-S 7-E
FISHER	**6**	1	1st PM 5-S 6-E
" "	**10**	1	1st PM 6-S 5-E
" "	**11**	1	1st PM 6-S 6-E
FISHPAW	**4**	1	1st PM 5-S 4-E
FLADERIOHAN	**10**	1	1st PM 6-S 5-E
FLEDDERIOHAN	**9**	2	1st PM 6-S 4-E
" "	**10**	1	1st PM 6-S 5-E
FLEDDERJOHAN	**10**	1	1st PM 6-S 5-E
FLEDDERJOHN	**9**	1	1st PM 6-S 4-E
FLEGAL	**12**	1	1st PM 6-S 7-E
FLEGEL	**12**	1	1st PM 6-S 7-E
FLEMMING	**5**	2	1st PM 5-S 5-E
FLOHR	**14**	1	1st PM 7-S 4-E
FLOWERS	**9**	1	1st PM 6-S 4-E
" "	**10**	1	1st PM 6-S 5-E
FOLKAMPF	**11**	1	1st PM 6-S 6-E
FONKMAN	**14**	1	1st PM 7-S 4-E
FONTS	**11**	1	1st PM 6-S 6-E
FOREMAN	**12**	2	1st PM 6-S 7-E
" "	**6**	1	1st PM 5-S 6-E
FORIS	**11**	1	1st PM 6-S 6-E
FORNEY	**10**	2	1st PM 6-S 5-E
" "	**5**	1	1st PM 5-S 5-E
FORNHOLT	**14**	1	1st PM 7-S 4-E
FORSYTHE	**6**	1	1st PM 5-S 6-E
FOSTER	**6**	1	1st PM 5-S 6-E
" "	**9**	1	1st PM 6-S 4-E
FOULKE	**1**	1	1st PM 4-S 4-E
FOWLER	**6**	1	1st PM 5-S 6-E
FRAME	**10**	1	1st PM 6-S 5-E
FRANKLIN	**9**	2	1st PM 6-S 4-E
FRANKS	**13**	2	1st PM 6-S 8-E
" "	**12**	1	1st PM 6-S 7-E
FRANTS	**11**	1	1st PM 6-S 6-E
FRAZIER	**6**	2	1st PM 5-S 6-E
FREAS	**11**	1	1st PM 6-S 6-E

Surname	Map Group	Parcels of Land	Meridian/Township/Range
FREDERICKS	**14**	1	1st PM 7-S 4-E
FREEMAN	**6**	1	1st PM 5-S 6-E
FREISNER	**5**	1	1st PM 5-S 5-E
FRELING	**14**	1	1st PM 7-S 4-E
FRENCH	**1**	8	1st PM 4-S 4-E
FREYMAN	**5**	1	1st PM 5-S 5-E
FRIEDLINE	**9**	1	1st PM 6-S 4-E
FRISCHE	**10**	3	1st PM 6-S 5-E
FRY	**6**	1	1st PM 5-S 6-E
FULLENKAMP	**14**	1	1st PM 7-S 4-E
FULLER	**10**	3	1st PM 6-S 5-E
FULTON	**3**	1	1st PM 4-S 6-E
FURNOW	**14**	1	1st PM 7-S 4-E
FURROW	**12**	1	1st PM 6-S 7-E
GANT	**8**	1	1st PM 5-S 8-E
GARBERRY	**14**	1	1st PM 7-S 4-E
GARDINER	**6**	3	1st PM 5-S 6-E
GARMIRE	**3**	2	1st PM 4-S 6-E
GARRETSONE	**5**	1	1st PM 5-S 5-E
GAST	**14**	2	1st PM 7-S 4-E
GAULHOUST	**9**	1	1st PM 6-S 4-E
GAUSEPOHL	**14**	2	1st PM 7-S 4-E
GAVER	**6**	1	1st PM 5-S 6-E
GEARHEART	**10**	5	1st PM 6-S 5-E
GEHVERS	**14**	1	1st PM 7-S 4-E
GEIER	**12**	2	1st PM 6-S 7-E
GEISLER	**11**	2	1st PM 6-S 6-E
GEYER	**12**	1	1st PM 6-S 7-E
GHORMLEY	**13**	1	1st PM 6-S 8-E
GIBESON	**12**	1	1st PM 6-S 7-E
GILBERT	**6**	1	1st PM 5-S 6-E
GILROY	**8**	2	1st PM 5-S 8-E
GLASER	**12**	1	1st PM 6-S 7-E
GODDARD	**5**	1	1st PM 5-S 5-E
" "	**6**	1	1st PM 5-S 6-E
GOLDING	**7**	1	1st PM 5-S 7-E
GOODENOW	**3**	1	1st PM 4-S 6-E
GOODSEL	**6**	1	1st PM 5-S 6-E
GORDAN	**12**	1	1st PM 6-S 7-E
GORDON	**9**	3	1st PM 6-S 4-E
" "	**5**	2	1st PM 5-S 5-E
GRABLE	**10**	1	1st PM 6-S 5-E
GRAHAM	**7**	2	1st PM 5-S 7-E
" "	**1**	1	1st PM 4-S 4-E
" "	**12**	1	1st PM 6-S 7-E
GRANER	**6**	1	1st PM 5-S 6-E
GRANT	**4**	2	1st PM 5-S 4-E
GRAY	**13**	4	1st PM 6-S 8-E
" "	**12**	1	1st PM 6-S 7-E
GREBER	**14**	2	1st PM 7-S 4-E
GREEN	**10**	4	1st PM 6-S 5-E
" "	**1**	2	1st PM 4-S 4-E
" "	**5**	1	1st PM 5-S 5-E
GREESHOPF	**14**	1	1st PM 7-S 4-E
GREGORY	**5**	1	1st PM 5-S 5-E
GREIDER	**3**	4	1st PM 4-S 6-E
GRINKEMEYER	**14**	1	1st PM 7-S 4-E
GRIZER	**6**	2	1st PM 5-S 6-E
GRONER	**6**	1	1st PM 5-S 6-E
GROSS	**12**	4	1st PM 6-S 7-E

Surname	Map Group	Parcels of Land	Meridian/Township/Range
GUDORF	**10**	1	1st PM 6-S 5-E
GUTHRIE	**2**	1	1st PM 4-S 5-E
" "	**3**	1	1st PM 4-S 6-E
GUTRIDGE	**6**	2	1st PM 5-S 6-E
GUYER	**12**	1	1st PM 6-S 7-E
HAGY	**7**	1	1st PM 5-S 7-E
HAHN	**12**	2	1st PM 6-S 7-E
HAINES	**10**	2	1st PM 6-S 5-E
" "	**5**	1	1st PM 5-S 5-E
HALL	**9**	2	1st PM 6-S 4-E
" "	**14**	2	1st PM 7-S 4-E
HALLER	**9**	3	1st PM 6-S 4-E
" "	**12**	1	1st PM 6-S 7-E
HAMER	**11**	1	1st PM 6-S 6-E
HAMILTON	**12**	2	1st PM 6-S 7-E
" "	**4**	1	1st PM 5-S 4-E
" "	**11**	1	1st PM 6-S 6-E
HAMMELL	**6**	2	1st PM 5-S 6-E
HANEY	**9**	1	1st PM 6-S 4-E
HANKINS	**10**	1	1st PM 6-S 5-E
HANKS	**13**	2	1st PM 6-S 8-E
HANSER	**6**	1	1st PM 5-S 6-E
HANSFELD	**14**	2	1st PM 7-S 4-E
HARBERT	**8**	1	1st PM 5-S 8-E
HARDEN	**5**	2	1st PM 5-S 5-E
HARDENBROOK	**14**	1	1st PM 7-S 4-E
HARMEL	**11**	1	1st PM 6-S 6-E
HARROD	**7**	13	1st PM 5-S 7-E
" "	**8**	6	1st PM 5-S 8-E
" "	**12**	1	1st PM 6-S 7-E
HARSHBARGER	**5**	2	1st PM 5-S 5-E
HARSHMAN	**11**	1	1st PM 6-S 6-E
HART	**5**	1	1st PM 5-S 5-E
HARTLEY	**12**	2	1st PM 6-S 7-E
HARVEY	**6**	5	1st PM 5-S 6-E
" "	**11**	3	1st PM 6-S 6-E
" "	**5**	1	1st PM 5-S 5-E
" "	**10**	1	1st PM 6-S 5-E
HASKILL	**5**	8	1st PM 5-S 5-E
HATCHER	**6**	1	1st PM 5-S 6-E
HATFIELD	**14**	1	1st PM 7-S 4-E
HATHAWAY	**8**	1	1st PM 5-S 8-E
" "	**12**	1	1st PM 6-S 7-E
HAUKINSON	**12**	1	1st PM 6-S 7-E
HAWTHORN	**5**	1	1st PM 5-S 5-E
" "	**9**	1	1st PM 6-S 4-E
HAWTHORNE	**9**	1	1st PM 6-S 4-E
HAY	**9**	2	1st PM 6-S 4-E
HAYS	**12**	1	1st PM 6-S 7-E
HAYWOOD	**6**	1	1st PM 5-S 6-E
HEADEPOHL	**11**	1	1st PM 6-S 6-E
HEATH	**14**	1	1st PM 7-S 4-E
HEBENSTREIT	**14**	1	1st PM 7-S 4-E
HEIDOCKER	**6**	1	1st PM 5-S 6-E
HEIGHTON	**4**	1	1st PM 5-S 4-E
HEIL	**6**	1	1st PM 5-S 6-E
HEINE	**11**	1	1st PM 6-S 6-E
HELFENSTEIN	**2**	7	1st PM 4-S 5-E
" "	**1**	3	1st PM 4-S 4-E
" "	**8**	1	1st PM 5-S 8-E

Surname	Map Group	Parcels of Land	Meridian/Township/Range
HELINLINGER	**12**	1	1st PM 6-S 7-E
HELM	**9**	3	1st PM 6-S 4-E
HELMINGES	**12**	1	1st PM 6-S 7-E
HELMLENGER	**12**	2	1st PM 6-S 7-E
HELMSING	**14**	1	1st PM 7-S 4-E
HEMMERT	**11**	1	1st PM 6-S 6-E
HENDERSHOT	**8**	1	1st PM 5-S 8-E
HENRICH	**4**	1	1st PM 5-S 4-E
HENRY	**12**	3	1st PM 6-S 7-E
" "	**7**	2	1st PM 5-S 7-E
" "	**8**	1	1st PM 5-S 8-E
HERBST	**12**	2	1st PM 6-S 7-E
HERGENROTHER	**14**	1	1st PM 7-S 4-E
HERMAN	**10**	1	1st PM 6-S 5-E
" "	**11**	1	1st PM 6-S 6-E
HERMES	**10**	1	1st PM 6-S 5-E
HEROFF	**11**	3	1st PM 6-S 6-E
HERTIG	**11**	1	1st PM 6-S 6-E
HERZING	**6**	2	1st PM 5-S 6-E
" "	**2**	1	1st PM 4-S 5-E
" "	**5**	1	1st PM 5-S 5-E
" "	**10**	1	1st PM 6-S 5-E
HESTER	**7**	1	1st PM 5-S 7-E
HEUSCH	**9**	1	1st PM 6-S 4-E
HEYSLER	**11**	2	1st PM 6-S 6-E
HIGHER	**2**	1	1st PM 4-S 5-E
HILLMANN	**14**	1	1st PM 7-S 4-E
HINDEL	**6**	1	1st PM 5-S 6-E
HINDERS	**14**	1	1st PM 7-S 4-E
HINKLE	**9**	5	1st PM 6-S 4-E
HIPPLE	**8**	1	1st PM 5-S 8-E
HITEMAN	**14**	1	1st PM 7-S 4-E
HITTEL	**6**	3	1st PM 5-S 6-E
" "	**10**	2	1st PM 6-S 5-E
" "	**7**	1	1st PM 5-S 7-E
HOBERG	**9**	1	1st PM 6-S 4-E
HODGES	**12**	1	1st PM 6-S 7-E
HOFFMAN	**8**	2	1st PM 5-S 8-E
" "	**7**	1	1st PM 5-S 7-E
HOGE	**10**	1	1st PM 6-S 5-E
HOHNE	**14**	1	1st PM 7-S 4-E
HOLBROOK	**6**	3	1st PM 5-S 6-E
HOLDRIDGE	**9**	3	1st PM 6-S 4-E
HOLLA	**14**	1	1st PM 7-S 4-E
HOLLINGSWORTH	**10**	1	1st PM 6-S 5-E
HOLLY	**8**	5	1st PM 5-S 8-E
HOLSINGER	**11**	1	1st PM 6-S 6-E
HOLTFOCHT	**14**	2	1st PM 7-S 4-E
HOLTZMAN	**3**	1	1st PM 4-S 6-E
HOOK	**9**	1	1st PM 6-S 4-E
HOOPES	**3**	2	1st PM 4-S 6-E
HOOVER	**1**	1	1st PM 4-S 4-E
HORMEL	**4**	1	1st PM 5-S 4-E
HORN	**8**	1	1st PM 5-S 8-E
HORSIMER	**6**	1	1st PM 5-S 6-E
HORTAS	**11**	1	1st PM 6-S 6-E
HOSNIRE	**6**	1	1st PM 5-S 6-E
HOTTES	**11**	1	1st PM 6-S 6-E
HOUCK	**11**	1	1st PM 6-S 6-E
HOUSE	**14**	2	1st PM 7-S 4-E

Surname	Map Group	Parcels of Land	Meridian/Township/Range		
HOUSTON	9	2	1st PM	6-S	4-E
HOVER	5	4	1st PM	5-S	5-E
" "	1	2	1st PM	4-S	4-E
" "	7	2	1st PM	5-S	7-E
" "	6	1	1st PM	5-S	6-E
HOWELL	7	8	1st PM	5-S	7-E
" "	4	1	1st PM	5-S	4-E
" "	5	1	1st PM	5-S	5-E
" "	6	1	1st PM	5-S	6-E
" "	11	1	1st PM	6-S	6-E
" "	12	1	1st PM	6-S	7-E
HUDSON	10	5	1st PM	6-S	5-E
" "	9	1	1st PM	6-S	4-E
HUFFMAN	5	1	1st PM	5-S	5-E
HUGEMAN	14	1	1st PM	7-S	4-E
HUKRIDE	14	1	1st PM	7-S	4-E
HULL	13	2	1st PM	6-S	8-E
HUNT	9	2	1st PM	6-S	4-E
HUNTER	12	1	1st PM	6-S	7-E
HURLEY	8	4	1st PM	5-S	8-E
" "	12	1	1st PM	6-S	7-E
" "	13	1	1st PM	6-S	8-E
HURTLE	14	1	1st PM	7-S	4-E
HUTCHEN	6	1	1st PM	5-S	6-E
HUTSON	10	1	1st PM	6-S	5-E
HUTZLER	11	1	1st PM	6-S	6-E
ICE	4	2	1st PM	5-S	4-E
INGLERIGHT	9	1	1st PM	6-S	4-E
INSKEEP	8	4	1st PM	5-S	8-E
JACKSON	10	1	1st PM	6-S	5-E
" "	11	1	1st PM	6-S	6-E
" "	14	1	1st PM	7-S	4-E
JACOBS	5	1	1st PM	5-S	5-E
" "	6	1	1st PM	5-S	6-E
JAY	4	1	1st PM	5-S	4-E
JEFFERY	4	3	1st PM	5-S	4-E
JEFFREY	4	2	1st PM	5-S	4-E
JEFFRIES	12	3	1st PM	6-S	7-E
JENKINS	6	1	1st PM	5-S	6-E
JETT	13	1	1st PM	6-S	8-E
JIAMS	1	1	1st PM	4-S	4-E
JOHNS	4	5	1st PM	5-S	4-E
JOHNSTON	6	3	1st PM	5-S	6-E
JONES	4	3	1st PM	5-S	4-E
" "	6	2	1st PM	5-S	6-E
" "	1	1	1st PM	4-S	4-E
" "	5	1	1st PM	5-S	5-E
" "	7	1	1st PM	5-S	7-E
JORDAN	14	2	1st PM	7-S	4-E
JOY	8	2	1st PM	5-S	8-E
JUDY	11	1	1st PM	6-S	6-E
JULIAN	10	1	1st PM	6-S	5-E
JULIEN	10	1	1st PM	6-S	5-E
JUSTICE	7	2	1st PM	5-S	7-E
KADIEBERT	11	1	1st PM	6-S	6-E
KAHLER	6	1	1st PM	5-S	6-E
KALLMEIER	10	2	1st PM	6-S	5-E
KATTERHEINRICH	10	2	1st PM	6-S	5-E
KATTERHENRICH	10	1	1st PM	6-S	5-E
KATTMAN	10	2	1st PM	6-S	5-E

Surname	Map Group	Parcels of Land	Meridian/Township/Range
KEAM	**8**	1	1st PM 5-S 8-E
KEENER	**11**	1	1st PM 6-S 6-E
KEEVER	**11**	1	1st PM 6-S 6-E
KELLER	**14**	2	1st PM 7-S 4-E
" "	**5**	1	1st PM 5-S 5-E
" "	**6**	1	1st PM 5-S 6-E
KEMPER	**3**	3	1st PM 4-S 6-E
" "	**2**	1	1st PM 4-S 5-E
KENEDY	**1**	1	1st PM 4-S 4-E
KENEFAK	**5**	1	1st PM 5-S 5-E
KENINGER	**6**	1	1st PM 5-S 6-E
KENT	**7**	4	1st PM 5-S 7-E
" "	**1**	2	1st PM 4-S 4-E
" "	**8**	2	1st PM 5-S 8-E
KENTNER	**11**	2	1st PM 6-S 6-E
" "	**6**	1	1st PM 5-S 6-E
KERNS	**8**	3	1st PM 5-S 8-E
KERR	**5**	1	1st PM 5-S 5-E
" "	**11**	1	1st PM 6-S 6-E
KIESEKAMP	**5**	2	1st PM 5-S 5-E
KINDLE	**13**	2	1st PM 6-S 8-E
KING	**8**	2	1st PM 5-S 8-E
" "	**13**	2	1st PM 6-S 8-E
" "	**12**	1	1st PM 6-S 7-E
KINNING	**9**	1	1st PM 6-S 4-E
KINTNER	**6**	1	1st PM 5-S 6-E
KIRKBRIDE	**7**	2	1st PM 5-S 7-E
KIRKPATRICK	**8**	3	1st PM 5-S 8-E
KISER	**5**	1	1st PM 5-S 5-E
" "	**14**	1	1st PM 7-S 4-E
KITE	**7**	1	1st PM 5-S 7-E
KLATTA	**14**	1	1st PM 7-S 4-E
KLINE	**6**	1	1st PM 5-S 6-E
" "	**8**	1	1st PM 5-S 8-E
" "	**13**	1	1st PM 6-S 8-E
KLIPFEL	**11**	3	1st PM 6-S 6-E
KLOAS	**14**	1	1st PM 7-S 4-E
KLOPF	**11**	2	1st PM 6-S 6-E
KLUE	**6**	1	1st PM 5-S 6-E
KLUIS	**14**	1	1st PM 7-S 4-E
KNARR	**11**	1	1st PM 6-S 6-E
KNECHT	**11**	3	1st PM 6-S 6-E
KNUPKE	**14**	1	1st PM 7-S 4-E
KOCH	**9**	1	1st PM 6-S 4-E
" "	**11**	1	1st PM 6-S 6-E
KOFMAN	**6**	1	1st PM 5-S 6-E
KOKENGE	**14**	1	1st PM 7-S 4-E
KOOK	**10**	1	1st PM 6-S 5-E
KOTTERHEINRICH	**10**	1	1st PM 6-S 5-E
KRAMER	**8**	2	1st PM 5-S 8-E
" "	**14**	1	1st PM 7-S 4-E
KRANER	**12**	2	1st PM 6-S 7-E
KRUSI	**10**	3	1st PM 6-S 5-E
KUCK	**10**	1	1st PM 6-S 5-E
KUHN	**11**	1	1st PM 6-S 6-E
KUNNEG	**9**	1	1st PM 6-S 4-E
KUNNING	**14**	1	1st PM 7-S 4-E
KUPER	**14**	1	1st PM 7-S 4-E
LAMB	**14**	2	1st PM 7-S 4-E
LANDCOMMER	**6**	1	1st PM 5-S 6-E

Surname	Map Group	Parcels of Land	Meridian/Township/Range		
LANDIS	**7**	1	1st PM	5-S	7-E
LANE	**12**	2	1st PM	6-S	7-E
" "	**7**	1	1st PM	5-S	7-E
LANKOM	**6**	1	1st PM	5-S	6-E
LAREW	**9**	1	1st PM	6-S	4-E
LAUER	**6**	1	1st PM	5-S	6-E
LAUGER	**14**	1	1st PM	7-S	4-E
LAURY	**6**	1	1st PM	5-S	6-E
LAYTON	**7**	1	1st PM	5-S	7-E
LEATHERMAN	**6**	2	1st PM	5-S	6-E
" "	**12**	2	1st PM	6-S	7-E
" "	**5**	1	1st PM	5-S	5-E
LEATHERS	**10**	3	1st PM	6-S	5-E
LEBEL	**11**	3	1st PM	6-S	6-E
LEMASTERS	**7**	2	1st PM	5-S	7-E
LEMKOHL	**14**	2	1st PM	7-S	4-E
LENNENEVER	**14**	1	1st PM	7-S	4-E
LENOX	**11**	1	1st PM	6-S	6-E
LEPPERT	**14**	1	1st PM	7-S	4-E
LEVERING	**6**	1	1st PM	5-S	6-E
LEVINGSTON	**8**	1	1st PM	5-S	8-E
LEWIS	**4**	2	1st PM	5-S	4-E
" "	**8**	1	1st PM	5-S	8-E
LIBLING	**6**	2	1st PM	5-S	6-E
LIGHTFOOT	**14**	1	1st PM	7-S	4-E
LINDER	**12**	1	1st PM	6-S	7-E
LINDLEY	**8**	1	1st PM	5-S	8-E
LINING	**14**	2	1st PM	7-S	4-E
LINTCH	**9**	4	1st PM	6-S	4-E
LISLE	**7**	2	1st PM	5-S	7-E
LLOYD	**4**	2	1st PM	5-S	4-E
LOCKART	**12**	1	1st PM	6-S	7-E
LOCKET	**14**	1	1st PM	7-S	4-E
LONG	**11**	1	1st PM	6-S	6-E
LONGWITH	**10**	2	1st PM	6-S	5-E
LONGWORTH	**9**	4	1st PM	6-S	4-E
" "	**10**	1	1st PM	6-S	5-E
LOONEY	**7**	1	1st PM	5-S	7-E
LOWREY	**6**	1	1st PM	5-S	6-E
LOWRY	**6**	1	1st PM	5-S	6-E
LUCAS	**10**	3	1st PM	6-S	5-E
" "	**6**	2	1st PM	5-S	6-E
LUERS	**14**	1	1st PM	7-S	4-E
LURES	**14**	1	1st PM	7-S	4-E
LUSK	**7**	9	1st PM	5-S	7-E
" "	**12**	1	1st PM	6-S	7-E
LUTTERBECK	**9**	1	1st PM	6-S	4-E
" "	**10**	1	1st PM	6-S	5-E
LUTTERBIEN	**10**	1	1st PM	6-S	5-E
LUTTRELL	**10**	1	1st PM	6-S	5-E
LYONS	**11**	1	1st PM	6-S	6-E
MACER	**14**	2	1st PM	7-S	4-E
MACKLIN	**10**	2	1st PM	6-S	5-E
MADDEN	**8**	6	1st PM	5-S	8-E
MAENS	**9**	2	1st PM	6-S	4-E
MAHEN	**8**	2	1st PM	5-S	8-E
MAHIN	**8**	7	1st PM	5-S	8-E
MAJOR	**14**	1	1st PM	7-S	4-E
MAJORS	**14**	2	1st PM	7-S	4-E
" "	**9**	1	1st PM	6-S	4-E

Surname	Map Group	Parcels of Land	Meridian/Township/Range		
MALAIM	**8**	1	1st PM	5-S	8-E
MALCOS	**14**	1	1st PM	7-S	4-E
MANNING	**12**	3	1st PM	6-S	7-E
MARKS	**6**	2	1st PM	5-S	6-E
MARQUIS	**13**	2	1st PM	6-S	8-E
MARSHALL	**5**	4	1st PM	5-S	5-E
" "	**11**	3	1st PM	6-S	6-E
" "	**9**	1	1st PM	6-S	4-E
MARTIN	**12**	2	1st PM	6-S	7-E
" "	**6**	1	1st PM	5-S	6-E
MARTZ	**2**	1	1st PM	4-S	5-E
MARZ	**13**	1	1st PM	6-S	8-E
MASTERS	**8**	1	1st PM	5-S	8-E
MATHENY	**6**	1	1st PM	5-S	6-E
MATHER	**11**	1	1st PM	6-S	6-E
MATHERS	**10**	2	1st PM	6-S	5-E
MCARTHUR	**6**	1	1st PM	5-S	6-E
MCCAHON	**5**	1	1st PM	5-S	5-E
MCCAIN	**4**	1	1st PM	5-S	4-E
MCCARTNEY	**6**	2	1st PM	5-S	6-E
MCCLEAN	**13**	2	1st PM	6-S	8-E
MCCLELLAN	**5**	1	1st PM	5-S	5-E
" "	**10**	1	1st PM	6-S	5-E
MCCONNEL	**5**	1	1st PM	5-S	5-E
MCCONNELL	**1**	3	1st PM	4-S	4-E
MCCORCLE	**9**	4	1st PM	6-S	4-E
MCCORMICK	**7**	1	1st PM	5-S	7-E
MCCOY	**1**	4	1st PM	4-S	4-E
" "	**8**	2	1st PM	5-S	8-E
MCCULLOUGH	**11**	2	1st PM	6-S	6-E
" "	**10**	1	1st PM	6-S	5-E
MCDONALD	**4**	3	1st PM	5-S	4-E
MCFARLAND	**5**	3	1st PM	5-S	5-E
MCGEEHAN	**8**	2	1st PM	5-S	8-E
MCGRADY	**3**	1	1st PM	4-S	6-E
MCINTIRE	**4**	1	1st PM	5-S	4-E
MCKEE	**5**	2	1st PM	5-S	5-E
MCKINNEY	**10**	1	1st PM	6-S	5-E
MCKNIGHT	**13**	2	1st PM	6-S	8-E
" "	**12**	1	1st PM	6-S	7-E
MCLAUGHLIN	**13**	2	1st PM	6-S	8-E
" "	**7**	1	1st PM	5-S	7-E
" "	**8**	1	1st PM	5-S	8-E
MCMILLIN	**11**	1	1st PM	6-S	6-E
" "	**12**	1	1st PM	6-S	7-E
MCNABB	**12**	1	1st PM	6-S	7-E
MCNAMUR	**11**	1	1st PM	6-S	6-E
MCNEIL	**6**	1	1st PM	5-S	6-E
MCPHERON	**8**	1	1st PM	5-S	8-E
MCVEIGH	**10**	1	1st PM	6-S	5-E
MCVICKER	**6**	1	1st PM	5-S	6-E
MEAD	**14**	1	1st PM	7-S	4-E
MEANS	**8**	2	1st PM	5-S	8-E
" "	**6**	1	1st PM	5-S	6-E
MECKSTOTT	**10**	1	1st PM	6-S	5-E
MECKSTROTT	**10**	1	1st PM	6-S	5-E
MEDBERY	**2**	1	1st PM	4-S	5-E
MEDEARIS	**7**	2	1st PM	5-S	7-E
MEFFERD	**12**	1	1st PM	6-S	7-E
MELCHER	**14**	1	1st PM	7-S	4-E

Surname	Map Group	Parcels of Land	Meridian/Township/Range
MELLINGER	**11**	2	1st PM 6-S 6-E
" "	**10**	1	1st PM 6-S 5-E
MESLOH	**14**	1	1st PM 7-S 4-E
MESSER	**9**	1	1st PM 6-S 4-E
METSKER	**14**	1	1st PM 7-S 4-E
MEYER	**14**	2	1st PM 7-S 4-E
MEYERS	**10**	1	1st PM 6-S 5-E
MICHAEL	**12**	2	1st PM 6-S 7-E
" "	**1**	1	1st PM 4-S 4-E
MIDDLEBECKE	**14**	1	1st PM 7-S 4-E
MILES	**8**	1	1st PM 5-S 8-E
MILLER	**6**	7	1st PM 5-S 6-E
" "	**7**	7	1st PM 5-S 7-E
" "	**11**	5	1st PM 6-S 6-E
" "	**14**	5	1st PM 7-S 4-E
" "	**8**	4	1st PM 5-S 8-E
" "	**12**	4	1st PM 6-S 7-E
" "	**5**	3	1st PM 5-S 5-E
" "	**10**	3	1st PM 6-S 5-E
" "	**1**	2	1st PM 4-S 4-E
" "	**2**	1	1st PM 4-S 5-E
" "	**9**	1	1st PM 6-S 4-E
MILLIGAN	**9**	1	1st PM 6-S 4-E
MINK	**12**	1	1st PM 6-S 7-E
MIRING	**14**	1	1st PM 7-S 4-E
MITCHELL	**9**	1	1st PM 6-S 4-E
MITTENDORF	**14**	1	1st PM 7-S 4-E
MITZ	**11**	1	1st PM 6-S 6-E
MIX	**8**	2	1st PM 5-S 8-E
" "	**12**	2	1st PM 6-S 7-E
" "	**7**	1	1st PM 5-S 7-E
MOEKER	**14**	1	1st PM 7-S 4-E
MOFFETT	**6**	2	1st PM 5-S 6-E
MOFFITT	**8**	1	1st PM 5-S 8-E
MOHR	**14**	3	1st PM 7-S 4-E
MOHRMAN	**9**	4	1st PM 6-S 4-E
MOJER	**14**	1	1st PM 7-S 4-E
MOKKARHIDER	**14**	1	1st PM 7-S 4-E
MONEYSMITH	**9**	2	1st PM 6-S 4-E
MONGER	**11**	1	1st PM 6-S 6-E
MONROE	**6**	1	1st PM 5-S 6-E
MONTER	**11**	2	1st PM 6-S 6-E
MOORCRAFT	**13**	1	1st PM 6-S 8-E
MOORE	**12**	5	1st PM 6-S 7-E
" "	**13**	3	1st PM 6-S 8-E
" "	**3**	1	1st PM 4-S 6-E
" "	**6**	1	1st PM 5-S 6-E
MOORMAN	**14**	1	1st PM 7-S 4-E
MOORMANN	**14**	1	1st PM 7-S 4-E
MORECRAFT	**8**	8	1st PM 5-S 8-E
" "	**13**	3	1st PM 6-S 8-E
MOREY	**5**	1	1st PM 5-S 5-E
MORGAN	**4**	1	1st PM 5-S 4-E
" "	**9**	1	1st PM 6-S 4-E
MORRIS	**7**	11	1st PM 5-S 7-E
" "	**8**	6	1st PM 5-S 8-E
" "	**12**	2	1st PM 6-S 7-E
MORROW	**6**	2	1st PM 5-S 6-E
" "	**8**	1	1st PM 5-S 8-E
MORTON	**14**	1	1st PM 7-S 4-E

Surname	Map Group	Parcels of Land	Meridian/Township/Range
MOSLER	**6**	1	1st PM 5-S 6-E
MOUNTS	**1**	1	1st PM 4-S 4-E
MOURER	**14**	1	1st PM 7-S 4-E
MULLER	**10**	2	1st PM 6-S 5-E
" "	**9**	1	1st PM 6-S 4-E
MUNDAY	**5**	2	1st PM 5-S 5-E
MURKER	**14**	1	1st PM 7-S 4-E
MURRAY	**13**	4	1st PM 6-S 8-E
" "	**9**	1	1st PM 6-S 4-E
MURRY	**9**	5	1st PM 6-S 4-E
" "	**4**	1	1st PM 5-S 4-E
MUSSELMAN	**7**	1	1st PM 5-S 7-E
MUSSER	**7**	1	1st PM 5-S 7-E
MYERS	**11**	3	1st PM 6-S 6-E
" "	**8**	1	1st PM 5-S 8-E
NAGLE	**11**	2	1st PM 6-S 6-E
" "	**14**	2	1st PM 7-S 4-E
NASON	**8**	1	1st PM 5-S 8-E
NAUMBURGER	**11**	1	1st PM 6-S 6-E
NEAL	**8**	1	1st PM 5-S 8-E
NEEDLES	**9**	1	1st PM 6-S 4-E
NEESE	**2**	8	1st PM 4-S 5-E
NEITER	**14**	1	1st PM 7-S 4-E
NELSON	**6**	1	1st PM 5-S 6-E
NERR	**11**	1	1st PM 6-S 6-E
NEWMAN	**12**	1	1st PM 6-S 7-E
NICHOLS	**6**	1	1st PM 5-S 6-E
NICKELL	**7**	1	1st PM 5-S 7-E
NIEHING	**9**	1	1st PM 6-S 4-E
NIEMAN	**14**	1	1st PM 7-S 4-E
NIETERT	**11**	1	1st PM 6-S 6-E
NIEWATZ	**9**	1	1st PM 6-S 4-E
NIPGEN	**12**	3	1st PM 6-S 7-E
NIPPGEN	**11**	1	1st PM 6-S 6-E
NOBLE	**1**	7	1st PM 4-S 4-E
" "	**4**	3	1st PM 5-S 4-E
NOGGLE	**10**	1	1st PM 6-S 5-E
NOKEL	**14**	1	1st PM 7-S 4-E
NOLAN	**14**	1	1st PM 7-S 4-E
NOLL	**1**	1	1st PM 4-S 4-E
NOROT	**12**	1	1st PM 6-S 7-E
NORRIS	**6**	1	1st PM 5-S 6-E
NORTH	**8**	2	1st PM 5-S 8-E
NORTON	**9**	1	1st PM 6-S 4-E
NURMEIER	**10**	1	1st PM 6-S 5-E
NUSMEIER	**10**	1	1st PM 6-S 5-E
NUSMEIRE	**10**	1	1st PM 6-S 5-E
NYE	**1**	1	1st PM 4-S 4-E
OAKLEY	**12**	1	1st PM 6-S 7-E
OAR	**7**	1	1st PM 5-S 7-E
OLIPHANT	**7**	1	1st PM 5-S 7-E
OLMAN	**14**	1	1st PM 7-S 4-E
ONERLA	**1**	1	1st PM 4-S 4-E
OPDYCKE	**9**	2	1st PM 6-S 4-E
" "	**14**	2	1st PM 7-S 4-E
OPDYKE	**9**	1	1st PM 6-S 4-E
" "	**14**	1	1st PM 7-S 4-E
ORTH	**10**	1	1st PM 6-S 5-E
ORTMAN	**14**	1	1st PM 7-S 4-E
ORTON	**4**	1	1st PM 5-S 4-E

Surname	Map Group	Parcels of Land	Meridian/Township/Range
OSBORN	4	1	1st PM 5-S 4-E
OSBORNE	8	2	1st PM 5-S 8-E
OSTERLOH	14	4	1st PM 7-S 4-E
OVERHALSER	3	1	1st PM 4-S 6-E
OVERLAY	1	1	1st PM 4-S 4-E
OVERLEY	4	1	1st PM 5-S 4-E
OXLY	12	2	1st PM 6-S 7-E
PAIRO	4	1	1st PM 5-S 4-E
PARLETT	6	1	1st PM 5-S 6-E
PARNELL	5	1	1st PM 5-S 5-E
PATRICK	6	1	1st PM 5-S 6-E
PATTERSON	13	5	1st PM 6-S 8-E
PATTON	10	2	1st PM 6-S 5-E
PAUL	14	1	1st PM 7-S 4-E
PEACHE	11	1	1st PM 6-S 6-E
PENCE	10	4	1st PM 6-S 5-E
PENESON	2	1	1st PM 4-S 5-E
PENING	14	1	1st PM 7-S 4-E
PENNY	4	1	1st PM 5-S 4-E
PETERS	5	1	1st PM 5-S 5-E
PETTIT	1	4	1st PM 4-S 4-E
PETTY	8	1	1st PM 5-S 8-E
PFAFF	6	1	1st PM 5-S 6-E
PHENEGAR	12	1	1st PM 6-S 7-E
PHILLIPS	5	4	1st PM 5-S 5-E
PICKEREL	4	1	1st PM 5-S 4-E
PIERCE	1	2	1st PM 4-S 4-E
" "	8	1	1st PM 5-S 8-E
PITMAN	14	1	1st PM 7-S 4-E
PLACE	2	1	1st PM 4-S 5-E
POLMANN	14	1	1st PM 7-S 4-E
POOL	6	2	1st PM 5-S 6-E
PORTER	7	2	1st PM 5-S 7-E
POST	6	1	1st PM 5-S 6-E
POWELL	11	2	1st PM 6-S 6-E
" "	7	1	1st PM 5-S 7-E
" "	10	1	1st PM 6-S 5-E
PRATT	4	4	1st PM 5-S 4-E
" "	8	1	1st PM 5-S 8-E
PRICTCHARD	7	1	1st PM 5-S 7-E
PRIMMER	5	1	1st PM 5-S 5-E
PRITCHARD	5	1	1st PM 5-S 5-E
PURCELL	12	1	1st PM 6-S 7-E
QURTMAN	14	1	1st PM 7-S 4-E
RAIN	5	1	1st PM 5-S 5-E
RAMSEY	14	1	1st PM 7-S 4-E
RASH	12	1	1st PM 6-S 7-E
RATHBURN	5	1	1st PM 5-S 5-E
REABURN	8	1	1st PM 5-S 8-E
REAMES	13	2	1st PM 6-S 8-E
REED	12	4	1st PM 6-S 7-E
" "	11	1	1st PM 6-S 6-E
REES	8	1	1st PM 5-S 8-E
REKEL	14	1	1st PM 7-S 4-E
RHODES	8	1	1st PM 5-S 8-E
RICE	5	1	1st PM 5-S 5-E
RICHARDSON	2	4	1st PM 4-S 5-E
" "	7	3	1st PM 5-S 7-E
" "	12	3	1st PM 6-S 7-E
" "	6	1	1st PM 5-S 6-E

Surname	Map Group	Parcels of Land	Meridian/Township/Range		
RIDLEY	**8**	2	1st PM	5-S	8-E
RIEMAN	**7**	1	1st PM	5-S	7-E
RILEY	**4**	1	1st PM	5-S	4-E
RINEHART	**12**	4	1st PM	6-S	7-E
RINGER	**5**	4	1st PM	5-S	5-E
RISBARGER	**11**	1	1st PM	6-S	6-E
RITCHEY	**6**	1	1st PM	5-S	6-E
RITTER	**10**	2	1st PM	6-S	5-E
ROACH	**2**	1	1st PM	4-S	5-E
ROBERTS	**10**	3	1st PM	6-S	5-E
ROBINS	**1**	2	1st PM	4-S	4-E
ROBINSON	**8**	7	1st PM	5-S	8-E
ROCK	**12**	4	1st PM	6-S	7-E
RODEKORTH	**14**	1	1st PM	7-S	4-E
ROELLE	**6**	1	1st PM	5-S	6-E
ROFLES	**14**	2	1st PM	7-S	4-E
ROGERS	**7**	1	1st PM	5-S	7-E
\\ "	**12**	1	1st PM	6-S	7-E
ROHENKOHL	**14**	1	1st PM	7-S	4-E
ROLFES	**15**	2	1st PM	8-S	4-E
ROLLINS	**11**	1	1st PM	6-S	6-E
RONEY	**6**	4	1st PM	5-S	6-E
ROOF	**14**	4	1st PM	7-S	4-E
ROOTS	**14**	1	1st PM	7-S	4-E
ROSS	**5**	1	1st PM	5-S	5-E
\\ "	**6**	1	1st PM	5-S	6-E
\\ "	**8**	1	1st PM	5-S	8-E
\\ "	**9**	1	1st PM	6-S	4-E
\\ "	**11**	1	1st PM	6-S	6-E
ROSTORFER	**12**	1	1st PM	6-S	7-E
ROTH	**11**	3	1st PM	6-S	6-E
ROTT	**12**	1	1st PM	6-S	7-E
ROUCH	**11**	1	1st PM	6-S	6-E
RUMAN	**7**	1	1st PM	5-S	7-E
RUNKLE	**12**	2	1st PM	6-S	7-E
RUNYAN	**12**	1	1st PM	6-S	7-E
RUNYON	**2**	1	1st PM	4-S	5-E
RUSSEL	**2**	3	1st PM	4-S	5-E
RUSSELL	**2**	1	1st PM	4-S	5-E
\\ "	**9**	1	1st PM	6-S	4-E
RYAN	**10**	3	1st PM	6-S	5-E
RYASON	**6**	2	1st PM	5-S	6-E
SACKETT	**14**	1	1st PM	7-S	4-E
SAMMETINGER	**11**	1	1st PM	6-S	6-E
SAMSON	**1**	2	1st PM	4-S	4-E
\\ "	**4**	1	1st PM	5-S	4-E
SATTERTHWAIT	**6**	1	1st PM	5-S	6-E
SAUM	**10**	2	1st PM	6-S	5-E
SAVIN	**6**	1	1st PM	5-S	6-E
SAWYER	**4**	2	1st PM	5-S	4-E
\\ "	**6**	2	1st PM	5-S	6-E
SCHAMMEL	**14**	1	1st PM	7-S	4-E
SCHARDELMANN	**14**	1	1st PM	7-S	4-E
SCHAUL	**11**	1	1st PM	6-S	6-E
SCHEMMEL	**11**	3	1st PM	6-S	6-E
SCHLICHTIG	**12**	1	1st PM	6-S	7-E
SCHLOSSER	**7**	2	1st PM	5-S	7-E
SCHOOLER	**7**	3	1st PM	5-S	7-E
\\ "	**8**	2	1st PM	5-S	8-E
SCHOULTE	**14**	1	1st PM	7-S	4-E

Surname	Map Group	Parcels of Land	Meridian/Township/Range		
SCHRER	**10**	3	1st PM	6-S	5-E
SCHROEDER	**14**	5	1st PM	7-S	4-E
SCHULZE	**14**	1	1st PM	7-S	4-E
SCHURE	**11**	1	1st PM	6-S	6-E
SCHWEINEFUSZ	**14**	1	1st PM	7-S	4-E
SCHWENKE	**9**	1	1st PM	6-S	4-E
SCOTT	**9**	7	1st PM	6-S	4-E
SEAMAR	**14**	2	1st PM	7-S	4-E
SEITER	**11**	2	1st PM	6-S	6-E
" "	**12**	2	1st PM	6-S	7-E
SEIVERT	**11**	1	1st PM	6-S	6-E
SELVY	**6**	1	1st PM	5-S	6-E
SERGES	**14**	1	1st PM	7-S	4-E
SESSIONS	**1**	1	1st PM	4-S	4-E
SHAEFFER	**6**	1	1st PM	5-S	6-E
" "	**11**	1	1st PM	6-S	6-E
SHAFER	**2**	1	1st PM	4-S	5-E
SHAFFER	**2**	4	1st PM	4-S	5-E
SHARER	**6**	1	1st PM	5-S	6-E
SHAUL	**13**	3	1st PM	6-S	8-E
SHAW	**6**	2	1st PM	5-S	6-E
" "	**7**	1	1st PM	5-S	7-E
" "	**8**	1	1st PM	5-S	8-E
SHEETS	**1**	2	1st PM	4-S	4-E
SHELBY	**7**	1	1st PM	5-S	7-E
" "	**12**	1	1st PM	6-S	7-E
SHELMITTER	**14**	2	1st PM	7-S	4-E
SHEPHERD	**9**	1	1st PM	6-S	4-E
" "	**12**	1	1st PM	6-S	7-E
SHEPPER	**14**	1	1st PM	7-S	4-E
SHERIDEN	**10**	1	1st PM	6-S	5-E
SHERMER	**11**	3	1st PM	6-S	6-E
SHIGLEY	**8**	1	1st PM	5-S	8-E
SHINN	**10**	1	1st PM	6-S	5-E
SHIRDEN	**10**	1	1st PM	6-S	5-E
SHOCKEY	**7**	2	1st PM	5-S	7-E
SHREDER	**6**	2	1st PM	5-S	6-E
SHULENBARG	**14**	1	1st PM	7-S	4-E
SHULL	**11**	1	1st PM	6-S	6-E
SIDES	**11**	1	1st PM	6-S	6-E
SIFORT	**11**	1	1st PM	6-S	6-E
SILLIN	**5**	1	1st PM	5-S	5-E
SIMES	**9**	1	1st PM	6-S	4-E
SKILLINGS	**13**	2	1st PM	6-S	8-E
SKILLMAN	**7**	1	1st PM	5-S	7-E
" "	**12**	1	1st PM	6-S	7-E
SKINNER	**6**	9	1st PM	5-S	6-E
" "	**5**	4	1st PM	5-S	5-E
" "	**7**	3	1st PM	5-S	7-E
SLATER	**5**	1	1st PM	5-S	5-E
" "	**7**	1	1st PM	5-S	7-E
SLOSS	**7**	1	1st PM	5-S	7-E
SMITH	**9**	12	1st PM	6-S	4-E
" "	**6**	7	1st PM	5-S	6-E
" "	**8**	2	1st PM	5-S	8-E
" "	**12**	2	1st PM	6-S	7-E
" "	**13**	2	1st PM	6-S	8-E
" "	**4**	1	1st PM	5-S	4-E
" "	**5**	1	1st PM	5-S	5-E
" "	**14**	1	1st PM	7-S	4-E

Surname	Map Group	Parcels of Land	Meridian/Township/Range
SNAVELY	**11**	1	1st PM 6-S 6-E
SNELLER	**10**	1	1st PM 6-S 5-E
SNIDER	**11**	2	1st PM 6-S 6-E
" "	**12**	1	1st PM 6-S 7-E
SNYDER	**11**	2	1st PM 6-S 6-E
SOLLMAN	**14**	3	1st PM 7-S 4-E
SOLMON	**14**	1	1st PM 7-S 4-E
SOURMANN	**14**	2	1st PM 7-S 4-E
SPALDING	**6**	1	1st PM 5-S 6-E
SPEES	**7**	6	1st PM 5-S 7-E
SPRAY	**11**	3	1st PM 6-S 6-E
" "	**10**	1	1st PM 6-S 5-E
SPREHEE	**14**	1	1st PM 7-S 4-E
SPROUL	**8**	3	1st PM 5-S 8-E
SPURRIER	**11**	2	1st PM 6-S 6-E
" "	**6**	1	1st PM 5-S 6-E
STALLO	**14**	9	1st PM 7-S 4-E
STARKEY	**8**	1	1st PM 5-S 8-E
STARRET	**13**	1	1st PM 6-S 8-E
STARRETT	**13**	1	1st PM 6-S 8-E
STATLER	**9**	2	1st PM 6-S 4-E
" "	**14**	2	1st PM 7-S 4-E
" "	**10**	1	1st PM 6-S 5-E
STAUTHITE	**9**	2	1st PM 6-S 4-E
STEBLETON	**3**	1	1st PM 4-S 6-E
STEEN	**9**	2	1st PM 6-S 4-E
STEINEMAN	**15**	1	1st PM 8-S 4-E
STEINEMANN	**14**	1	1st PM 7-S 4-E
STEINMANN	**14**	1	1st PM 7-S 4-E
STELTZER	**14**	2	1st PM 7-S 4-E
STEVENS	**6**	1	1st PM 5-S 6-E
" "	**7**	1	1st PM 5-S 7-E
" "	**11**	1	1st PM 6-S 6-E
STEWART	**8**	1	1st PM 5-S 8-E
STILES	**7**	3	1st PM 5-S 7-E
" "	**12**	1	1st PM 6-S 7-E
STILL	**5**	1	1st PM 5-S 5-E
STILLNAG	**10**	1	1st PM 6-S 5-E
STINE	**14**	1	1st PM 7-S 4-E
STOCKDALE	**11**	2	1st PM 6-S 6-E
STOCKER	**9**	1	1st PM 6-S 4-E
STODDARD	**5**	12	1st PM 5-S 5-E
" "	**6**	10	1st PM 5-S 6-E
" "	**7**	7	1st PM 5-S 7-E
" "	**12**	2	1st PM 6-S 7-E
" "	**2**	1	1st PM 4-S 5-E
" "	**11**	1	1st PM 6-S 6-E
STOKER	**9**	4	1st PM 6-S 4-E
STONEROCK	**4**	2	1st PM 5-S 4-E
STORCK	**14**	2	1st PM 7-S 4-E
STORTS	**2**	2	1st PM 4-S 5-E
STOUT	**9**	3	1st PM 6-S 4-E
STRASBURG	**9**	3	1st PM 6-S 4-E
STRAWSBURG	**12**	2	1st PM 6-S 7-E
STRICKER	**6**	1	1st PM 5-S 6-E
STRICKLE	**6**	1	1st PM 5-S 6-E
STRICKLER	**12**	1	1st PM 6-S 7-E
STROH	**10**	3	1st PM 6-S 5-E
STUBBE	**14**	1	1st PM 7-S 4-E
STUBBS	**9**	1	1st PM 6-S 4-E

Surname	Map Group	Parcels of Land	Meridian/Township/Range
STUDEBAKER	7	1	1st PM 5-S 7-E
STUKEY	2	1	1st PM 4-S 5-E
STURGEON	9	1	1st PM 6-S 4-E
SULLIVAN	4	2	1st PM 5-S 4-E
" "	5	2	1st PM 5-S 5-E
SUNDERLAND	14	2	1st PM 7-S 4-E
" "	2	1	1st PM 4-S 5-E
" "	4	1	1st PM 5-S 4-E
SURMANN	14	1	1st PM 7-S 4-E
SUTER	11	1	1st PM 6-S 6-E
SUTTON	2	1	1st PM 4-S 5-E
" "	4	1	1st PM 5-S 4-E
SWEARINGEN	11	2	1st PM 6-S 6-E
SWICKARD	12	3	1st PM 6-S 7-E
SWINEHART	3	3	1st PM 4-S 6-E
SWISHER	7	1	1st PM 5-S 7-E
TABA	14	1	1st PM 7-S 4-E
TAFE	4	1	1st PM 5-S 4-E
TAM	6	4	1st PM 5-S 6-E
TAMPLETON	8	2	1st PM 5-S 8-E
TANGEMANN	14	1	1st PM 7-S 4-E
TAUBEN	14	2	1st PM 7-S 4-E
TAYLOR	2	2	1st PM 4-S 5-E
" "	11	2	1st PM 6-S 6-E
TEMPLETON	6	2	1st PM 5-S 6-E
TERWILLEGER	5	2	1st PM 5-S 5-E
TERWILLIGER	5	2	1st PM 5-S 5-E
THAYER	8	1	1st PM 5-S 8-E
THERSTICKER	12	1	1st PM 6-S 7-E
THIMANN	14	2	1st PM 7-S 4-E
THOMAS	8	3	1st PM 5-S 8-E
" "	6	1	1st PM 5-S 6-E
THORN	5	2	1st PM 5-S 5-E
THROCKMORTON	6	1	1st PM 5-S 6-E
TINDALL	4	1	1st PM 5-S 4-E
TINGLE	6	1	1st PM 5-S 6-E
TIPPIE	1	4	1st PM 4-S 4-E
TOBIAS	11	5	1st PM 6-S 6-E
" "	10	2	1st PM 6-S 5-E
" "	4	1	1st PM 5-S 4-E
" "	12	1	1st PM 6-S 7-E
TODD	11	1	1st PM 6-S 6-E
TOLMAN	8	3	1st PM 5-S 8-E
TOMAN	14	1	1st PM 7-S 4-E
TOMON	14	1	1st PM 7-S 4-E
TONG	12	1	1st PM 6-S 7-E
TONGAMAN	9	1	1st PM 6-S 4-E
" "	14	1	1st PM 7-S 4-E
TREBEIN	11	2	1st PM 6-S 6-E
TRESHER	12	1	1st PM 6-S 7-E
TRINT	13	1	1st PM 6-S 8-E
TROYER	3	1	1st PM 4-S 6-E
TRUMBO	12	1	1st PM 6-S 7-E
TUCKER	10	2	1st PM 6-S 5-E
" "	14	1	1st PM 7-S 4-E
TUNEMANN	14	1	1st PM 7-S 4-E
TUPP	14	1	1st PM 7-S 4-E
TURNER	8	3	1st PM 5-S 8-E
TYRRELL	4	1	1st PM 5-S 4-E
UPTON	1	2	1st PM 4-S 4-E

Surname	Map Group	Parcels of Land	Meridian/Township/Range
VAN ANTWERP	**11**	2	1st PM 6-S 6-E
VAN BLARACOM	**11**	3	1st PM 6-S 6-E
" "	**6**	1	1st PM 5-S 6-E
VAN BLARICOM	**11**	1	1st PM 6-S 6-E
VAN GUNDY	**1**	1	1st PM 4-S 4-E
VAN HORNE	**11**	11	1st PM 6-S 6-E
" "	**6**	9	1st PM 5-S 6-E
" "	**5**	3	1st PM 5-S 5-E
VAN NORTWICK	**5**	1	1st PM 5-S 5-E
VAN NUYS	**4**	1	1st PM 5-S 4-E
VANARSDAL	**4**	2	1st PM 5-S 4-E
VANCE	**10**	1	1st PM 6-S 5-E
VANDERVEER	**10**	4	1st PM 6-S 5-E
VANFLEET	**7**	2	1st PM 5-S 7-E
VANNUYS	**4**	1	1st PM 5-S 4-E
VAUGHAN	**7**	3	1st PM 5-S 7-E
VEHORN	**14**	1	1st PM 7-S 4-E
VENNEMANN	**10**	3	1st PM 6-S 5-E
VERTH	**11**	1	1st PM 6-S 6-E
VICKER	**6**	1	1st PM 5-S 6-E
VINSON	**9**	2	1st PM 6-S 4-E
VINTER	**14**	1	1st PM 7-S 4-E
VOEGE	**9**	1	1st PM 6-S 4-E
VOLL	**11**	1	1st PM 6-S 6-E
VOORHIS	**14**	2	1st PM 7-S 4-E
" "	**11**	1	1st PM 6-S 6-E
WAGGONER	**11**	2	1st PM 6-S 6-E
WAITE	**7**	2	1st PM 5-S 7-E
" "	**5**	1	1st PM 5-S 5-E
WALCK	**12**	1	1st PM 6-S 7-E
WALKE	**14**	1	1st PM 7-S 4-E
WALKER	**5**	3	1st PM 5-S 5-E
WALLACE	**14**	1	1st PM 7-S 4-E
WALTER	**5**	3	1st PM 5-S 5-E
WALTON	**7**	1	1st PM 5-S 7-E
WARLING	**12**	1	1st PM 6-S 7-E
WATERS	**9**	2	1st PM 6-S 4-E
WATKIN	**9**	1	1st PM 6-S 4-E
WATSON	**13**	1	1st PM 6-S 8-E
WATT	**12**	2	1st PM 6-S 7-E
" "	**7**	1	1st PM 5-S 7-E
WATTON	**7**	1	1st PM 5-S 7-E
WAYMIRE	**11**	2	1st PM 6-S 6-E
WAYNER	**11**	2	1st PM 6-S 6-E
WEAVER	**5**	2	1st PM 5-S 5-E
" "	**2**	1	1st PM 4-S 5-E
" "	**13**	1	1st PM 6-S 8-E
WEIMART	**12**	1	1st PM 6-S 7-E
WELDEHR	**14**	2	1st PM 7-S 4-E
WELDELN	**14**	1	1st PM 7-S 4-E
WELLER	**10**	2	1st PM 6-S 5-E
WELLMAN	**10**	4	1st PM 6-S 5-E
" "	**14**	2	1st PM 7-S 4-E
WELLMANN	**14**	1	1st PM 7-S 4-E
WELLS	**8**	3	1st PM 5-S 8-E
" "	**4**	1	1st PM 5-S 4-E
WELTY	**4**	1	1st PM 5-S 4-E
WERST	**12**	2	1st PM 6-S 7-E
" "	**11**	1	1st PM 6-S 6-E
WESJOHN	**14**	1	1st PM 7-S 4-E

Surname	Map Group	Parcels of Land	Meridian/Township/Range		
WEST	**5**	2	1st PM	5-S	5-E
WETSTONE	**12**	1	1st PM	6-S	7-E
WETTERER	**14**	1	1st PM	7-S	4-E
WHEATLAND	**1**	1	1st PM	4-S	4-E
WHEELER	**6**	7	1st PM	5-S	6-E
" "	**5**	2	1st PM	5-S	5-E
WHETSTONE	**2**	5	1st PM	4-S	5-E
" "	**5**	1	1st PM	5-S	5-E
" "	**8**	1	1st PM	5-S	8-E
" "	**12**	1	1st PM	6-S	7-E
WICHER	**14**	1	1st PM	7-S	4-E
WICHMANN	**14**	1	1st PM	7-S	4-E
WICKMAN	**14**	1	1st PM	7-S	4-E
WIEMEYER	**14**	1	1st PM	7-S	4-E
WIENNER	**14**	1	1st PM	7-S	4-E
WIERWILLE	**9**	1	1st PM	6-S	4-E
WILCOX	**8**	2	1st PM	5-S	8-E
WILDENBREW	**9**	1	1st PM	6-S	4-E
WILDS	**6**	11	1st PM	5-S	6-E
WILEY	**10**	2	1st PM	6-S	5-E
WILHELM	**11**	1	1st PM	6-S	6-E
WILKINS	**9**	6	1st PM	6-S	4-E
" "	**10**	2	1st PM	6-S	5-E
WILLIAMS	**5**	6	1st PM	5-S	5-E
" "	**6**	6	1st PM	5-S	6-E
" "	**8**	6	1st PM	5-S	8-E
" "	**12**	3	1st PM	6-S	7-E
" "	**13**	3	1st PM	6-S	8-E
" "	**4**	2	1st PM	5-S	4-E
" "	**7**	1	1st PM	5-S	7-E
" "	**9**	1	1st PM	6-S	4-E
" "	**11**	1	1st PM	6-S	6-E
WILSON	**5**	2	1st PM	5-S	5-E
" "	**3**	1	1st PM	4-S	6-E
" "	**12**	1	1st PM	6-S	7-E
WIMERT	**6**	1	1st PM	5-S	6-E
" "	**11**	1	1st PM	6-S	6-E
WINDELER	**14**	1	1st PM	7-S	4-E
WINGET	**6**	1	1st PM	5-S	6-E
WINTHORT	**14**	1	1st PM	7-S	4-E
WISE	**11**	1	1st PM	6-S	6-E
WISS	**12**	2	1st PM	6-S	7-E
WITHAM	**8**	3	1st PM	5-S	8-E
WOOD	**6**	2	1st PM	5-S	6-E
" "	**4**	1	1st PM	5-S	4-E
WOODBURY	**8**	2	1st PM	5-S	8-E
WOODRUFF	**10**	4	1st PM	6-S	5-E
WORMANN	**14**	2	1st PM	7-S	4-E
WRIGHT	**6**	2	1st PM	5-S	6-E
" "	**12**	2	1st PM	6-S	7-E
WULF	**6**	1	1st PM	5-S	6-E
WUPPENHARST	**9**	1	1st PM	6-S	4-E
" "	**14**	1	1st PM	7-S	4-E
WYLAND	**4**	3	1st PM	5-S	4-E
YOAKAM	**2**	1	1st PM	4-S	5-E
YORK	**10**	1	1st PM	6-S	5-E
YOSTING	**12**	1	1st PM	6-S	7-E
YOUNG	**4**	2	1st PM	5-S	4-E
" "	**10**	2	1st PM	6-S	5-E
" "	**6**	1	1st PM	5-S	6-E

Surname	Map Group	Parcels of Land	Meridian/Township/Range
YOUNKER	**14**	1	1st PM 7-S 4-E
ZANGLEIN	**11**	2	1st PM 6-S 6-E
ZEHNER	**8**	2	1st PM 5-S 8-E
" "	**7**	1	1st PM 5-S 7-E
ZINK	**6**	1	1st PM 5-S 6-E
ZINN	**6**	1	1st PM 5-S 6-E

– Part II –

Township Map Groups

Map Group 1: Index to Land Patents

Township 4-South Range 4-East (1st PM)

After you locate an individual in this Index, take note of the Section and Section Part then proceed to the Land Patent map on the pages immediately following. You should have no difficulty locating the corresponding parcel of land.

The "For More Info" Column will lead you to more information about the underlying Patents. See the Legend at right, and the "How to Use this Book" chapter, for more information.

```
                        LEGEND
              "For More Info . . . " column
A = Authority (Legislative Act, See Appendix "A")
B = Block or Lot (location in Section unknown)
C = Cancelled Patent
F = Fractional Section
G = Group  (Multi-Patentee Patent, see Appendix "C")
V = Overlaps another Parcel
R = Re-Issued (Parcel patented more than once)

(A & G items require you to look in the Appendixes referred
to above. All other Letter-designations followed by a number
require you to locate line-items in this index that possess
the ID number found after the letter).
```

ID	Individual in Patent	Sec.	Sec. Part	Date Issued	Other Counties	For More Info . . .
17	ADGATE, Charles H	20	NW	1837-03-20		A1
37	BEEM, John A	33	E½SW	1852-06-01		A1
33	CARMEAN, James	25	E½SE	1849-02-01		A1
34	" "	25	SENE	1849-02-01		A1
66	CHAMBERLIN, Thomas T	25	SENW	1848-06-01		A1
65	" "	25	NENW	1848-08-01		A1
38	COCHRUN, John	35	NE	1835-04-09		A1 F
1	CONOVER, Alexander G	23	E½NW	1846-10-01		A1
3	" "	23	W½NW	1846-10-01		A1
2	" "	23	N½SW	1846-11-05		A1
4	" "	23	W½SE	1850-07-01		A1
69	FINDLY, William	27	N½NE	1850-07-01		A1
59	FOULKE, Theophilus	35	W½SW	1852-06-01		A1 F
11	FRENCH, Asa	29	S½S½	1835-09-15		A1 F
10	" "	29	NWSE	1837-03-16		A1
12	" "	29	SWNE	1837-03-16		A1
19	FRENCH, Daniel	32	N½NW	1835-09-15		A1 F
21	FRENCH, David C	32	W½NW	1835-09-15		A1 F
20	" "	31	E½NE	1837-03-15		A1
25	FRENCH, Ezekiel	31	E½NW	1837-03-16		A1 F
31	FRENCH, Isaac	32	NWSW	1836-02-15		A1
29	GRAHAM, Henring	31	SWNE	1837-03-20		A1
70	GREEN, William	19	S½	1837-03-18		A1
71	" "	29	NW	1837-03-18		A1
49	HELFENSTEIN, Mary	29	SENE	1837-03-16		A1 F R68
51	" "	32	N½NE	1837-03-16		A1 F
50	" "	32	E½NE	1840-11-10		A1 F
26	HOOVER, Ezekiel	21	S½	1837-03-18		A1
27	HOVER, Ezekiel	19	NW	1837-03-20		A1
45	HOVER, Joseph	20	NE	1837-03-18		A1
39	JIAMS, John	20	SW	1837-03-18		A1
13	JONES, Austin	31	SW	1837-03-20		A1
63	KENEDY, Thomas	19	NE	1837-03-18		A1
77	KENT, Zardus	21	NW	1837-03-18		A1
78	KENT, Zeno	21	NE	1837-03-18		A1
60	MCCONNELL, Thomas J	23	E½NE	1846-10-01		A1
62	" "	23	W½NE	1846-10-01		A1
61	" "	23	E½SE	1846-11-05		A1
5	MCCOY, Alexander	27	S½SE	1851-02-01		A1
6	" "	27	SENW	1853-06-01		A1
40	MCCOY, John	27	NESE	1850-07-01		A1
41	" "	27	S½NE	1850-07-01		A1
9	MICHAEL, Andrew	31	W½NW	1837-03-16		A1
16	MILLER, Branson J	35	E½NW	1835-10-09		A1 F
15	" "	20	SE	1837-03-18		A1
46	MOUNTS, Joseph	33	SESE	1853-06-01		A1

ID	Individual in Patent	Sec.	Sec. Part	Date Issued	Other Counties	For More Info . . .
14	NOBLE, Benjamin	33	NESE	1852-06-01		A1
18	NOBLE, Charles	32	W½NE	1837-03-16		A1 F
23	NOBLE, Elisha	32	E½NW	1837-03-16		A1 F
24	" "	32	E½SE	1837-03-18		A1
42	NOBLE, John	29	W½SW	1837-03-16		A1 F
43	" "	32	W½SE	1837-03-18		A1
48	NOBLE, Leonard	33	W½SW	1852-06-01		A1
28	NOLL, George	25	NWNE	1849-02-01		A1
53	NYE, Nathan	25	SWSW	1848-08-01		A1
76	ONERLA, Zacharias	32	SWSW	1837-03-20		A1
72	OVERLAY, William	32	E½SW	1835-12-24		A1
55	PETTIT, Samuel	25	E½SW	1846-10-01		A1
57	" "	25	W½SE	1846-10-01		A1
56	" "	25	NWNW	1850-07-01		A1
58	" "	35	SE	1850-07-01		A1 F
47	PIERCE, Joseph	25	SWNE	1848-08-01		A1
64	PIERCE, Thomas	35	E½SW	1849-02-01		A1 F
35	ROBINS, James	29	N½NE	1837-03-18		A1
36	" "	29	NESW	1837-03-18		A1 F
7	SAMSON, Amos	35	NW	1835-10-09		A1 F
8	" "	35	SW	1835-10-09		A1 F
30	SESSIONS, Horace	33	N½	1856-03-10		A1 F
22	SHEETS, David	31	SE	1837-03-20		A1
44	SHEETS, John P	23	S½SW	1850-07-01		A1
52	TIPPIE, Michael	36	SWNW	1835-10-08		A1
73	TIPPIE, William	25	NENE	1848-08-01		A1
74	" "	25	NWSW	1849-02-01		A1
75	" "	25	SWNW	1850-07-01		A1
67	UPTON, Thomas	29	NES½	1835-10-07		A1 F
68	" "	29	SENE	1835-10-07		A1 R49
32	VAN GUNDY, JACOB	29	SWSW	1835-10-09		A1
54	WHEATLAND, Phebe	31	NWNE	1837-03-16		A1

Patent Map

T4-S R4-E
1st PM Meridian

Map Group 1

Township Statistics

Parcels Mapped	:	78
Number of Patents	:	74
Number of Individuals	:	52
Patentees Identified	:	52
Number of Surnames	:	38
Multi-Patentee Parcels	:	0
Oldest Patent Date	:	4/9/1835
Most Recent Patent	:	3/10/1856
Block/Lot Parcels	:	1
Parcels Re - Issued	:	1
Parcels that Overlap	:	0
Cities and Towns	:	1
Cemeteries	:	4

Note: the area contained in this map amounts to far less than a full Township. Therefore, its contents are completely on this single page (instead of a "normal" 2-page spread).

Legend

— Patent Boundary

— Section Boundary

No Patents Found (or Outside County)

1., 2., 3., ... Lot Numbers (when beside a name)

[ ] Group Number (see Appendix "C")

Scale: Section = 1 mile X 1 mile (generally, with some exceptions)

N

Van Wert County

Auglaize County

Allen County

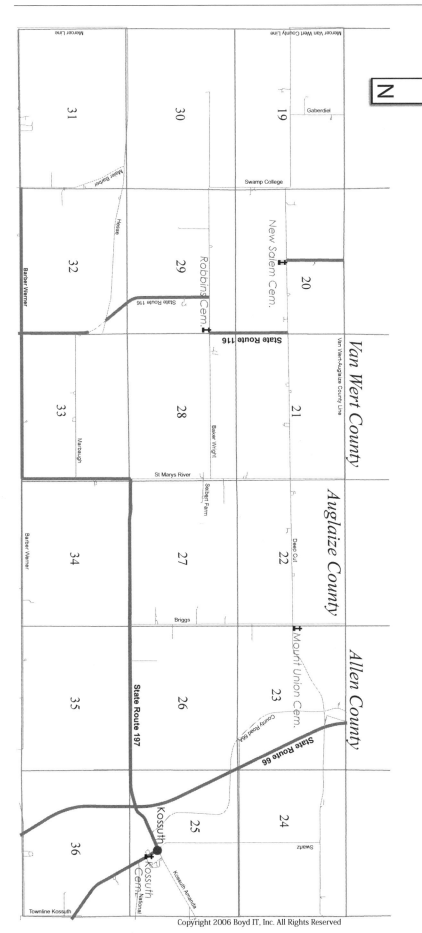

Note: the area contained in this map amounts to far less than a full Township. Therefore, its contents are completely on this single page (instead of a "normal" 2-page spread).

Cities & Towns
Kossuth

Cemeteries
Kossuth Cemetery
Mount Union Cemetery
New Salem Cemetery
Robbins Cemetery

Legend

———————	Section Lines
═══════	Interstates
━━━━━━━	Highways
————————	Other Roads
●	Cities/Towns
✝	Cemeteries

Scale: Section = 1 mile X 1 mile
(generally, with some exceptions)

Historical Map

T4-S R4-E
1st PM Meridian

Map Group 1

Note: the area contained in this map amounts to far less than a full Township. Therefore, its contents are completely on this single page (instead of a "normal" 2-page spread).

Cities & Towns
Kossuth

Cemeteries
Kossuth Cemetery
Mount Union Cemetery
New Salem Cemetery
Robbins Cemetery

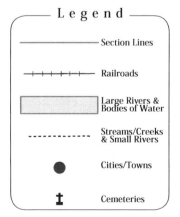

Legend

Section Lines

┼┼┼┼┼ Railroads

Large Rivers & Bodies of Water

Streams/Creeks & Small Rivers

● Cities/Towns

✝ Cemeteries

Scale: Section = 1 mile X 1 mile
(there are some exceptions)

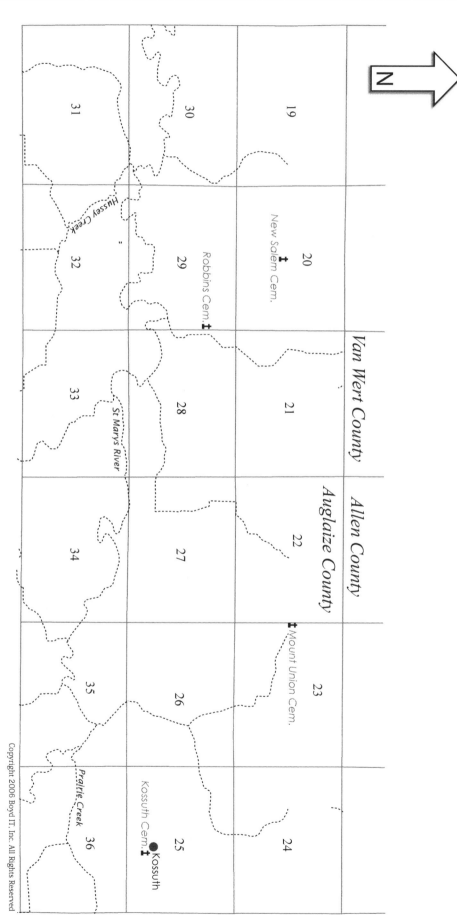

Map Group 2: Index to Land Patents

Township 4-South Range 5-East (1st PM)

After you locate an individual in this Index, take note of the Section and Section Part then proceed to the Land Patent map on the pages immediately following. You should have no difficulty locating the corresponding parcel of land.

The "For More Info" Column will lead you to more information about the underlying Patents. See the Legend at right, and the "How to Use this Book" chapter, for more information.

```
                        LEGEND
              "For More Info . . . " column
A = Authority (Legislative Act, See Appendix "A")
B = Block or Lot (location in Section unknown)
C = Cancelled Patent
F = Fractional Section
G = Group  (Multi-Patentee Patent, see Appendix "C")
V = Overlaps another Parcel
R = Re-Issued (Parcel patented more than once)

(A & G items require you to look in the Appendixes referred
to above. All other Letter-designations followed by a number
require you to locate line-items in this index that possess
the ID number found after the letter).
```

ID	Individual in Patent	Sec.	Sec. Part	Date Issued	Other Counties	For More Info . . .
119	BAKER, John	25	N½SE	1848-06-01		A1
120	" "	25	S½NE	1848-06-01		A1
144	BARR, William	36	S½NW	1835-09-15		A1
145	" "	36	SW	1835-09-15		A1
140	BERRYMAN, Thomas	22	S½S½	1826-09-20		A1 F
131	BLISS, Oramel H	27	S½SE	1846-10-01		A1 F
105	BOWER, Jacob	23	N½NE	1852-06-01		A1
142	CHAMBERLIN, Thomas T	19	SESE	1850-07-01		A1
143	" "	31	NWNW	1850-07-01		A1 F
82	CIRCLE, Abraham	29	NW	1852-06-01		A1
83	CIRKLE, Abraham	21	SE	1852-06-01		A1
136	COCHRAN, Simon	33	NWSE	1852-06-01		A1 F
113	CROSIER, James	27	NES½	1826-05-10		A1 F
114	" "	27	SE	1826-05-10		A1 F
115	CROZIER, James	35	SEW½	1835-10-09		A1 F
121	CROZIER, John	35	NW	1828-01-03		A1 F
112	CULP, James A	25	S½SE	1848-08-01		A1
146	DENISTON, William	19	SW	1850-07-01		A1
147	" "	19	SWSE	1850-07-01		A1
81	GUTHRIE, Abelard	34	SWNE	1840-10-10		A1 F
95	HELFENSTEIN, Edward	34	SE	1837-03-20		A1
96	" "	35	SE	1837-03-20		A1
97	" "	35	SENE	1838-09-04		A1
98	" "	35	SWNE	1838-09-04		A1
94	" "	34	S½SW	1840-10-10		A1 F
117	HELFENSTEIN, John A	34	NESW	1840-10-10		A1 F
118	" "	34	SENW	1840-10-10		A1 F
133	HERZING, Philip	36	S½NE	1838-09-04		A1 F
124	HIGHER, Martin	34	SENE	1835-10-09		A1
100	KEMPER, Elijah	36	SE	1837-03-18		A1
125	MARTZ, Michael	31	E½NW	1850-07-01		A1
126	MEDBERY, Nathaniel	27	S½NW	1846-10-01		A1 F
148	MILLER, William	33	E½SE	1852-06-01		A1
86	NEESE, Ambrose	23	E½SW	1852-06-01		A1
87	" "	23	NWSE	1852-06-01		A1
106	NEESE, Jacob	21	E½NW	1852-06-01		A1
107	" "	21	E½SW	1852-06-01		A1
108	" "	23	SENW	1852-06-01		A1
109	" "	23	SWNE	1852-06-01		A1
110	" "	23	W½SW	1852-06-01		A1
134	NEESE, Samuel	25	W½NW	1851-06-02		A1 F
111	PENESON, Jacob	29	NWNE	1852-06-01		A1
123	PLACE, Leonard	27	NWSW	1852-06-01		A1
92	RICHARDSON, David	31	NWNE	1852-06-01		A1
101	RICHARDSON, George W	33	NENE	1852-06-01		A1
102	" "	33	SENE	1852-06-01		A1

ID	Individual in Patent	Sec.	Sec. Part	Date Issued	Other Counties	For More Info . . .
132	RICHARDSON, Perry	29	SESW	1850-07-01		A1
149	ROACH, William	23	SENE	1854-12-15		A1
122	RUNYON, Joseph	25	N½NE	1850-07-01		A1
88	RUSSEL, Andrew	22	E½NE	1822-04-08		A1 F
89	" "	22	NWSE	1822-08-06		A1 F
90	" "	26	SW	1822-08-06		A1 F
91	RUSSELL, Andrew	22	W½NE	1822-04-08		A1 F
128	SHAFER, Nicholas	23	SWSE	1852-06-01		A1
79	SHAFFER, Aaron	21	SWNW	1852-06-01		A1
80	" "	21	W½SW	1852-06-01		A1
130	SHAFFER, Nicholas	23	SESE	1851-06-02		A1
129	" "	23	NESE	1852-06-01		A1
103	STODDARD, Henry	35	SW	1834-01-30		A1 V150
84	STORTS, Abraham	29	E½SE	1853-06-01		A1
85	" "	29	SWSE	1853-06-01		A1
99	STUKEY, Eli H	19	NWSE	1853-06-01		A1
93	SUNDERLAND, Dy	27	NE	1824-08-09		A1 F
141	SUTTON, Thomas	27	N½NW	1846-10-01		A1 F
150	TAYLOR, William	35	NESW	1835-10-08		A1 V103
151	" "	35	NEW½	1835-10-08		A1 F
127	WEAVER, Newton	21	NE	1852-06-01		A1
104	WHETSTONE, Henry	33	SWSE	1854-12-15		A1 F
135	WHETSTONE, Samuel	27	NESW	1846-10-01		A1
138	WHETSTONE, Simon	27	SESW	1849-02-01		A1
139	" "	27	SWSW	1850-07-01		A1
137	" "	27	E½SE	1854-12-15		A1 F
116	YOAKAM, James	23	W½NW	1852-06-01		A1

Patent Map

T4-S   R5-E
1st PM Meridian

Map Group 2

N

Township Statistics

Parcels Mapped	:	73
Number of Patents	:	66
Number of Individuals	:	49
Patentees Identified	:	49
Number of Surnames	:	40
Multi-Patentee Parcels	:	0
Oldest Patent Date	:	4/8/1822
Most Recent Patent	:	12/15/1854
Block/Lot Parcels	:	3
Parcels Re - Issued	:	0
Parcels that Overlap	:	2
Cities and Towns	:	0
Cemeteries	:	2

Note: the area contained in this map amounts to far less than a full Township. Therefore, its contents are completely on this single page (instead of a "normal" 2-page spread).

Legend

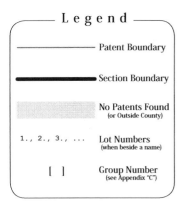

—————— Patent Boundary

━━━━━━ Section Boundary

░░░░░░ No Patents Found
(or Outside County)

1., 2., 3., ...   Lot Numbers
(when beside a name)

[ ]   Group Number
(see Appendix "C")

Scale: Section = 1 mile X 1 mile
(generally, with some exceptions)

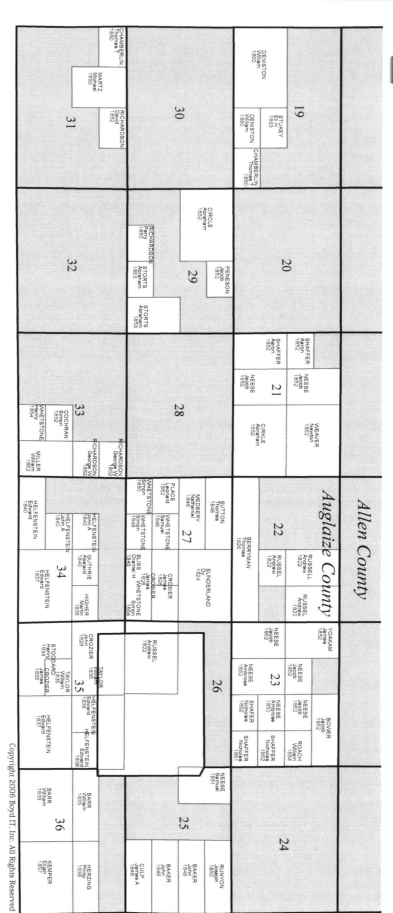

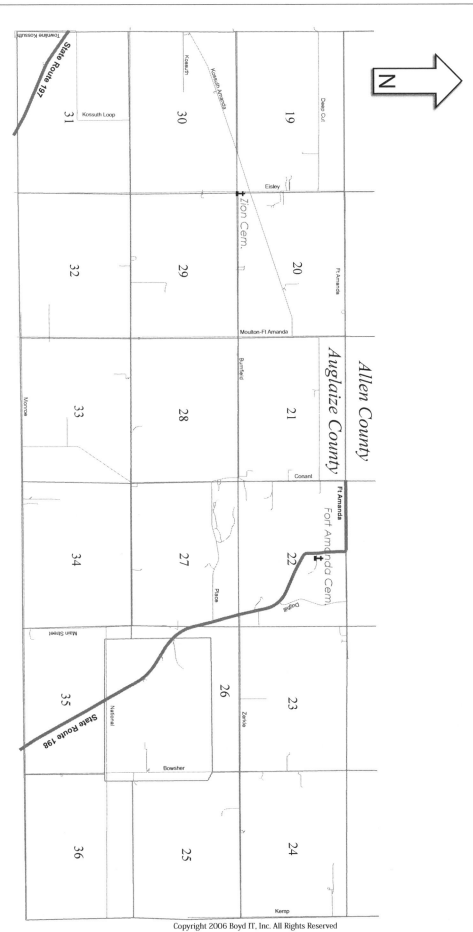

Road Map

T4-S R5-E
1st PM Meridian

M a p   G r o u p   2

Note: the area contained in this map amounts to far less than a full Township. Therefore, its contents are completely on this single page (instead of a "normal" 2-page spread).

Cities & Towns
None

Cemeteries
Fort Amanda Cemetery
Zion Cemetery

L e g e n d

———— Section Lines

═══ Interstates

▬▬▬ Highways

——— Other Roads

● Cities/Towns

✝ Cemeteries

Scale: Section = 1 mile X 1 mile
(generally, with some exceptions)

Historical Map

T4-S R5-E
1st PM Meridian

Map Group 2

Note: the area contained in this map amounts to far less than a full Township. Therefore, its contents are completely on this single page (instead of a "normal" 2-page spread).

Cities & Towns
None

Cemeteries
Fort Amanda Cemetery
Zion Cemetery

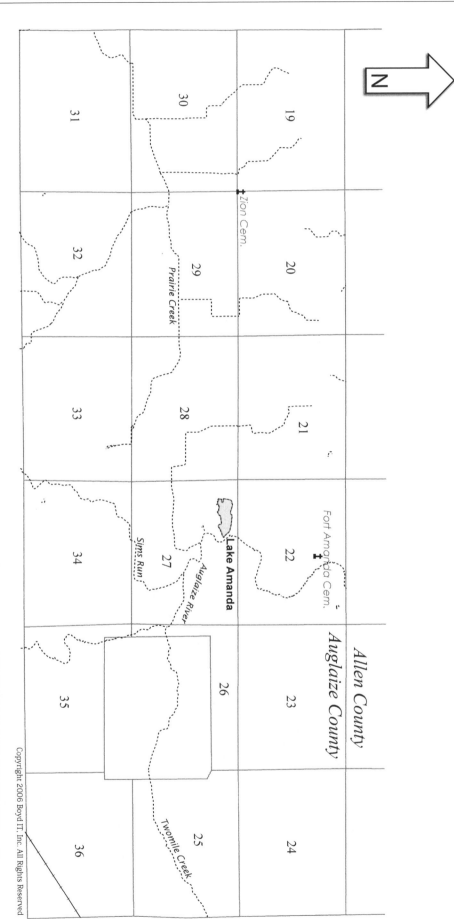

Legend

	Section Lines
┼┼┼┼┼	Railroads
▭	Large Rivers & Bodies of Water
- - - -	Streams/Creeks & Small Rivers
●	Cities/Towns
✝	Cemeteries

Scale: Section = 1 mile X 1 mile
(there are some exceptions)

Map Group 3: Index to Land Patents

Township 4-South Range 6-East (1st PM)

After you locate an individual in this Index, take note of the Section and Section Part then proceed to the Land Patent map on the pages immediately following. You should have no difficulty locating the corresponding parcel of land.

The "For More Info" Column will lead you to more information about the underlying Patents. See the Legend at right, and the "How to Use this Book" chapter, for more information.

```
                    LEGEND
           "For More Info . . . " column
A = Authority (Legislative Act, See Appendix "A")
B = Block or Lot (location in Section unknown)
C = Cancelled Patent
F = Fractional Section
G = Group  (Multi-Patentee Patent, see Appendix "C")
V = Overlaps another Parcel
R = Re-Issued (Parcel patented more than once)

(A & G items require you to look in the Appendixes referred
to above. All other Letter-designations followed by a number
require you to locate line-items in this index that possess
the ID number found after the letter).
```

ID	Individual in Patent	Sec.	Sec. Part	Date Issued	Other Counties	For More Info . . .
158	ANTHONY, David	32	NWSE	1837-11-21		A1
159	" "	32	SWSW	1837-11-21		A1
185	BELKNAP, Jonas	36	E½SW	1837-03-15		A1
186	" "	36	W½SE	1837-03-15		A1
164	BELNAP, George	35	S½SW	1837-03-16		A1
165	BINKLEY, George S	34	NW	1837-03-18		A1
196	BONER, Samuel	31	N½NW	1835-09-15		A1
188	BROWN, Leonard A	35	W½NE	1836-02-15		A1
179	BRUMFIELD, John	33	SW	1837-03-18		A1
155	CAMPBELL, Archibald	35	SE	1836-02-15		A1
156	" "	36	W½SW	1836-02-15		A1
197	CLARK, Samuel M	33	SENW	1837-08-21		A1
180	CONKEL, John	34	W½SW	1837-03-20		A1
193	COWAN, Miles	36	SENE	1836-02-15		A1
191	CRETCHER, Mathew	35	E½NE	1837-03-16		A1
192	" "	36	W½NW	1837-03-16		A1 C R183
154	DAVIS, Anthony	36	E½SE	1837-03-15		A1
168	DEALONG, Jacob	34	E½NE	1837-03-18		A1
169	DELONG, Jacob	34	NESE	1837-03-18		A1
170	" "	34	SESE	1837-03-18		A1
171	" "	34	W½SE	1837-03-18		A1
172	" "	35	N½SW	1837-03-18		A1
173	" "	35	S½NW	1837-03-18		A1
190	DOUGHERTY, Margaret	33	NENW	1837-08-21		A1
187	FULTON, Joseph	34	E½SW	1837-03-20		A1
198	GARMIRE, William	32	E½SE	1837-03-18		A1
199	" "	32	SWSE	1837-03-18		A1
189	GOODENOW, Levi	35	N½NW	1837-03-16		A1
162	GREIDER, Frederick	31	E½SE	1835-10-07		A1
163	" "	32	NWSW	1835-10-07		A1
174	GREIDER, Jacob	31	S½NE	1835-10-07		A1
175	" "	32	SWNW	1835-10-07		A1
152	GUTHRIE, Abelard	36	NENE	1840-10-10		A1 F
176	HOLTZMAN, John A	32	E½SW	1837-03-18		A1
177	HOOPES, John B	31	N½NE	1835-10-07		A1
178	" "	32	NWNW	1835-10-07		A1
157	KEMPER, Daniel	31	W½SE	1837-03-18		A1
166	KEMPER, Isaac	33	E½	1837-03-18		A1
195	KEMPER, Robert	31	SW	1837-03-18		A1 F
167	MCGRADY, Isaac	32	E½NW	1837-03-20		A1
161	MOORE, Enoch	31	S½NW	1838-09-04		A1 F
153	OVERHALSER, Adam	33	W½NW	1835-12-24		A1
160	STEBLETON, David	34	W½NE	1837-03-18		A1
181	SWINEHART, John	36	NWNE	1837-03-15		A1 F
182	" "	36	SWNE	1837-03-15		A1 F
183	" "	36	W½NW	1837-03-15		A1 F R192

ID	Individual in Patent	Sec.	Sec. Part	Date Issued	Other Counties	For More Info . . .
194	TROYER, Moses	32	NE	1837-03-18		A1
184	WILSON, John	36	E½NW	1857-04-08		A1

Patent Map

T4-S R6-E
1st PM Meridian

Map Group 3

Township Statistics

Parcels Mapped	48
Number of Patents	42
Number of Individuals	34
Patentees Identified	34
Number of Surnames	31
Multi-Patentee Parcels	0
Oldest Patent Date	9/15/1835
Most Recent Patent	4/8/1857
Block/Lot Parcels	0
Parcels Re - Issued	1
Parcels that Overlap	0
Cities and Towns	2
Cemeteries	0

Note: the area contained in this map amounts to far less than a full Township. Therefore, its contents are completely on this single page (instead of a "normal" 2-page spread).

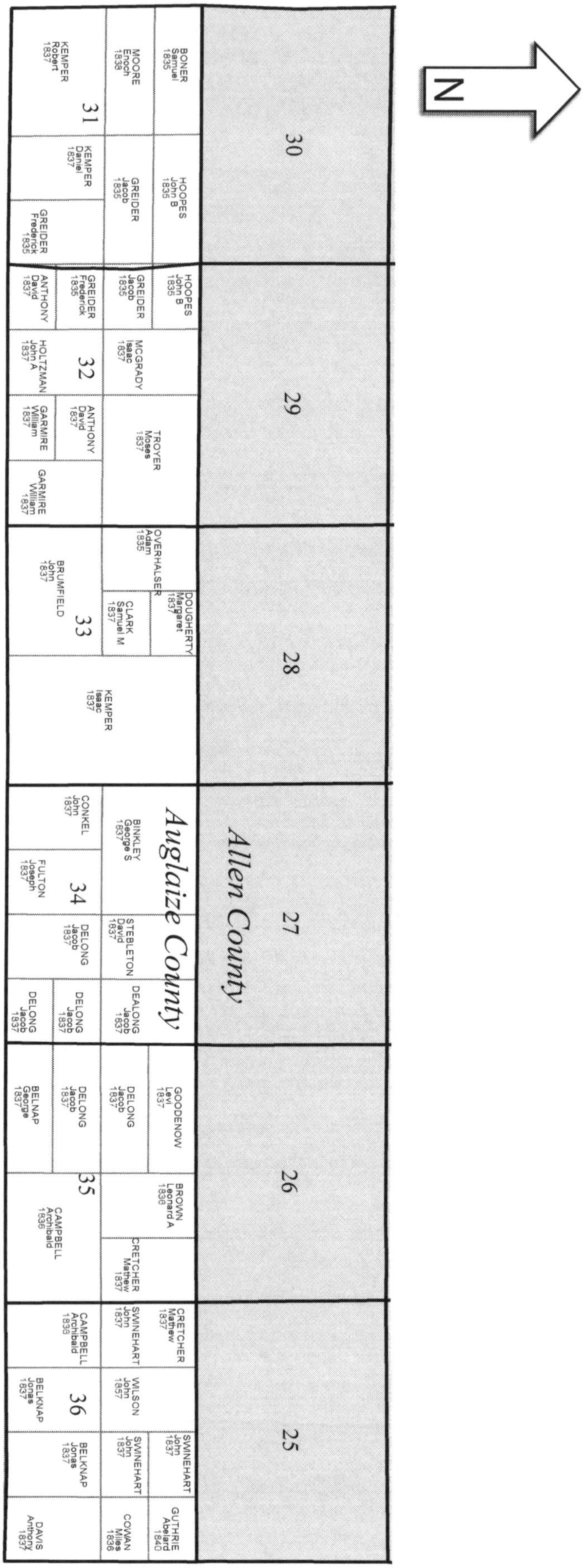
N
30
31
BONER Samuel 1835
MOORE Enoch 1836
KEMPER Robert 1837
HOOPES John B 1835
GREIDER Jacob 1835
KEMPER Daniel 1837
GREIDER Frederick 1835
29
32
HOOPES John B 1835
GREIDER Jacob 1835
GREIDER Frederick 1835
ANTHONY David 1837
MCGRADY Isaac 1837
HOLTZMAN John A 1837
TROYER Moses 1837
ANTHONY David 1837
GARMIRE William 1837
GARMIRE William 1837
28
33
DOUGHERTY Margaret 1837
OVERHALSER Adam 1835
CLARK Samuel M 1837
BRUMFIELD John 1837
KEMPER Isaac 1837
27
34
Allen County
Auglaize County
BINKLEY George S 1837
CONKEL John 1837
FULTON Joseph 1837
STEBLETON David 1837
DELONG Jacob 1837
DEALONG Jacob 1837
DELONG Jacob 1837
DELONG Jacob 1837
26
35
GOODENOW Levi 1837
DELONG Jacob 1837
DELONG Jacob 1837
BELNAP George 1837
BROWN Leonard A 1836
CAMPBELL Archibald 1836
CRETCHER Mathew 1837
25
36
CRETCHER Mathew 1837
SWINEHART John 1837
CAMPBELL Archibald 1836
WILSON John 1857
BELKNAP Jonas 1837
SWINEHART John 1837
SWINEHART John 1837
BELKNAP Jonas 1837
GUTHRIE Abelard 1840
COWAN Miles 1836
DAVIS Anthony 1837

Legend

- Patent Boundary
- Section Boundary
- No Patents Found (or Outside County)
- 1., 2., 3., ... Lot Numbers (when beside a name)
- [ ] Group Number (see Appendix "C")

Scale: Section = 1 mile X 1 mile
(generally, with some exceptions)

Road Map

T4-S R6-E
1st PM Meridian

M a p   G r o u p   3

Note: the area contained in this map amounts to far less than a full Township. Therefore, its contents are completely on this single page (instead of a "normal" 2-page spread).

Cities & Towns
Cridersville
Green Acres

Cemeteries
None

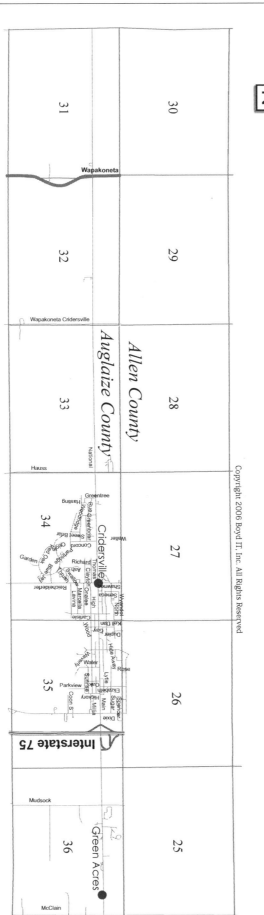

L e g e n d

————— Section Lines

═════ Interstates

▬▬▬▬ Highways

——— Other Roads

● Cities/Towns

✝ Cemeteries

Scale: Section = 1 mile X 1 mile
(generally, with some exceptions)

Historical Map

T4-S R6-E
1st PM Meridian

Map Group 3

Note: the area contained in this map amounts to far less than a full Township. Therefore, its contents are completely on this single page (instead of a "normal" 2-page spread).

Cities & Towns
Cridersville
Green Acres

Cemeteries
None

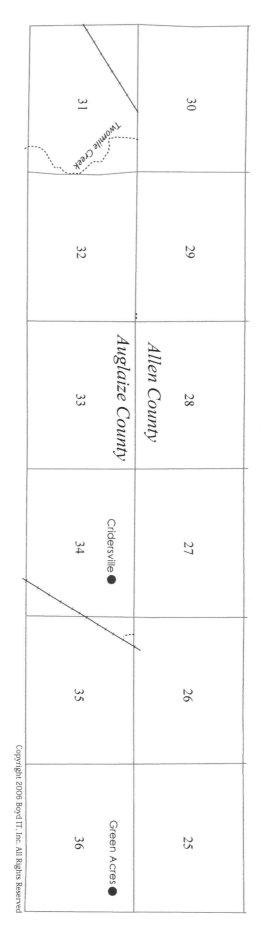

Legend

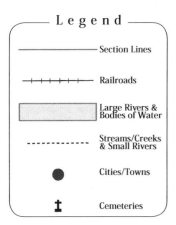

――――― Section Lines

┼┼┼┼┼┼ Railroads

▭ Large Rivers & Bodies of Water

- - - - - - Streams/Creeks & Small Rivers

● Cities/Towns

† Cemeteries

Scale: Section = 1 mile X 1 mile
(there are some exceptions)

Map Group 4: Index to Land Patents

Township 5-South Range 4-East (1st PM)

After you locate an individual in this Index, take note of the Section and Section Part then proceed to the Land Patent map on the pages immediately following. You should have no difficulty locating the corresponding parcel of land.

The "For More Info" Column will lead you to more information about the underlying Patents. See the Legend at right, and the "How to Use this Book" chapter, for more information.

ID	Individual in Patent	Sec.	Sec. Part	Date Issued	Other Counties	For More Info . . .
290	APGAR, Peter	31	W½SE	1850-07-01		A1
304	ARMSTRONG, Thomas	15	SWS½	1829-04-02		A1 F
205	BATCHELER, Almond L	27	SENW	1850-07-01		A1 F
289	BLISS, Oramel H	27	E½NW	1846-10-01		A1
256	BOSCHE, John F	11	W½SW	1852-06-01		A1 F
261	" "	17	NENW	1852-06-01		A1
262	" "	19	E½NE	1852-06-01		A1
263	" "	19	E½NW	1852-06-01		A1 F
265	" "	25	W½SW	1852-06-01		A1
266	" "	31	E½NW	1852-06-01		A1 F
267	" "	31	NWNW	1852-06-01		A1 F
257	" "	13	NESW	1853-06-01		A1
258	" "	13	SENE	1853-06-01		A1
259	" "	13	W½NE	1853-06-01		A1
260	" "	17	E½NE	1853-06-01		A1
264	" "	25	E½SW	1853-06-01		A1
254	BOYLES, John	21	SWNE	1848-08-01		A1
229	BRIGHT, Isaac E	17	W½NW	1852-06-01		A1
285	BROADWELL, Lewis	33	NESW	1849-02-01		A1
286	" "	33	NWSW	1849-02-01		A1
284	" "	33	E½NW	1850-07-01		A1
281	BROWNELL, L R	15	E½	1821-09-06		A1 G19 F
275	BUSH, Joseph	31	W½NE	1850-07-01		A1
209	COVERT, Burgon	12	W½NW	1835-10-16		A1 F
239	CREIGHTON, James	15	SENW	1849-08-10		A1
294	CREIGHTON, Samuel	15	NENW	1852-06-01		A1
255	DENNEY, John	23	W½NE	1848-06-01		A1
276	DENNEY, Joseph	35	NWNW	1848-06-01		A1
277	" "	35	SWNW	1850-07-01		A1
295	DENNEY, Samuel	25	NWNE	1848-06-01		A1
299	DENNEY, Solomon	25	E½NW	1846-10-01		A1
300	"	25	SWNW	1846-10-01		A1
307	DENNEY, William	23	E½NW	1850-07-01		A1
301	DENNY, Solomon	25	NWNW	1835-10-08		A1
292	DOTY, Picket	11	NESW	1856-04-15		A1
278	DOUTE, Joseph	21	SENW	1852-06-01		A1
305	DOUTE, Thomas	21	NWNE	1852-06-01		A1
230	DUNGAN, Isaiah	22	W½NW	1824-08-09		A1 F
251	DYE, Jane	15	N½SW	1850-07-01		A1 F
240	ELLIOTT, James	27	NESW	1850-07-01		A1
226	ESPY, Henry P	6	E½NW	1837-03-20		A1
227	" "	7	W½	1837-03-20		A1
302	FALES, Stephen	6	NE	1837-03-20		A1
207	FISHPAW, Aquilla	17	S½	1852-06-01		A1
308	GRANT, William	1	N½SW	1852-06-01		A1 F
309	" "	1	S½SW	1852-06-01		A1 F

ID	Individual in Patent	Sec.	Sec. Part	Date Issued	Other Counties	For More Info . . .
219	HAMILTON, David P	27	W½NW	1850-07-01		A1 F
293	HEIGHTON, Robert	29	SWSW	1835-10-08		A1
224	HENRICH, George	19	E½SE	1852-06-01		A1
200	HORMEL, Adam	19	W½SE	1852-06-01		A1
279	HOWELL, Joseph	25	W½SE	1850-07-01		A1
235	ICE, Jacob	11	SESE	1848-08-01		A1
234	" "	11	NESE	1853-06-01		A1
310	JAY, William	22	W½SW	1827-01-30		A1 F
242	JEFFERY, James	22	E½SW	1835-10-08		A1
243	" "	22	W½SE	1835-10-08		A1
241	" "	22	E½SE	1835-10-16		A1
244	JEFFREY, James	23	NWSW	1849-08-10		A1
245	" "	23	SWSW	1850-07-01		A1
231	JOHNS, Israel	15	NES½	1829-11-02		A1 F
232	" "	15	S½SE	1848-06-01		A1 F
233	" "	15	W½NE	1848-08-01		A1 F
268	JOHNS, John	14	NWNW	1829-11-02		A1 F R303
269	" "	15	NENE	1829-11-02		A1 F
236	JONES, Jacob	3	NENE	1852-06-01		A1 F
237	" "	3	SENE	1853-06-01		A1 F
280	JONES, Joseph	3	NWNE	1849-02-01		A1
218	LEWIS, Cyrus C	11	SESW	1848-08-01		A1 F
238	LEWIS, Jacob	11	W½SE	1849-02-01		A1 F
201	LLOYD, Alexander D	21	N½NW	1852-06-01		A1
202	" "	21	SWNW	1852-06-01		A1
246	MCCAIN, James L	27	W½NE	1850-07-01		A1 F
203	MCDONALD, Alexander	6	SW	1837-03-20		A1 F
204	" "	6	SWNW	1837-03-20		A1 F
311	MCDONALD, William	6	SE	1837-03-20		A1
313	MCINTIRE, William R	1	S½SW	1852-06-01		A1 F
282	MORGAN, Lawrence	31	W½SW	1850-07-01		A1
212	MURRY, Charles	34	SWNW	1822-04-08		A1
213	NOBLE, Charles	9	E½NW	1852-06-01		A1
214	" "	9	SE	1852-06-01		A1
215	" "	9	W½NE	1852-06-01		A1
222	ORTON, Elisha B	1	E½NE	1850-07-01		A1 F
225	OSBORN, Henry	3	SWNE	1852-06-01		A1 F
312	OVERLEY, William	33	SESW	1848-08-01		A1
216	PAIRO, Charles W	6	NWNW	1852-06-01		A1 F
303	PENNY, Theophilus T	14	NWNW	1832-11-05		A1 R268
270	PICKEREL, John	22	E½NW	1833-11-27		A1
220	PRATT, Dudley	1	SWNE	1848-06-01		A1 F
221	" "	1	W½NW	1851-02-01		A1 F
298	PRATT, Seth	1	NWNE	1848-06-01		A1 F
297	" "	1	E½NW	1850-07-01		A1 F
250	RILEY, James W	15	SENE	1846-10-01		A1 F
206	SAMSON, Amos	2	N½NE	1835-10-09		A1
314	SAWYER, William	23	E½NE	1848-06-01		A1
315	" "	29	NWNW	1853-06-01		A1
228	SMITH, Henry	11	NENE	1852-06-01		A1 F
247	STONEROCK, James	15	NWNW	1852-06-01		A1
248	" "	15	SWNW	1852-06-01		A1
210	SULLIVAN, Carter	25	E½NE	1852-06-01		A1
211	" "	25	SWNE	1852-06-01		A1
316	SUNDERLAND, William	34	W½NE	1827-01-30		A1 F
317	SUTTON, William	27	SESW	1849-08-10		A1
283	TAFE, Lawrence	31	SWNW	1852-06-01		A1 F
223	TINDALL, Enoch	11	SENE	1835-10-08		A1
272	TOBIAS, Jonathan	31	NESW	1851-02-01		A1 F
208	TYRRELL, Benjamin	34	SESW	1822-04-08		A1
291	VAN NUYS, PETER M	21	E½SE	1835-10-09		A1
288	VANARSDAL, Lucus	34	SW	1821-09-06		A1 F
287	" "	34	E½NW	1822-08-06		A1 F
249	VANNUYS, James	21	E½NE	1832-03-03		A1
217	WELLS, Clark W	3	W½NW	1856-04-15		A1
296	WELTY, Samuel	31	SESW	1850-07-01		A1 F
252	WILLIAMS, Jesse	1	E½SW	1835-10-07		A1 F
253	" "	1	SE	1835-10-07		A1
306	WOOD, Truman	1	NW	1877-08-30		A2 C F
271	WYLAND, John	22	W½NE	1826-05-10		A1 F
274	WYLAND, Jonathan	22	E½NW	1821-09-06		A1
273	" "	15	S½	1826-05-10		A1 F
281	YOUNG, Robert	15	E½	1821-09-06		A1 G19 F

ID	Individual in Patent	Sec.	Sec. Part	Date Issued	Other Counties	For More Info . . .
318	YOUNG, William	33	SWSW	1848-08-01		A1

Patent Map

T5-S R4-E
1st PM Meridian

Map Group 4

Township Statistics

Parcels Mapped	:	119
Number of Patents	:	113
Number of Individuals	:	83
Patentees Identified	:	82
Number of Surnames	:	70
Multi-Patentee Parcels	:	1
Oldest Patent Date	:	9/6/1821
Most Recent Patent	:	8/30/1877
Block/Lot Parcels	:	2
Parcels Re - Issued	:	1
Parcels that Overlap	:	0
Cities and Towns	:	0
Cemeteries	:	2

WELLS Clark W 1856	JONES Joseph 1849	JONES Jacob 1852
	OSBORN Henry 1852	JONES Jacob 1853
3		

SAMSON Amos 1835
2

PRATT Dudley 1851	WOOD Truman 1847		PRATT Seth 1848	
	MCINTIRE William R 1852	PRATT Seth 1850	PRATT Dudley 1848	ORTON Elisha B 1850
GRANT William 1852		**1**	
		WILLIAMS Jesse 1835	
GRANT William 1852	WILLIAMS Jesse 1835		

10

	SMITH Henry 1852	COVERT Burgon 1835
11	TINDALL Enoch 1835	
BOSCHE John F 1852	DOTY Picket 1856	LEWIS Jacob 1849	ICE Jacob 1853
	LEWIS Cyrus C 1848		ICE Jacob 1848

12

STONEROCK James 1852	CREIGHTON Samuel 1852	JOHNS Israel 1848	JOHNS John 1829
STONEROCK James 1852	CREIGHTON James 1849	**15**	RILEY James W 1846
		BROWNELL [19] L R 1821	JOHNS Israel 1829
DYE Jane 1850			
ARMSTRONG Thomas 1829	WYLAND Jonathan 1826	JOHNS Israel 1848	

JOHNS John 1829	PENNY Theophilus T 1832
14	

	BOSCHE John F 1853
	BOSCHE John F 1853
BOSCHE John F 1853	**13**

DUNGAN Isaiah 1824	WYLAND John 1826	
	WYLAND Jonathan 1821	**22**	PICKEREL John 1833
JAY William 1827	JEFFERY James 1835	
	JEFFERY James 1835	JEFFERY James 1835

	DENNEY John 1848
DENNEY William 1850	SAWYER William 1848
JEFFREY James 1849	
	23
JEFFREY James 1850	

24

HAMILTON David P 1850	MCCAIN James L 1850
BATCHELER Almond L 1850 BLISS Oramel H 1846	
ELLIOTT James 1850	**27**
SUTTON William 1849	

26

DENNY Solomon 1835		DENNEY Samuel 1848	
DENNEY Solomon 1846	DENNEY Solomon 1846	SULLIVAN Carter 1852	SULLIVAN Carter 1852
BOSCHE John F 1852	**25**	HOWELL Joseph 1850	
	BOSCHE John F 1853		

	SUNDERLAND William 1827
MURRY Charles 1822	VANARSDAL Lucus 1822
34	
VANARSDAL Lucus 1821	
	TYRRELL Benjamin 1822

DENNEY Joseph 1848
DENNEY Joseph 1850
35

36

Helpful Hints

1. This Map's INDEX can be found on the preceding pages.

2. Refer to Map "C" to see where this Township lies within Auglaize County, Ohio.

3. Numbers within square brackets [ ] denote a multi-patentee land parcel (multi-owner). Refer to Appendix "C" for a full list of members in this group.

4. Areas that look to be crowded with Patentees usually indicate multiple sales of the same parcel (Re-issues) or Overlapping parcels. See this Township's Index for an explanation of these and other circumstances that might explain "odd" groupings of Patentees on this map.

Legend

———	Patent Boundary
▬▬▬	Section Boundary
░░░	No Patents Found (or Outside County)
1., 2., 3., ...	Lot Numbers (when beside a name)
[ ]	Group Number (see Appendix "C")

Scale: Section = 1 mile X 1 mile (generally, with some exceptions)

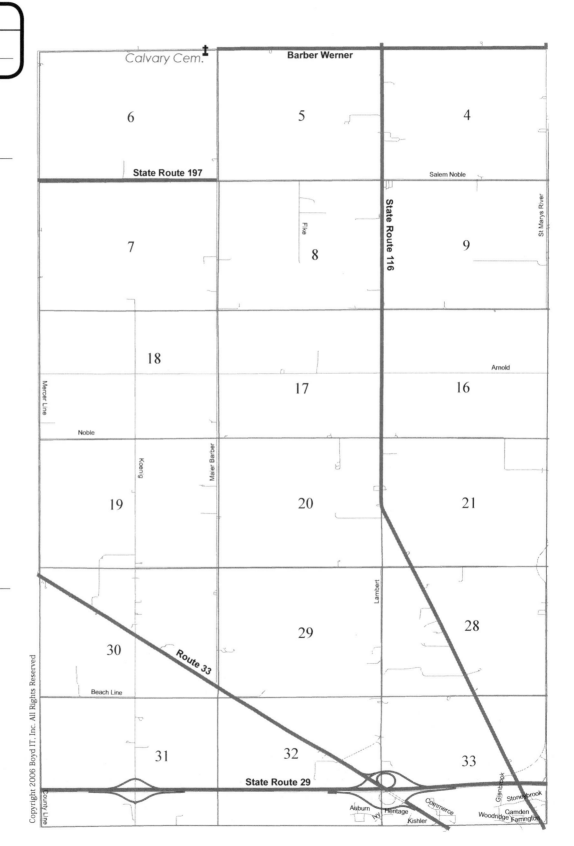

Road Map

T5-S R4-E
1st PM Meridian

Map Group 4

Cities & Towns
None

Cemeteries
Calvary Cemetery
Pratt Cemetery

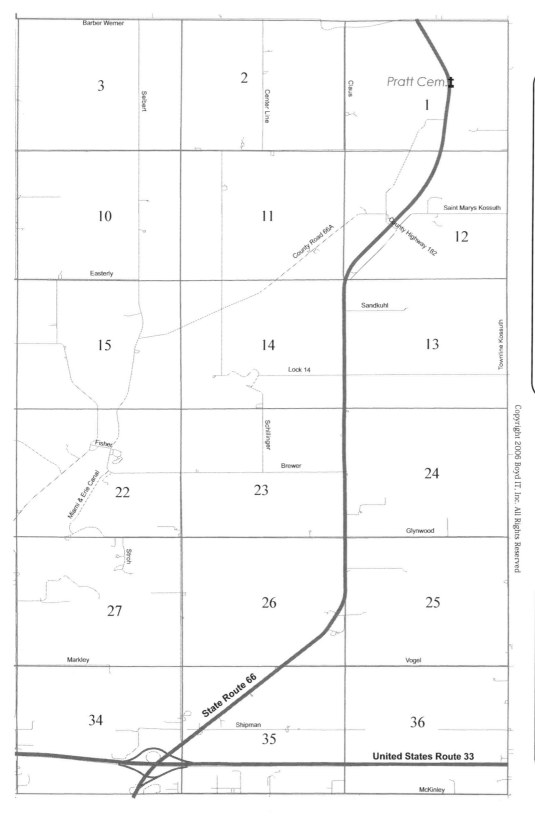

Helpful Hints

1. This road map has a number of uses, but primarily it is to help you: a) find the present location of land owned by your ancestors (at least the general area), b) find cemeteries and city-centers, and c) estimate the route/roads used by Census-takers & tax-assessors.

2. If you plan to travel to Auglaize County to locate cemeteries or land parcels, please pick up a modern travel map for the area before you do. Mapping old land parcels on modern maps is not as exact a science as you might think. Just the slightest variations in public land survey coordinates, estimates of parcel boundaries, or road-map deviations can greatly alter a map's representation of how a road either does or doesn't cross a particular parcel of land.

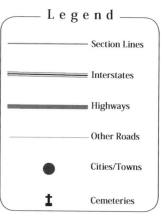

L e g e n d

———————	Section Lines
═══════	Interstates
▬▬▬▬▬	Highways
—————	Other Roads
●	Cities/Towns
⚓	Cemeteries

Scale: Section = 1 mile X 1 mile
(generally, with some exceptions)

Historical Map

T5-S R4-E
1st PM Meridian

Map Group 4

Cities & Towns
None

Cemeteries
Calvary Cemetery
Pratt Cemetery

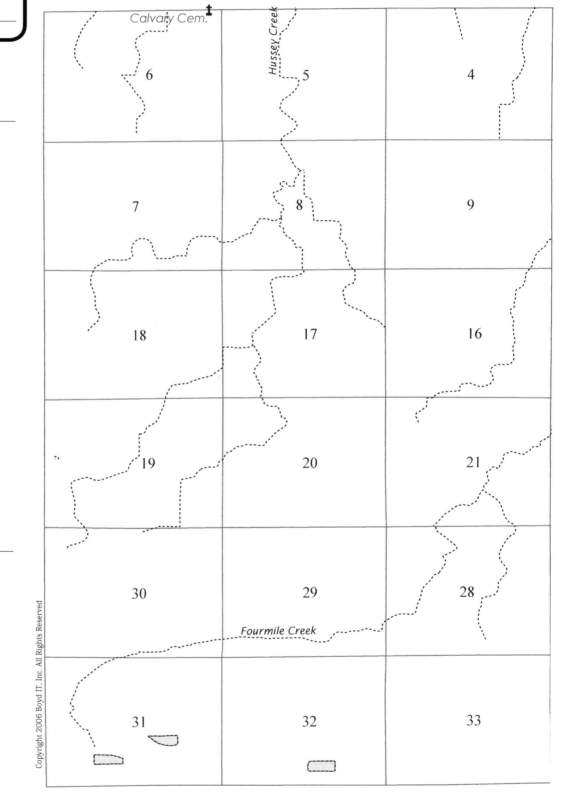

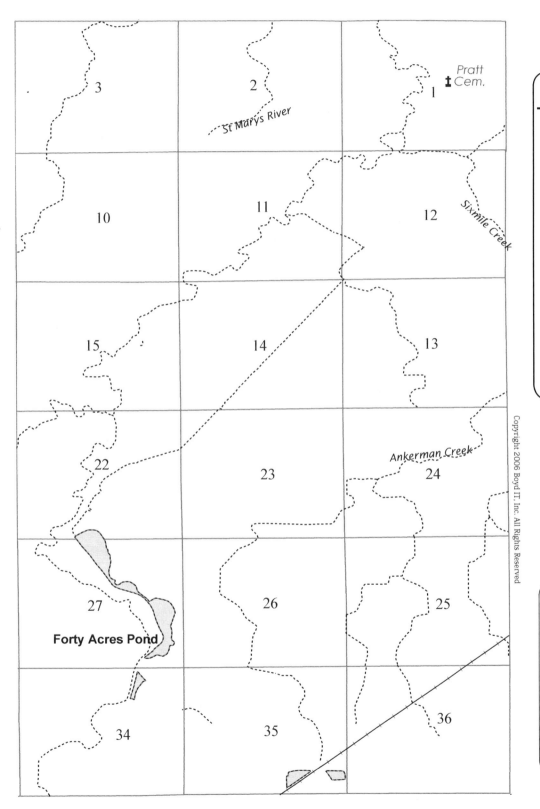

Pratt
Cem.

3

2

St Marys River

1

10

11

12

Sixmile Creek

15

14

13

22

23

Ankerman Creek

24

27

26

25

Forty Acres Pond

34

35

36

Helpful Hints

1. This Map takes a different look at the same Congressional Township displayed in the preceding two maps. It presents features that can help you better envision the historical development of the area: a) Water-bodies (lakes & ponds), b) Water-courses (rivers, streams, etc.), c) Railroads, d) City/town center-points (where they were oftentimes located when first settled), and e) Cemeteries.

2. Using this "Historical" map in tandem with this Township's Patent Map and Road Map, may lead you to some interesting discoveries. You will often find roads, towns, cemeteries, and waterways are named after nearby landowners: sometimes those names will be the ones you are researching. See how many of these research gems you can find here in Auglaize County.

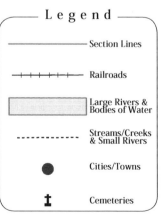

L e g e n d

——————— Section Lines

+–+–+–+–+–+–+ Railroads

Large Rivers &
Bodies of Water

– – – – – – – Streams/Creeks
& Small Rivers

● Cities/Towns

✝ Cemeteries

Scale: Section = 1 mile X 1 mile
(there are some exceptions)

Map Group 5: Index to Land Patents

Township 5-South Range 5-East (1st PM)

After you locate an individual in this Index, take note of the Section and Section Part then proceed to the Land Patent map on the pages immediately following. You should have no difficulty locating the corresponding parcel of land.

The "For More Info" Column will lead you to more information about the underlying Patents. See the Legend at right, and the "How to Use this Book" chapter, for more information.

```
                        LEGEND
            "For More Info . . . " column
A = Authority (Legislative Act, See Appendix "A")
B = Block or Lot (location in Section unknown)
C = Cancelled Patent
F = Fractional Section
G = Group  (Multi-Patentee Patent, see Appendix "C")
V = Overlaps another Parcel
R = Re-Issued (Parcel patented more than once)

(A & G items require you to look in the Appendixes referred
to above. All other Letter-designations followed by a number
require you to locate line-items in this index that possess
the ID number found after the letter).
```

ID	Individual in Patent	Sec.	Sec. Part	Date Issued	Other Counties	For More Info . . .
361	APPLE, Henry	26	SESE	1835-10-09		A1
359	AYERS, Grover	35	SENW	1837-03-20		A1 G6
358	" "	35	SWNE	1837-03-20		A1
403	AYERS, Jeremiah	35	NWSE	1837-03-20		A1 G7
391	BAKER, Jacob	2	W½SE	1837-03-18		A1
390	"	10	SENW	1837-03-20		A1 C
363	BARNES, Henry	1	W½SW	1837-03-18		A1
364	" "	11	NE	1837-03-18		A1
365	" "	2	E½SE	1837-03-18		A1
346	BARNEY, Elijah G	3	SW	1840-10-10		A1 F
326	BARRINGTON, Alexander	31	SW	1851-12-10		A1 F
463	BARRINGTON, Richard R	31	SE	1850-07-01		A1
491	BEARD, William	23	NWNW	1835-10-09		A1 F
492	BLAND, William	31	NWNW	1852-06-01		A1 F
493	" "	31	S½NW	1852-06-01		A1 F
453	BONSER, Nathaniel	26	W½SE	1835-10-09		A1
442	BORTON, Josiah	24	N½SW	1835-09-15		A1
443	" "	24	SESW	1835-09-15		A1
412	BOSCHE, John F	19	S½NE	1852-06-01		A1
413	" "	19	W½NW	1853-06-01		A1 F
494	BOTKINS, William	11	SWSW	1837-03-16		A1 F
446	BREES, Lewis	15	NW	1835-10-09		A1 F
447	" "	15	NWNE	1835-10-09		A1
458	BREHANT, Peter	36	SWNW	1835-10-09		A1
348	BROCK, Francis	36	SENE	1834-01-30		A1
347	" "	36	SE	1835-10-08		A1
349	" "	36	SWNE	1835-10-08		A1
448	BUB, Michael	17	N½SE	1852-06-01		A1
384	CAMPBELL, Homer M	13	NESE	1837-03-20		A1
385	" "	13	NW	1837-03-20		A1
386	" "	13	S½NE	1837-03-20		A1
407	CARL, John	9	NESW	1853-06-01		A1
408	CARSWELL, John	15	SE	1835-10-09		A1 F
409	" "	15	SW	1835-10-09		A1 F
422	CARY, John W	25	SESW	1834-01-30		A1 G27
423	" "	25	SWSE	1834-01-30		A1 G27 F
470	CHAMBERLIN, Samuel	22	E½	1837-03-20		A1
471	" "	26	NW	1837-03-20		A1
472	" "	27	E½	1837-03-20		A1
473	" "	27	N½SW	1837-03-20		A1 F
395	CHANEY, James	1	E½SW	1836-02-15		A1
396	" "	1	W½SE	1836-02-15		A1
410	CLAUSON, John	10	NESE	1835-10-16		A1
444	CLAWSON, Josiah	2	SWSW	1834-01-30		A1
483	CLAWSON, Thomas	10	NENE	1837-03-16		A1
445	CLOSSON, Josiah	10	SENE	1853-12-15		A1

ID	Individual in Patent	Sec.	Sec. Part	Date Issued	Other Counties	For More Info . . .
456	COLLINS, Oliver C	23	SWNW	1837-03-20		A1
457	" "	26	NESE	1837-03-20		A1
481	CREMEEN, Smith	5	W½SE	1850-07-01		A1
340	CRISTY, Cornelius	22	SW	1837-03-20		A1 F
343	CROFT, David	26	NENE	1834-01-30		A1
344	" "	26	NWNE	1834-01-30		A1 F
495	CROWDER, William	35	SENE	1836-02-15		A1
426	CUMMINS, Joseph	24	NW	1837-03-20		A1
345	DAVIS, David Y	1	NW	1835-09-15		A1
449	DUMBROFF, Michael	35	SWNW	1838-09-04		A1
387	ELLIOTT, Hugh	34	NE	1837-03-20		A1
400	ELLIOTT, James	36	E½SW	1835-10-08		A1
401	" "	36	SWSW	1837-03-18		A1
399	" "	27	S½SW	1845-06-01		A1 F
411	ELLIS, John	3	W½SE	1837-11-21		A1
496	EWEN, William	23	NES½	1835-10-09		A1
497	" "	23	SENE	1835-10-09		A1
392	FLEMMING, Jacob	14	E½NW	1837-03-20		A1
393	" "	14	NE	1837-03-20		A1
339	FORNEY, Christian	12	W½SE	1837-03-20		A1
353	FREISNER, Frederick	21	E½NW	1851-06-02		A1
414	FREYMAN, John G	25	SESE	1835-10-09		A1
334	GARRETSONE, Arnold	33	E½NE	1852-06-01		A1
486	GODDARD, Thomas V	25	NENE	1835-10-08		A1
422	GORDON, James	25	SESW	1834-01-30		A1 G27
423	" "	25	SWSE	1834-01-30		A1 G27 F
498	GREEN, William	34	S½SW	1837-11-21		A1 F
360	GREGORY, Harrison	3	W½NE	1837-03-18		A1
406	HAINES, Job	2	NE	1837-03-18		A1
404	HARDEN, Jesse	34	N½SW	1837-03-20		A1 F
405	" "	34	NW	1837-03-20		A1 F
427	HARSHBARGER, Joseph	15	W½	1853-09-01		A1 F
428	" "	9	S½SW	1853-09-01		A1
342	HART, Daniel M	34	SE	1837-03-20		A1
329	HARVEY, Ambrose	12	NWNE	1838-09-04		A1
429	HASKILL, Joseph	10	SWSE	1834-01-30		A1 F
430	" "	23	SWNE	1834-01-30		A1 F
431	" "	23	SWSE	1834-01-30		A1
432	" "	25	E½NW	1834-01-30		A1
433	" "	25	NESW	1834-01-30		A1
434	" "	25	NWNW	1834-01-30		A1
435	" "	25	NWSE	1834-01-30		A1
436	" "	25	W½NE	1834-01-30		A1 F
415	HAWTHORN, John	33	W½SW	1850-07-01		A1
459	HERZING, Philip	35	NENW	1838-09-04		A1
437	HOVER, Joseph	13	SESE	1838-09-04		A1
438	" "	13	W½SE	1838-09-04		A1
439	" "	15	NESW	1840-04-04		A1
440	" "	15	SENW	1840-04-04		A1 F
402	HOWELL, James	19	W½SE	1852-06-01		A1
354	HUFFMAN, George	19	E½SE	1849-02-01		A1
341	JACOBS, Daniel	13	N½NE	1837-03-20		A1
485	JONES, Thomas	23	E½SW	1835-10-09		A1
319	KELLER, Abraham	23	N½NE	1837-03-20		A1
500	KENEFAK, William	19	NWNE	1852-06-01		A1
468	KERR, Robert	25	NESE	1835-10-16		A1
403	KIESEKAMP, Henry	35	NWSE	1837-03-20		A1 G7
359	" "	35	SENW	1837-03-20		A1 G6
394	KISER, Jacob	22	E½NW	1837-03-18		A1 F
450	LEATHERMAN, Michael	23	SESE	1844-09-10		A1 F R380
474	MARSHALL, Samuel	14	NWNW	1835-10-08		A1
475	" "	14	NWSW	1835-10-08		A1 F
476	" "	14	SESW	1835-10-08		A1 F
477	" "	15	NE	1835-10-08		A1 F
333	MCCAHON, Archibald	35	E½SW	1837-03-20		A1
416	MCCLELLAN, John	23	SENW	1835-10-09		A1 F
370	MCCONNEL, Henry	27	NW	1837-03-20		A1 F
398	MCFARLAND, James E	33	W½SE	1850-07-01		A1
397	" "	31	E½NE	1852-06-01		A1
499	MCFARLAND, William H	33	E½SE	1850-07-01		A1
331	MCKEE, Andrew	11	SE	1837-03-18		A1
332	" "	12	SW	1837-03-18		A1
336	MILLER, Charles S	35	W½SW	1837-03-20		A1 R362

ID	Individual in Patent	Sec.	Sec. Part	Date Issued	Other Counties	For More Info . . .
337	MILLER, Charles W	17	NW	1853-06-01		A1
338	" "	17	W½NE	1853-06-01		A1
501	MOREY, William P	12	E½NE	1837-03-18		A1
454	MUNDAY, Nicholas	12	E½NW	1837-11-21		A1
455	"	12	SWNE	1837-11-21		A1
335	PARNELL, Charles	11	NENW	1835-10-08		A1
502	PETERS, William	36	NWNW	1835-10-09		A1
419	PHILLIPS, John	33	NW	1852-06-01		A1
420	" "	33	W½NE	1852-06-01		A1
418	" "	21	E½SE	1853-06-01		A1
421	" "	9	E½SE	1853-06-01		A1
322	PRIMMER, Adam	13	SW	1837-03-20		A1
441	PRITCHARD, Joseph	33	E½SW	1850-07-01		A1
350	RAIN, Francis	12	W½NW	1838-09-04		A1
383	RATHBURN, Hiram	21	NENE	1850-07-01		A1
503	RICE, William	23	W½SW	1837-03-20		A1
451	RINGER, Michael	10	NW	1837-03-20		A1 F
452	" "	10	NWNE	1837-03-20		A1 F
504	RINGER, William	10	SWNE	1837-03-20		A1
505	" "	3	NW	1837-03-20		A1 F
484	ROSS, Thomas D	19	W½SW	1852-06-01		A1 F
417	SILLIN, John P	12	E½SE	1837-03-18		A1
464	SKINNER, Robert J	2	NESW	1834-01-30		A1
465	" "	2	SESW	1834-01-30		A1
467	" "	25	SWNW	1834-01-30		A1 G64
466	" "	36	NENE	1834-01-30		A1
469	SLATER, Robert	9	E½NE	1852-06-01		A1
330	SMITH, Amos	3	E½NE	1835-10-16		A1
506	STILL, William	14	SESE	1837-03-20		A1
371	STODDARD, Henry	10	SESE	1834-01-30		A1 F
372	" "	11	NESW	1834-01-30		A1
373	" "	11	NWSW	1834-01-30		A1
374	" "	11	SENW	1834-01-30		A1
375	" "	14	SWSW	1834-01-30		A1
376	" "	15	E½	1834-01-30		A1 F
377	" "	2	NWSW	1834-01-30		A1
378	" "	2	W½NW	1834-01-30		A1
379	" "	23	NENW	1834-01-30		A1 F
380	" "	23	SESE	1834-01-30		A1 R450
381	" "	24	SWSW	1834-01-30		A1
382	" "	26	SWNE	1834-01-30		A1
351	SULLIVAN, Franklin	31	NENW	1852-06-01		A1 F
352	" "	31	W½NE	1852-06-01		A1
388	TERWILLEGER, Isaac	11	NWNW	1835-10-08		A1 F
389	" "	11	SWNW	1835-10-08		A1 F
460	TERWILLIGER, Phillip	2	NENW	1835-10-09		A1 F
461	" "	2	SENW	1835-10-09		A1 F
467	THORN, Henry B	25	SWNW	1834-01-30		A1 G64
362	" "	35	W½SW	1835-10-08		A1 R336
482	VAN HORNE, THOMAS B	36	NWNE	1834-01-30		A1 F
489	VAN HORNE, WILLIAM A	25	SENE	1835-10-08		A1 F
490	" "	36	E½NW	1835-10-09		A1
462	VAN NORTWICK, PHILLIP	36	NWSW	1835-10-08		A1
424	WAITE, John	24	E½	1836-02-15		A1
479	WALKER, Samuel	11	SESW	1837-08-21		A1
478	" "	10	NWSE	1837-11-21		A1
480	" "	5	NWSW	1853-06-01		A1
355	WALTER, George	14	NESE	1837-03-20		A1
356	" "	14	SWSE	1837-03-20		A1
357	" "	35	N½NE	1837-03-20		A1
323	WEAVER, Adam	26	SW	1837-03-18		A1
324	" "	35	NWNW	1837-03-18		A1
425	WEST, Jonathan	35	E½SE	1835-09-15		A1 G68
425	WEST, Thomas J	35	E½SE	1835-09-15		A1 G68
507	WEST, William	35	SWSE	1837-03-15		A1
327	WHEELER, Almon	9	NENW	1852-06-01		A1
328	" "	9	NWNE	1852-06-01		A1
325	WHETSTONE, Adonijah	3	E½SE	1836-02-15		A1 G69
325	WHETSTONE, Elizabeth	3	E½SE	1836-02-15		A1 G69
325	WHETSTONE, John	3	E½SE	1836-02-15		A1 G69
325	WHETSTONE, Mary J	3	E½SE	1836-02-15		A1 G69
366	WILLIAMS, Henry D	14	NESW	1840-10-10		A1
367	" "	14	NWSE	1840-10-10		A1

ID	Individual in Patent	Sec.	Sec. Part	Date Issued	Other Counties	For More Info . . .
368	WILLIAMS, Henry D (Cont'd)	14	SWNW	1840-10-10		A1 F
369	" "	14	W½NW	1844-08-01		A1 F
487	WILLIAMS, Thomas	15	NWSE	1835-10-09		A1 F
488	" "	15	SWNE	1835-10-09		A1 F
320	WILSON, Abraham	10	N½SW	1837-08-21		A1 F
321	" "	10	S½SW	1837-08-21		A1 F

Patent Map

T5-S R5-E
1st PM Meridian

Map Group 5

Township Statistics

Parcels Mapped	:	189
Number of Patents	:	169
Number of Individuals	:	118
Patentees Identified	:	114
Number of Surnames	:	104
Multi-Patentee Parcels	:	7
Oldest Patent Date	:	1/30/1834
Most Recent Patent	:	12/15/1853
Block/Lot Parcels	:	1
Parcels Re-Issued	:	2
Parcels that Overlap	:	0
Cities and Towns	:	5
Cemeteries	:	6

6	5	4
	WALKER Samuel 1853 — CREMEEN Smith 1850	
7	8	WHEELER Almon 1852 / WHEELER Almon 1852 — 9 — SLATER Robert 1852 / CARL John 1853 / HARSHBARGER Joseph 1853 / PHILLIPS John 1853
18	MILLER Charles W 1853 / MILLER Charles W 1853 — 17 — BUB Michael 1852	16
BOSCHE John F 1853 / KENEFAK William 1852 / 19 / BOSCHE John F 1852 / ROSS Thomas D 1852 / HOWELL James 1852 / HUFFMAN George 1849	20	FREISNER Frederick 1851 — RATHBURN Hiram 1850 / 21 / PHILLIPS John 1853
30	29	28
BLAND William 1852 / SULLIVAN Franklin 1852 / SULLIVAN Franklin 1852 / BLAND William 1852 / 31 / MCFARLAND James E 1852 / BARRINGTON Alexander 1851 / BARRINGTON Richard R 1850	32	PHILLIPS John 1852 / PHILLIPS John 1852 / 33 / GARRETSONE Arnold 1852 / HAWTHORN John 1850 / PRITCHARD Joseph 1850 / MCFARLAND James E 1850 / MCFARLAND William H 1850

Section 3
RINGER William 1837

GREGORY Harrison 1837

SMITH Amos 1835

BARNEY Elijah G 1840

ELLIS John 1837

WHETSTONE [69] Adonijah 1836

Section 2
STODDARD Henry 1834

TERWILLIGER Phillip 1835

TERWILLIGER Phillip 1835

HAINES Job 1837

STODDARD Henry 1834

SKINNER Robert J 1834

BAKER Jacob 1837

CLAWSON Josiah 1834

SKINNER Robert J 1834

BARNES Henry 1837

Section 1
DAVIS David Y 1835

BARNES Henry 1837

CHANEY James 1836

CHANEY James 1836

Section 10
RINGER Michael 1837

RINGER Michael 1837

BAKER Jacob 1837

RINGER William 1837

CLAWSON Thomas 1837

CLOSSON Josiah 1853

WILSON Abraham 1837

WALKER Samuel 1837

CLAUSON John 1835

WILSON Abraham 1837

HASKILL Joseph 1834

STODDARD Henry 1834

Section 11
TERWILLEGER Isaac 1835

TERWILLEGER Isaac 1835

STODDARD Henry 1834

STODDARD Henry 1834

STODDARD Henry 1834

BOTKINS William 1837

WALKER Samuel 1837

PARNELL Charles 1835

BARNES Henry 1837

MCKEE Andrew 1837

Section 12
RAIN Francis 1838

MUNDAY Nicholas 1837

MUNDAY Nicholas 1837

MOREY William P 1837

FORNEY Christian 1837

SILLIN John P 1837

HARVEY Ambrose 1838

MCKEE Andrew 1837

Section 15
BREES Lewis 1835

BREES Lewis 1835

HOVER Joseph 1840

HARSHBARGER Joseph 1853

HOVER Joseph 1840

CARSWELL John 1835

MARSHALL Samuel 1835

WILLIAMS Thomas 1835

WILLIAMS Thomas 1835

CARSWELL John 1835

Section 14
WILLIAMS Henry D 1844

MARSHALL Samuel 1835

WILLIAMS Henry D 1840

FLEMMING Jacob 1837

MARSHALL Samuel 1835

STODDARD Henry 1834

WILLIAMS Henry D 1840

WALTER George 1837

MARSHALL Samuel 1835

WALTER George 1837

STILL William 1837

STODDARD Henry 1834

FLEMMING Jacob 1837

Section 13
CAMPBELL Homer M 1837

CAMPBELL Homer M 1837

PRIMMER Adam 1837

JACOBS Daniel 1837

HOVER Joseph 1838

CAMPBELL Homer M 1837

HOVER Joseph 1838

Section 22
KISER Jacob 1837

CHAMBERLIN Samuel 1837

CRISTY Cornelius 1837

Section 23
BEARD William 1835

STODDARD Henry 1834

COLLINS Oliver C 1837

MCCLELLAN John 1835

HASKILL Joseph 1834

RICE William 1837

JONES Thomas 1835

HASKILL Joseph 1834

KELLER Abraham 1837

EWEN William 1835

EWEN William 1835

LEATHERMAN Michael 1844 STODDARD Henry 1834

STODDARD Henry 1834

Section 24
CUMMINS Joseph 1837

WAITE John 1836

BORTON Josiah 1835

BORTON Josiah 1835

Section 27
MCCONNEL Henry 1837

CHAMBERLIN Samuel 1837

CHAMBERLIN Samuel 1837

ELLIOTT James 1845

Section 26
CHAMBERLIN Samuel 1837

STODDARD Henry 1834

WEAVER Adam 1837

CROFT David 1834

BONSER Nathaniel 1835

CROFT David 1834

COLLINS Oliver C 1837

APPLE Henry 1835

Section 25
HASKILL Joseph 1834

SKINNER [64] Robert J 1834

HASKILL Joseph 1834

HASKILL Joseph 1834

HASKILL Joseph 1834

CARY [27] John W 1834

HASKILL Joseph 1834

GODDARD Thomas V 1835

HORNE William A Van 1835

CARY [27] John W 1834

KERR Robert 1835

FREYMAN John G 1835

Section 34
HARDEN Jesse 1837

ELLIOTT Hugh 1837

HARDEN Jesse 1837

HART Daniel M 1837

GREEN William 1837

Section 35
WEAVER Adam 1837

HERZING Philip 1838

DUMBROFF Michael 1838

AYERS [6] Grover 1837

MILLER Charles S 1837

THORN Henry B 1835

WALTER George 1837

AYERS Grover 1837

CROWDER William 1836

AYERS [7] Jeremiah 1837

MCCAHON Archibald 1837

WEST William 1837

WEST [68] Jonathan 1835

Section 36
PETERS William 1835

BREHANT Peter 1835

NORTWICK Phillip Van 1837

ELLIOTT James 1837

ELLIOTT James 1835

HORNE Thomas B Van 1834

HORNE William A Van 1835

BROCK Francis 1835

BROCK Francis 1835

SKINNER Robert J 1834

BROCK Francis 1834

Copyright 2006 Boyd IT, Inc. All Rights Reserved

Helpful Hints

1. This Map's INDEX can be found on the preceding pages.

2. Refer to Map "C" to see where this Township lies within Auglaize County, Ohio.

3. Numbers within square brackets [ ] denote a multi-patentee land parcel (multi-owner). Refer to Appendix "C" for a full list of members in this group.

4. Areas that look to be crowded with Patentees usually indicate multiple sales of the same parcel (Re-issues) or Overlapping parcels. See this Township's Index for an explanation of these and other circumstances that might explain "odd" groupings of Patentees on this map.

Legend

————— Patent Boundary

━━━━━ Section Boundary

▨ No Patents Found (or Outside County)

1., 2., 3., ... Lot Numbers (when beside a name)

[ ] Group Number (see Appendix "C")

Scale: Section = 1 mile X 1 mile
(generally, with some exceptions)

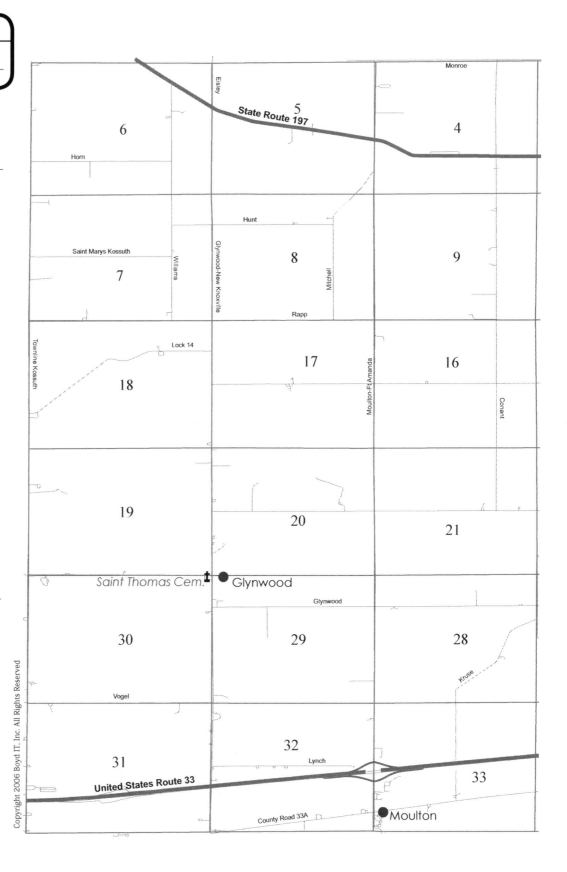

Road Map

T5-S R5-E
1st PM Meridian

Map Group 5

Cities & Towns
Bay (historical)
Buckland
Glynwood
Moulton
Pusheta Town (historical)

Cemeteries
Buckland Cemetery
Crow Cemetery
Jacob Baker Cemetery
Julion Cemetery
Saint Thomas Cemetery
Zion Cemetery

Copyright 2006 Boyd IT. Inc. All Rights Reserved

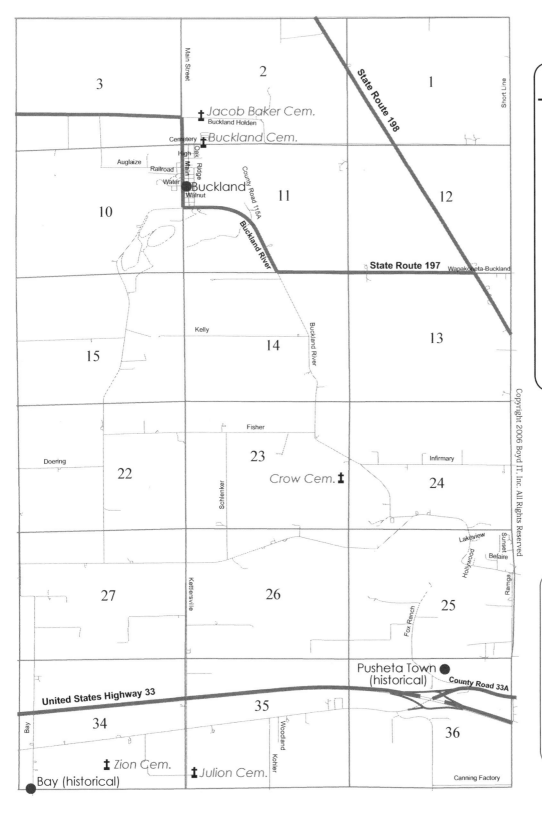

3

2

Main Street

State Route 198

1

Short Line

✝ *Jacob Baker Cem.*
Buckland Holden

Cemetery ✝ *Buckland Cem.*

High

Auglaize

Railroad

Oak

Main

Ridge

Water

● Buckland
Walnut

County Road 115A

11

12

10

Buckland River

State Route 197   Wapakoneta-Buckland

Kelly

15

14

Buckland River

13

Fisher

Doering

23

Crow Cem. ✝

Infirmary

22

Schlenker

24

Lakeview

Sunset

Belaire

Hollywood

Ranga

27

Kettlersville

26

Fox Ranch

25

Pusheta Town
(historical) ●   County Road 33A

United States Highway 33

35

Bay

34

Woodland

Kohler

36

✝ *Zion Cem.*

✝ *Julion Cem.*

Canning Factory

● Bay (historical)

Helpful Hints

1. This road map has a number of uses, but primarily it is to help you: a) find the present location of land owned by your ancestors (at least the general area), b) find cemeteries and city-centers, and c) estimate the route/roads used by Census-takers & tax-assessors.

2. If you plan to travel to Auglaize County to locate cemeteries or land parcels, please pick up a modern travel map for the area before you do. Mapping old land parcels on modern maps is not as exact a science as you might think. Just the slightest variations in public land survey coordinates, estimates of parcel boundaries, or road-map deviations can greatly alter a map's representation of how a road either does or doesn't cross a particular parcel of land.

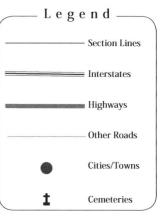

L e g e n d

——————— Section Lines

════════ Interstates

━━━━━━━ Highways

————— Other Roads

● Cities/Towns

✝ Cemeteries

Scale: Section = 1 mile X 1 mile
(generally, with some exceptions)

Historical Map

T5-S R5-E
1st PM Meridian

Map Group 5

Cities & Towns
Bay (historical)
Buckland
Glynwood
Moulton
Pusheta Town (historical)

Cemeteries
Buckland Cemetery
Crow Cemetery
Jacob Baker Cemetery
Julion Cemetery
Saint Thomas Cemetery
Zion Cemetery

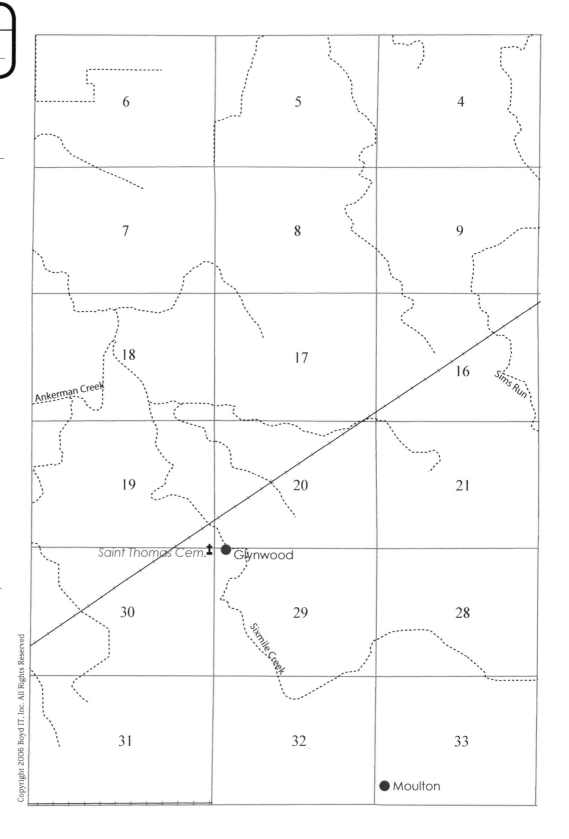

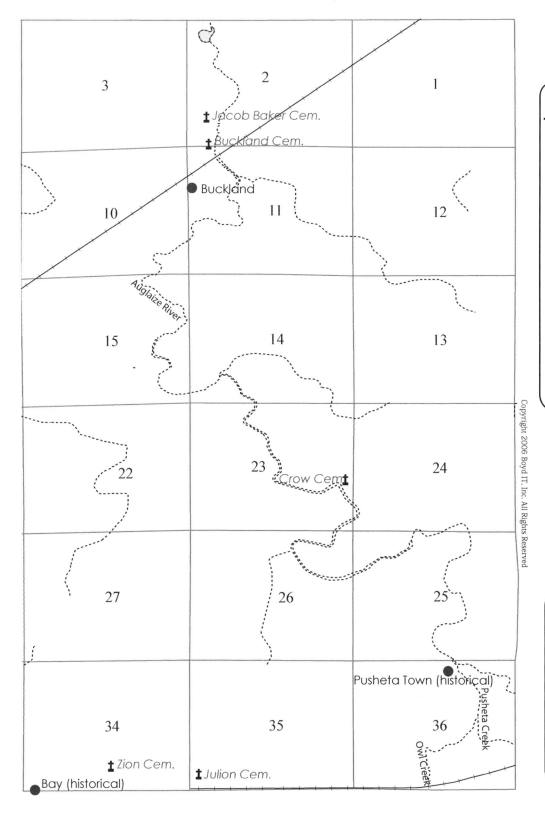

3

2

1

‡ Jacob Baker Cem.

‡ Buckland Cem.

● Buckland

10

11

12

Auglaize River

15

14

13

22

23

Crow Cem ‡

24

27

26

25

Pusheta Town (historical)

Pusheta Creek

34

35

36

Owl Creek

‡ Zion Cem.

‡ Julion Cem.

● Bay (historical)

Helpful Hints

1. This Map takes a different look at the same Congressional Township displayed in the preceding two maps. It presents features that can help you better envision the historical development of the area: a) Water-bodies (lakes & ponds), b) Water-courses (rivers, streams, etc.), c) Railroads, d) City/town center-points (where they were oftentimes located when first settled), and e) Cemeteries.

2. Using this "Historical" map in tandem with this Township's Patent Map and Road Map, may lead you to some interesting discoveries. You will often find roads, towns, cemeteries, and waterways are named after nearby landowners: sometimes those names will be the ones you are researching. See how many of these research gems you can find here in Auglaize County.

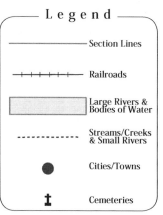

Legend

————————	Section Lines
┼┼┼┼┼┼┼	Railroads
�_____	Large Rivers & Bodies of Water
- - - - - -	Streams/Creeks & Small Rivers
●	Cities/Towns
‡	Cemeteries

Scale: Section = 1 mile X 1 mile
(there are some exceptions)

Map Group 6: Index to Land Patents
Township 5-South Range 6-East (1st PM)

After you locate an individual in this Index, take note of the Section and Section Part then proceed to the Land Patent map on the pages immediately following. You should have no difficulty locating the corresponding parcel of land.

The "For More Info" Column will lead you to more information about the underlying Patents. See the Legend at right, and the "How to Use this Book" chapter, for more information.

```
                        LEGEND
                "For More Info . . ." column
A = Authority (Legislative Act, See Appendix "A")
B = Block or Lot (location in Section unknown)
C = Cancelled Patent
F = Fractional Section
G = Group (Multi-Patentee Patent, see Appendix "C")
V = Overlaps another Parcel
R = Re-Issued (Parcel patented more than once)

(A & G items require you to look in the Appendixes referred
to above. All other Letter-designations followed by a number
require you to locate line-items in this index that possess
the ID number found after the letter).
```

ID	Individual in Patent	Sec.	Sec. Part	Date Issued	Other Counties	For More Info . . .
680	ARMSTRONG, John M	16	SWSW	1844-09-10		A1
792	ARMSTRONG, William	16	NW	1844-09-10		A1
793	" "	16	NWSW	1844-09-10		A1
545	ARTHUR, Daniel M	4	E½NW	1837-03-18		A1
546	"	5	NENE	1837-03-18		A1 F
700	ARTHUR, Joseph G	5	N½NW	1837-03-16		A1 F
701	" "	5	SENW	1837-03-16		A1 F
702	" "	5	W½NE	1837-03-18		A1
743	AUGHENBAUGH, Peter	29	NWSW	1834-01-30		A1 G3
744	AUGHENBOUGH, Peter	29	NESE	1834-01-30		A1 G4
745	" "	29	NWSE	1834-01-30		A1 G4
654	AYRES, Jeremiah	29	SESE	1834-01-30		A1 G9
655	" "	15	E½SW	1835-10-07		A1 G8
651	" "	27	SWNW	1835-10-07		A1
650	" "	20	SWSE	1835-10-08		A1
652	" "	33	E½NE	1835-10-08		A1
653	" "	33	NWNE	1835-10-08		A1
528	BAKER, Benjamin M	18	E½NE	1835-10-09		A1
529	" "	18	SWNE	1837-11-21		A1
728	BAKER, Melyn	8	SW	1835-10-09		A1
729	BAKER, Melyn D	8	E½NE	1837-03-16		A1
730	" "	8	NWNE	1837-03-16		A1
577	BALTZELL, George	19	E½SE	1835-10-09		A1
714	BARLETT, Joshua	23	N½NW	1835-10-07		A1 R561
744	BARNETT, Joseph	29	NESE	1834-01-30		A1 G4
745	" "	29	NWSE	1834-01-30		A1 G4
743	" "	29	NWSW	1834-01-30		A1 G3
695	" "	29	S½SW	1834-01-30		A1 G11 F
696	" "	29	SWSE	1834-01-30		A1 G11
697	" "	32	NE	1834-01-30		A1 G11
698	" "	32	NW	1834-01-30		A1 G11
657	BASS, John	6	SENW	1836-02-15		A1
578	BEAR, George	6	S½NE	1835-10-16		A1
659	BEIDLEMAN, John	20	SESE	1835-10-08		A1
658	" "	20	NWSE	1835-10-09		A1
542	BITLER, Daniel	35	NENE	1835-10-07		A1
753	BLANCK, Phillip	27	W½SW	1837-02-07		A1
660	BOB, John	17	NENE	1837-08-21		A1
550	BOBP, David	11	W½NW	1837-03-20		A1
622	BOOKER, Jacob	35	SENW	1835-10-16		A1
634	BORDEN, James	23	NESE	1836-02-15		A1
635	" "	23	NWSE	1836-02-25		A1
636	" "	24	W½NW	1837-03-18		A1
579	BORTON, George	14	SWSE	1835-10-07		A1
580	" "	23	NWNE	1835-10-07		A1
615	BORTON, Isaac	14	SESE	1837-03-20		A1

ID	Individual in Patent	Sec.	Sec. Part	Date Issued	Other Counties	For More Info . . .
616	BORTON, Isaac (Cont'd)	26	W½SE	1837-03-20		A1
717	BORTON, Josiah	26	E½SE	1835-10-09		A1
718	" "	36	E½NW	1835-10-09		A1
716	" "	26	E½NE	1837-03-20		A1
663	BOTHE, John C	30	NENW	1838-09-04		A1
664	" "	30	NWNE	1838-09-04		A1 F
665	" "	30	NWNW	1838-09-04		A1
666	" "	30	SWNW	1838-09-04		A1
521	BOWDENTISSEL, Anton	23	E½SW	1835-10-07		A1
572	BROCK, Francis	31	SWNW	1834-01-30		A1
581	BROWN, George	21	NWNE	1836-02-25		A1
661	BUCHANNAN, John	10	SW	1837-03-20		A1 G21
662	" "	10	W½SE	1837-03-20		A1 G21
582	BURK, George	4	W½SE	1840-04-04		A1 G22
801	BURK, William T	4	SESE	1838-09-04		A1
582	" "	4	W½SE	1840-04-04		A1 G22
795	BUTTERWORTH, William	33	E½SW	1835-10-08		A1
567	CARY, Ephraim	22	E½SW	1835-10-09		A1
525	CASE, Benjamin	7	E½SW	1835-10-16		A1
746	CATRON, Peter	35	SESE	1835-10-09		A1
747	" "	35	W½SE	1835-10-09		A1
802	CATROW, Zephaniah	35	NENW	1835-09-15		A1
803	" "	35	NWNE	1835-09-15		A1
804	" "	35	S½NE	1835-10-09		A1 V756
637	CHANEY, James	8	W½NW	1835-10-09		A1
648	CHANEY, James S	6	E½SE	1835-10-16		A1
649	" "	7	E½NE	1835-10-16		A1
551	CLAYTON, David	3	W½NW	1837-03-18		A1 F
552	" "	4	NE	1837-03-18		A1 F
584	CONRAD, George	15	W½NE	1836-02-15		A1
583	" "	15	SENW	1836-02-25		A1
623	COOK, Jacob	23	SWSW	1835-10-07		A1
779	CRAWFORD, Thomas	7	SE	1835-10-16		A1
778	" "	7	NWSW	1837-03-20		A1 F
780	" "	7	SWSW	1837-03-20		A1 F
638	CUNNINGHAM, James	10	E½SE	1837-03-20		A1
639	" "	11	E½NW	1837-03-20		A1
667	CUNNINGHAM, John	10	W½NW	1837-08-21		A1
526	CURL, Benjamin	23	S½SE	1836-02-25		A1
699	DARR, Joseph	19	E½NW	1835-09-15		A1
519	DAVIS, Anthony	13	E½SW	1835-10-07		A1
520	" "	13	SWSW	1835-10-07		A1
518	" "	1	N½NE	1837-03-15		A1 F
570	DEIHL, Eustace	34	SE	1835-10-08		A1
668	DEKLAR, John	27	SESW	1840-10-10		A1
781	DEPRES, Thomas J	24	NESW	1835-10-08		A1
722	DIEAHL, Lewis	27	NWSE	1840-10-10		A1
571	DUMBROFF, Eva	15	SWSW	1836-02-15		A1 G33
554	EDMISTON, David	1	E½NW	1837-03-18		A1
555	" "	1	W½SW	1837-03-18		A1
640	ELLIOTT, James	26	W½NW	1840-10-10		A1
585	EMERICK, George	36	SE	1835-10-07		A1
556	EMMERT, David	26	SENW	1840-10-10		A1
796	EPART, William	21	W½NW	1835-09-15		A1
586	ESPY, George	15	W½SE	1835-10-08		A1
587	" "	21	E½SW	1835-10-08		A1
558	FAIRFIELD, David	13	SE	1835-10-08		A1
557	" "	13	NWNW	1835-10-16		A1
559	" "	13	SWNW	1835-10-16		A1
614	FISHER, Ignatz	21	NENW	1840-10-10		A1
669	FOREMAN, John	3	SE	1837-03-18		A1
566	FORSYTHE, Elijah	14	NE	1835-10-08		A1
670	FOSTER, John	2	W½NW	1837-03-18		A1
671	FOWLER, John	2	W½SW	1837-03-18		A1
661	FRAZIER, John	10	SW	1837-03-20		A1 G21
662	" "	10	W½SE	1837-03-20		A1 G21
681	FREEMAN, John M	33	W½SE	1835-10-08		A1
723	FRY, Lorentz	23	NWSW	1836-02-15		A1
631	GARDINER, James B	30	S½	1834-01-30		A1 F
632	" "	30	SE	1834-01-30		A1
633	" "	31	N½NW	1834-01-30		A1 F
612	GAVER, Hiram	16	NE	1844-09-10		A1
673	GILBERT, John	17	W½NE	1835-09-15		A1

ID	Individual in Patent	Sec.	Sec. Part	Date Issued	Other Counties	For More Info . . .
784	GODDARD, Thomas V	30	W½	1834-01-30		A1 F
774	GOODSEL, Sebastian	22	E½SE	1835-10-07		A1
538	GRANER, Christopher	33	W½NW	1835-10-08		A1
625	GRIZER, Jacob	35	W½NW	1835-12-24		A1 G42
624	" "	27	SENE	1840-10-10		A1
539	GRONER, Christopher	13	NWSW	1840-10-10		A1
733	GUTRIDGE, Milton R	12	NWNW	1837-03-18		A1
734	" "	12	SWNW	1837-03-18		A1
748	HAMMELL, Peter	31	NWNW	1834-01-30		A1 F
749	" "	30	NE	1835-10-09		A1 G43
750	HANSER, Philip	3	E½NW	1837-03-20		A1
510	HARVEY, Ambrose	6	NENW	1837-08-21		A1 F
511	" "	6	NWNW	1837-08-21		A1 F
512	" "	6	NWSW	1837-08-21		A1
513	" "	6	SWNW	1837-08-21		A1 F
514	" "	6	SWSW	1837-08-21		A1
676	HATCHER, John L	19	W½NE	1837-03-18		A1 G45
703	HAYWOOD, Joseph	9	SE	1835-09-15		A1
600	HEIDOCKER, Henry	26	W½SW	1835-10-07		A1
541	HEIL, Conrad	26	NESW	1837-08-21		A1
751	HERZING, Philip	19	NENE	1838-09-04		A1
571	HERZING, Phillip	15	SWSW	1836-02-15		A1 G33
626	HINDEL, Jacob	10	NE	1837-03-20		A1
628	HITTEL, Jacob	34	E½SW	1834-01-30		A1
629	" "	34	W½SW	1834-01-30		A1
627	" "	19	W½NW	1840-10-10		A1 F
593	HOLBROOK, George W	15	NWSW	1837-03-18		A1
594	" "	15	W½NW	1837-03-18		A1
595	" "	19	SENE	1837-03-18		A1
625	HORSIMER, Henry	35	W½NW	1835-12-24		A1 G42
601	HOSNIRE, Henry	26	SESW	1836-02-15		A1
704	HOVER, Joseph	2	NWNE	1837-03-20		A1
749	HOWELL, Samuel	30	NE	1835-10-09		A1 G43
674	HUTCHEN, John	25	NW	1835-10-16		A1
782	JACOBS, Thomas K	16	SE	1844-09-10		A1
568	JENKINS, Ephraim S	8	SWNE	1838-09-04		A1
641	JOHNSTON, James	22	W½NW	1834-01-30		A1
642	" "	22	W½SW	1834-01-30		A1
656	JOHNSTON, Job	34	NE	1835-10-08		A1
757	JONES, Richard	2	E½SE	1837-03-16		A1
758	" "	2	NWSE	1837-03-16		A1
724	KAHLER, Lorentz	27	NENE	1835-10-07		A1
675	KELLER, John	11	S½NE	1835-10-07		A1 V707
705	KENINGER, Joseph	22	W½SE	1835-10-07		A1
725	KENTNER, Martin	35	NESE	1835-10-08		A1
726	KINTNER, Martin	36	N½NE	1835-09-15		A1
588	KLINE, George	23	E½NE	1836-02-15		A1
741	KLUE, Nicholas	27	SENW	1835-10-07		A1
527	KOFMAN, Benjamin	19	E½SW	1835-10-07		A1
727	LANDCOMMER, Matthias	27	W½NE	1835-10-07		A1
573	LANKOM, Francis H	15	NENW	1836-02-15		A1
754	LAUER, Phillip	33	SWNE	1835-10-08		A1 G52
677	LAURY, John	1	E½SE	1835-10-07		A1
731	LEATHERMAN, Michael	18	NESW	1844-09-10		A1
732	" "	18	SESE	1844-09-10		A1
569	LEVERING, Esther	6	E½SW	1835-09-15		A1
589	LIBLING, George	27	NENW	1835-10-07		A1
590	" "	27	NESW	1835-10-07		A1
678	LOWREY, John	1	W½SE	1837-03-15		A1
679	LOWRY, John	1	S½NE	1835-09-15		A1
619	LUCAS, Israel	36	S½NE	1835-10-07		A1
620	" "	36	W½SW	1835-10-08		A1
646	MARKS, James	5	S½SE	1835-10-16		A1
645	" "	4	SW	1837-03-16		A1
523	MARTIN, Archelaus	18	W½SW	1835-10-16		A1
759	MATHENY, Richard	17	NW	1835-10-09		A1
547	MCARTHUR, Daniel	4	W½NW	1837-03-16		A1
798	MCCARTNEY, William	7	NWNW	1837-03-20		A1
799	" "	7	SWNW	1837-03-20		A1
591	MCNEIL, George	2	SWSE	1837-03-18		A1
647	MCVICKER, James	18	SESW	1835-10-07		A1
800	MEANS, William	34	NW	1835-10-08		A1
509	MILLER, Adam W	27	E½SE	1835-10-16		A1

ID	Individual in Patent	Sec.	Sec. Part	Date Issued	Other Counties	For More Info . . .
522	MILLER, Anton	26	W½NE	1837-08-21		A1
707	MILLER, Joseph	11	NE	1835-10-08		A1 V675
708	" "	11	S½	1835-10-08		A1
709	" "	14	W½NW	1835-10-08		A1
710	" "	15	E½NE	1835-10-16		A1
770	MILLER, Samuel	25	SW	1835-10-09		A1
516	MOFFETT, Andrew	17	E½SW	1835-10-16		A1
517	" "	17	W½SE	1835-10-16		A1
682	MONROE, John	3	NE	1837-03-18		A1 F
533	MOORE, Charles A	17	SWSW	1838-09-04		A1
548	MORROW, Daniel	23	SWNE	1836-02-25		A1
760	MORROW, Richard	23	S½NW	1836-02-25		A1
613	MOSLER, Ignatius	27	SWSE	1835-10-16		A1
721	NELSON, Levi	10	E½NW	1837-03-20		A1
676	NICHOLS, Isaac	19	W½NE	1837-03-18		A1 G45
683	NORRIS, John	22	E½NE	1835-10-08		A1
715	PARLETT, Joshua	36	W½NW	1835-10-09		A1
565	PATRICK, Edward F	24	W½SW	1835-10-07		A1
752	PFAFF, Philip	17	SENE	1837-08-21		A1
597	POOL, Guy W	32	SW	1835-10-08		A1 G59
598	" "	32	W½SE	1835-10-08		A1 G59
621	POST, Israel	19	W½SE	1835-10-09		A1
655	RICHARDSON, William	15	E½SW	1835-10-07		A1 G8
508	RITCHEY, Adam	8	E½NW	1835-10-16		A1
574	ROELLE, Francis	35	SW	1835-10-09		A1
536	RONEY, Charles	7	NENW	1835-10-07		A1 G60
537	" "	7	W½NE	1835-10-07		A1 G60
775	RONEY, Silas	6	N½NE	1837-03-18		A1 F
536	RONEY, Thomas	7	NENW	1835-10-07		A1 G60
537	" "	7	W½NE	1835-10-07		A1 G60
783	" "	7	SENW	1837-03-15		A1
560	ROSS, David	20	E½SW	1835-10-09		A1
617	RYASON, Isaac	3	E½SW	1837-03-20		A1
618	" "	3	W½SW	1837-03-20		A1
524	SATTERTHWAIT, Barclay A	16	E½SW	1844-09-10		A1
684	SAVIN, John	26	NENW	1835-10-07		A1
711	SAWYER, Joseph	29	NENE	1835-10-08		A1
712	" "	29	W½NE	1835-10-08		A1
720	SELVY, Leonard	25	SE	1835-10-07		A1
553	SHAEFFER, David D	21	E½NE	1835-10-07		A1
561	SHARER, David	23	N½NW	1864-02-10		A1 R714
643	SHAW, James M	4	NESE	1840-10-10		A1
740	SHAW, Neal	1	W½NW	1836-02-15		A1
575	SHREDER, Francis W	20	NESE	1837-03-15		A1
576	" "	20	SWNE	1837-03-15		A1
761	SKINNER, Robert J	14	W½SW	1834-01-30		A1
762	" "	15	E½SE	1834-01-30		A1
763	" "	21	W½SW	1834-01-30		A1
764	" "	24	E½SE	1834-01-30		A1
765	" "	25	W½NE	1834-01-30		A1
767	" "	31	SENW	1834-01-30		A1
768	" "	33	E½NW	1834-01-30		A1
766	" "	30	E½	1835-10-08		A1 F
769	" "	12	W½SW	1835-10-09		A1 G65
515	SMITH, Ammi	6	W½SE	1835-10-16		A1
530	SMITH, Casper	20	SENW	1837-03-16		A1
531	SMITH, Catharine	20	NWNE	1837-03-15		A1
532	SMITH, Catherine	20	NENW	1837-08-21		A1
549	SMITH, Daniel	17	SESE	1837-03-16		A1
719	SMITH, Kasper	20	E½NE	1835-09-15		A1
742	SMITH, Oliver	8	SE	1835-10-16		A1
794	SPALDING, William B	27	NWNW	1835-10-09		A1
754	SPURRIER, Beal	33	SWNE	1835-10-08		A1 G52
563	STEVENS, Ebenezer D	13	NE	1835-10-08		A1
602	STODDARD, Henry	14	E½NW	1834-01-30		A1
603	" "	14	E½SW	1834-01-30		A1
604	" "	21	E½SE	1834-01-30		A1
605	" "	21	W½SE	1834-01-30		A1
606	" "	22	E½NW	1834-01-30		A1
607	" "	22	W½NE	1834-01-30		A1
608	" "	24	W½SE	1834-01-30		A1
609	" "	25	E½NE	1834-01-30		A1
610	" "	31	S½NE	1834-01-30		A1

ID	Individual in Patent	Sec.	Sec. Part	Date Issued	Other Counties	For More Info . . .
611	STODDARD, Henry (Cont'd)	31	W½SW	1834-01-30		A1
592	STRICKER, George	9	E½NE	1837-11-21		A1
540	STRICKLE, Christopher	14	N½SE	1836-02-15		A1
654	TAM, John	29	SESE	1834-01-30		A1 G9
685	" "	24	NE	1835-10-08		A1
687	" "	24	SENW	1835-10-09		A1
686	" "	24	NENW	1835-10-16		A1
543	TEMPLETON, Daniel G	5	SW	1835-09-15		A1
544	" "	5	SWNW	1835-09-15		A1
797	THOMAS, William J	20	W½SW	1835-09-15		A1
772	THROCKMORTON, Samuel	21	SENW	1837-03-16		A1
771	TINGLE, Samuel P	2	E½NE	1837-03-15		A1
773	VAN BLARACOM, SAMUEL	33	E½SE	1835-10-08		A1
777	VAN HORNE, THOMAS B	33	W½SW	1835-10-08		A1
788	VAN HORNE, WILLIAM A	29	SENE	1835-10-08		A1 F
789	" "	31	E½SW	1835-10-08		A1
790	" "	31	SE	1835-10-08		A1
791	" "	32	E½SE	1835-10-08		A1
769	" "	12	W½SW	1835-10-09		A1 G65
785	" "	13	E½NW	1835-10-16		A1
786	" "	2	E½NW	1835-12-24		A1
787	" "	2	E½SW	1835-12-24		A1
644	VICKER, James M	18	NESE	1837-03-15		A1
562	WHEELER, Ebenezar	9	W½NW	1837-03-16		A1
564	WHEELER, Ebenezer	9	E½NW	1837-03-16		A1
738	WHEELER, Moses	18	NWNE	1835-10-07		A1
737	" "	18	E½NW	1835-10-16		A1
736	WHEELER, Moses M	18	W½SE	1837-03-18		A1
735	" "	17	NWSW	1837-08-21		A1
776	WHEELER, Stephen M	20	W½NW	1837-08-21		A1
744	WILDS, Jonathan K	29	NESE	1834-01-30		A1 G4
745	" "	29	NWSE	1834-01-30		A1 G4
743	" "	29	NWSW	1834-01-30		A1 G3
695	" "	29	S½SW	1834-01-30		A1 G11 F
696	" "	29	SWSE	1834-01-30		A1 G11
693	" "	31	NENE	1834-01-30		A1
694	" "	31	NWNE	1834-01-30		A1
697	" "	32	NE	1834-01-30		A1 G11
698	" "	32	NW	1834-01-30		A1 G11
597	" "	32	SW	1835-10-08		A1 G59
598	" "	32	W½SE	1835-10-08		A1 G59
596	WILLIAMS, George W	1	E½SW	1837-03-16		A1
599	WILLIAMS, Henry D	2	SWNE	1838-09-04		A1
688	WILLIAMS, John	12	E½	1835-10-08		A1
690	" "	12	E½SW	1835-10-08		A1
689	" "	12	E½NW	1836-02-25		A1
691	" "	9	W½NE	1837-08-21		A1
692	WIMERT, John	36	E½SW	1835-10-07		A1
755	WINGET, Reuben	5	N½SE	1835-10-16		A1
534	WOOD, Charles F	29	E½NW	1834-04-09		A1
535	" "	29	W½NW	1834-04-09		A1
739	WRIGHT, Nathan	18	W½NW	1835-10-16		A1
756	WRIGHT, Reuben	35	SENE	1837-03-16		A1 V804
672	WULF, John G	21	SWNE	1835-09-15		A1
706	YOUNG, Joseph M	9	SW	1837-08-21		A1
713	ZINK, Joseph	17	NESE	1837-03-16		A1
630	ZINN, Jacob	24	SESW	1836-02-15		A1

Patent Map

T5-S R6-E
1st PM Meridian

Map Group 6

Township Statistics

Parcels Mapped	:	297
Number of Patents	:	273
Number of Individuals	:	201
Patentees Identified	:	199
Number of Surnames	:	169
Multi-Patentee Parcels	:	22
Oldest Patent Date	:	1/30/1834
Most Recent Patent	:	2/10/1864
Block/Lot Parcels	:	0
Parcels Re - Issued	:	1
Parcels that Overlap	:	4
Cities and Towns	:	2
Cemeteries	:	11

HARVEY Ambrose 1837
HARVEY Ambrose 1837
RONEY Silas 1837
ARTHUR Joseph G 1837
ARTHUR Joseph G 1837
ARTHUR Daniel M 1837
MCARTHUR Daniel 1837
CLAYTON David 1837

HARVEY Ambrose 1837
BASS John 1836
BEAR George 1835
TEMPLETON Daniel G 1835
ARTHUR Joseph G 1837
5
ARTHUR Daniel M 1837

HARVEY Ambrose 1837
6
SMITH Ammi 1835
TEMPLETON Daniel G 1835
WINGET Reuben 1835
4
BURK [22] George 1840
SHAW James M 1840

HARVEY Ambrose 1837
LEVERING Esther 1835
CHANEY James S 1835
MARKS James 1835
MARKS James 1837
BURK William T 1838

MCCARTNEY William 1837
RONEY [60] Charles 1835
RONEY [60] Charles 1835
CHANEY James 1835
BAKER Melyn D 1837
WHEELER Ebenezar 1837
WILLIAMS John 1837

MCCARTNEY William 1837
RONEY Thomas 1837
7
CHANEY James S 1835
RITCHEY Adam 1835
JENKINS Ephraim S 1838
BAKER Melyn D 1837
WHEELER Ebenezer 1837
9
STRICKER George 1837

CRAWFORD Thomas 1837
CRAWFORD Thomas 1835
8
BAKER Melyn 1835
SMITH Oliver 1835
YOUNG Joseph M 1837
HAYWOOD Joseph 1835

CRAWFORD Thomas 1837
CASE Benjamin 1835

WRIGHT Nathan 1835
WHEELER Moses 1835
WHEELER Moses 1835
MATHENY Richard 1835
GILBERT John 1835
BOB John 1837
ARMSTRONG William 1844
GAVER Hiram 1844

18
BAKER Benjamin M 1837
BAKER Benjamin M 1835
17
PFAFF Philip 1837
16

MARTIN Archelaus 1835
LEATHERMAN Michael 1844
WHEELER Moses M 1837
VICKER James M 1837
WHEELER Moses M 1837
MOFFETT Andrew 1835
ZINK Joseph 1837
ARMSTRONG William 1844
SATTERTHWAIT Barclay A 1844
JACOBS Thomas K 1844

MCVICKER James 1835
LEATHERMAN Michael 1844
MOORE Charles A 1838
MOFFETT Andrew 1835
SMITH Daniel 1837
ARMSTRONG John M 1844

HITTEL Jacob 1840
HATCHER [45] John L 1837
HERZING Philip 1838
WHEELER Stephen M 1837
SMITH Catherine 1837
SMITH Catharine 1837
EPART William 1835
FISHER Ignatz 1840
BROWN George 1836

DARR Joseph 1835
19
HOLBROOK George W 1837
SMITH Casper 1837
SHREDER Francis W 1837
SMITH Kasper 1835
THROCKMORTON Samuel 1837
WULF John G 1835
SHAEFFER David D 1835

POST Israel 1835
THOMAS William J 1835
20
BEIDLEMAN John 1835
SHREDER Francis W 1837
SKINNER Robert J 1834
21
STODDARD Henry 1834

KOFMAN Benjamin 1835
BALTZELL George 1835
ROSS David 1835
AYRES Jeremiah 1835
BEIDLEMAN John 1835
ESPY George 1835
STODDARD Henry 1834

BOTHE John C 1838
BOTHE John C 1838
BOTHE John C 1838
WOOD Charles F 1834
SAWYER Joseph 1835
SAWYER Joseph 1835

BOTHE John C 1838
HAMMELL [43] Peter 1835
WOOD Charles F 1834
29
HORNE William A Van 1835
28

GODDARD Thomas V 1834
30
SKINNER Robert J 1835
AUGHENBAUGH [3] Peter 1834
AUGHENBOUGH [4] Peter 1834

GARDINER James B 1834
GARDINER James B 1834
BARNETT [11] Joseph 1834
BARNETT [11] Joseph 1834
AYRES [9] Jeremiah 1834

HAMMELL Peter 1834
GARDINER James B 1834
WILDS Jonathan K 1834
WILDS Jonathan K 1834
GRANER Christopher 1835
AYRES Jeremiah 1835

BROCK Francis 1834
SKINNER Robert J 1834
STODDARD Henry 1834
BARNETT [11] Joseph 1834
BARNETT [11] Joseph 1834
SKINNER Robert J 1834
LAUER [52] Phillip 1835
AYRES Jeremiah 1835

STODDARD Henry 1834
31
HORNE William A Van 1835
HORNE William A Van 1835
POOL [59] Guy W 1835
POOL [59] Guy W 1835
HORNE William A Van 1835
HORNE Thomas B Van 1835
33
FREEMAN John M 1835
BUTTERWORTH William 1835
BLARACOM Samuel Van 1835

Section 3:
CLAYTON David 1837
HANSER Philip 1837
MONROE John 1837
RYASON Isaac 1837
3
FOREMAN John 1837
RYASON Isaac 1837

Section 2:
FOSTER John 1837
HORNE William A Van 1835
WILLIAMS Henry D 1838
TINGLE Samuel P 1837
FOWLER John 1837
2
JONES Richard 1837
HORNE William A Van 1835
MCNEIL George 1837
JONES Richard 1837

Section 1:
HOVER Joseph 1837
SHAW Neal 1836
DAVIS Anthony 1837
EDMISTON David 1837
LOWRY John 1835
EDMISTON David 1837
1
LOWREY John 1837
WILLIAMS George W 1837
LAURY John 1835

Section 10:
CUNNINGHAM John 1837
NELSON Levi 1837
HINDEL Jacob 1837
10
BUCHANNAN [21] John 1837
BUCHANNAN [21] John 1837
CUNNINGHAM James 1837

Section 11:
BOBP David 1837
CUNNINGHAM James 1837
MILLER Joseph 1835
KELLER John 1835
11
MILLER Joseph 1835

Section 12:
GUTRIDGE Milton R 1837
GUTRIDGE Milton R 1837
WILLIAMS John 1836
WILLIAMS John 1835
SKINNER [65] Robert J 1835
12
WILLIAMS John 1835

Section 15:
HOLBROOK George W 1837
LANKOM Francis H 1836
CONRAD George 1836
CONRAD George 1836
MILLER Joseph 1835
15
HOLBROOK George W 1837
AYRES [8] Jeremiah 1835
ESPY George 1835
DUMBROFF [33] Eva 1836
SKINNER Robert J 1834

Section 14:
MILLER Joseph 1835
STODDARD Henry 1834
FORSYTHE Elijah 1835
SKINNER Robert J 1834
14
STRICKLE Christopher 1836
STODDARD Henry 1834
BORTON George 1835
BORTON Isaac 1837

Section 13:
FAIRFIELD David 1835
HORNE William A Van 1835
STEVENS Ebenezer D 1835
FAIRFIELD David 1835
GRONER Christopher 1840
13
FAIRFIELD David 1835
DAVIS Anthony 1835
DAVIS Anthony 1835

Section 22:
JOHNSTON James 1834
STODDARD Henry 1834
STODDARD Henry 1834
NORRIS John 1835
22
KENINGER Joseph 1835
JOHNSTON James 1834
CARY Ephraim 1835
GOODSEL Sebastian 1835

Section 23:
BARLETT Joshua 1835
SHARER David 1864
BORTON George 1835
MORROW Richard 1836
MORROW Daniel 1836
KLINE George 1836
FRY Lorentz 1836
23
BORDEN James 1836
BORDEN James 1836
COOK Jacob 1835
BOWDENTISSEL Anton 1835
CURL Benjamin 1836

Section 24:
BORDEN James 1837
TAM John 1835
TAM John 1835
TAM John 1835
24
PATRICK Edward F 1835
DEPRES Thomas J 1835
STODDARD Henry 1834
ZINN Jacob 1836
SKINNER Robert J 1834

Section 27:
SPALDING William B 1835
LIBLING George 1835
LANDCOMMER Matthias 1835
KAHLER Lorentz 1835
AYRES Jeremiah 1835
KLUE Nicholas 1835
27
GRIZER Jacob 1840
BLANCK Phillip 1837
LIBLING George 1835
DIEAHL Lewis 1840
DEKLAR John 1840
MOSLER Ignatius 1835
MILLER Adam W 1835

Section 26:
ELLIOTT James 1840
SAVIN John 1835
MILLER Anton 1837
EMMERT David 1840
26
BORTON Josiah 1837
HEIDOCKER Henry 1835
HEIL Conrad 1837
BORTON Isaac 1837
HOSNIRE Henry 1836
BORTON Josiah 1835

Section 25:
HUTCHEN John 1835
SKINNER Robert J 1834
STODDARD Henry 1834
25
MILLER Samuel 1835
SELVY Leonard 1835

Section 34:
MEANS William 1835
JOHNSTON Job 1835
34
HITTEL Jacob 1834
HITTEL Jacob 1834
DEIHL Eustace 1835

Section 35:
GRIZER [42] Jacob 1835
CATROW Zephaniah 1835
CATROW Zephaniah 1835
BITLER Daniel 1835
BOOKER Jacob 1835
CATROW Zephaniah 1835
WRIGHT Reuben 1837
ROELLE Francis 1835
35
CATRON Peter 1835
KENTNER Martin 1835
CATRON Peter 1835

Section 36:
PARLETT Joshua 1835
KINTNER Martin 1835
BORTON Josiah 1835
LUCAS Israel 1835
LUCAS Israel 1835
36
WIMERT John 1835
EMERICK George 1835

Helpful Hints

1. This Map's INDEX can be found on the preceding pages.

2. Refer to Map "C" to see where this Township lies within Auglaize County, Ohio.

3. Numbers within square brackets [ ] denote a multi-patentee land parcel (multi-owner). Refer to Appendix "C" for a full list of members in this group.

4. Areas that look to be crowded with Patentees usually indicate multiple sales of the same parcel (Re-issues) or Overlapping parcels. See this Township's Index for an explanation of these and other circumstances that might explain "odd" groupings of Patentees on this map.

Legend

——— Patent Boundary

━━━ Section Boundary

▨ No Patents Found (or Outside County)

1., 2., 3., ... Lot Numbers (when beside a name)

[ ] Group Number (see Appendix "C")

Scale: Section = 1 mile X 1 mile (generally, with some exceptions)

95

Road Map

T5-S R6-E
1st PM Meridian

Map Group 6

Cities & Towns

Sherwood Forest (subdivision)
Wapakoneta

Cemeteries

Bethel Cemetery
Conner-Kaiser Cemetery
Craft Cemetery
Evergreen Cemetery
Greenlawn Cemetery
Old Saint Josephs Cemetery
Reinhart Cemetery
Saint Joseph Cemetery
Stevely Cemetery
Tam Cemetery
Wheeler Cemetery

Ritchie

Wheeler Cem.

| 6 | 5 | 4 |

Buckland Holden

Stevely Cem.

| 7 | 8 | 9 |

Wapakoneta-Buckland

| 18 | 17 | 16 |

Linzee

Rosewood
Bluegrass
Infirmary

Springfield

| 19 | 20 | 21 |

Kah
Commancheta Tr
Apache
Navajo
Cherokee
Redskin
Redskin Trail

Sherwood Forest
(subdivision)

Brewfield

Magnolia
Dogwood
Cottonwood
Dearborn
Center
Stinebaugh
Cole

| 30 | 29 | 28 |

Evergreen Cem.

Quaker Run Village

Old Saint Josephs Cem.

Pearl

Wapakoneta

Greenlawn Cem.

| 31 | 32 | 33 |

3

Reichelderfer

2

Freymuth

1

‡ Bethel Cem.

Seitz

10

Dixie

11

12

Craft Cem. ‡

Interstate 75

Golden Bridge

13

Hengstler

14

Conner-Kaiser Cem. ‡

Haus

15

Mudsock

State Route 67

Tam Cem. ‡

22

Brown

Blackhoof Creek

24

23

Blank

Bachman

27

26

25

Middle

Reinhart Cem. ‡

34

35

36

‡ Saint Joseph Cem.

United States Route 33

Town Line—Line Town

Helpful Hints

1. This road map has a number of uses, but primarily it is to help you: a) find the present location of land owned by your ancestors (at least the general area), b) find cemeteries and city-centers, and c) estimate the route/roads used by Census-takers & tax-assessors.

2. If you plan to travel to Auglaize County to locate cemeteries or land parcels, please pick up a modern travel map for the area before you do. Mapping old land parcels on modern maps is not as exact a science as you might think. Just the slightest variations in public land survey coordinates, estimates of parcel boundaries, or road-map deviations can greatly alter a map's representation of how a road either does or doesn't cross a particular parcel of land.

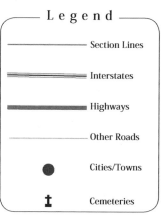

L e g e n d

———————— Section Lines

════════ Interstates

━━━━━━━━ Highways

———————— Other Roads

● Cities/Towns

‡ Cemeteries

Scale: Section = 1 mile X 1 mile
(generally, with some exceptions)

97

Historical Map

T5-S R6-E
1st PM Meridian

Map Group 6

Cities & Towns
Sherwood Forest (subdivision)
Wapakoneta

Cemeteries
Bethel Cemetery
Conner-Kaiser Cemetery
Craft Cemetery
Evergreen Cemetery
Greenlawn Cemetery
Old Saint Josephs Cemetery
Reinhart Cemetery
Saint Joseph Cemetery
Stevely Cemetery
Tam Cemetery
Wheeler Cemetery

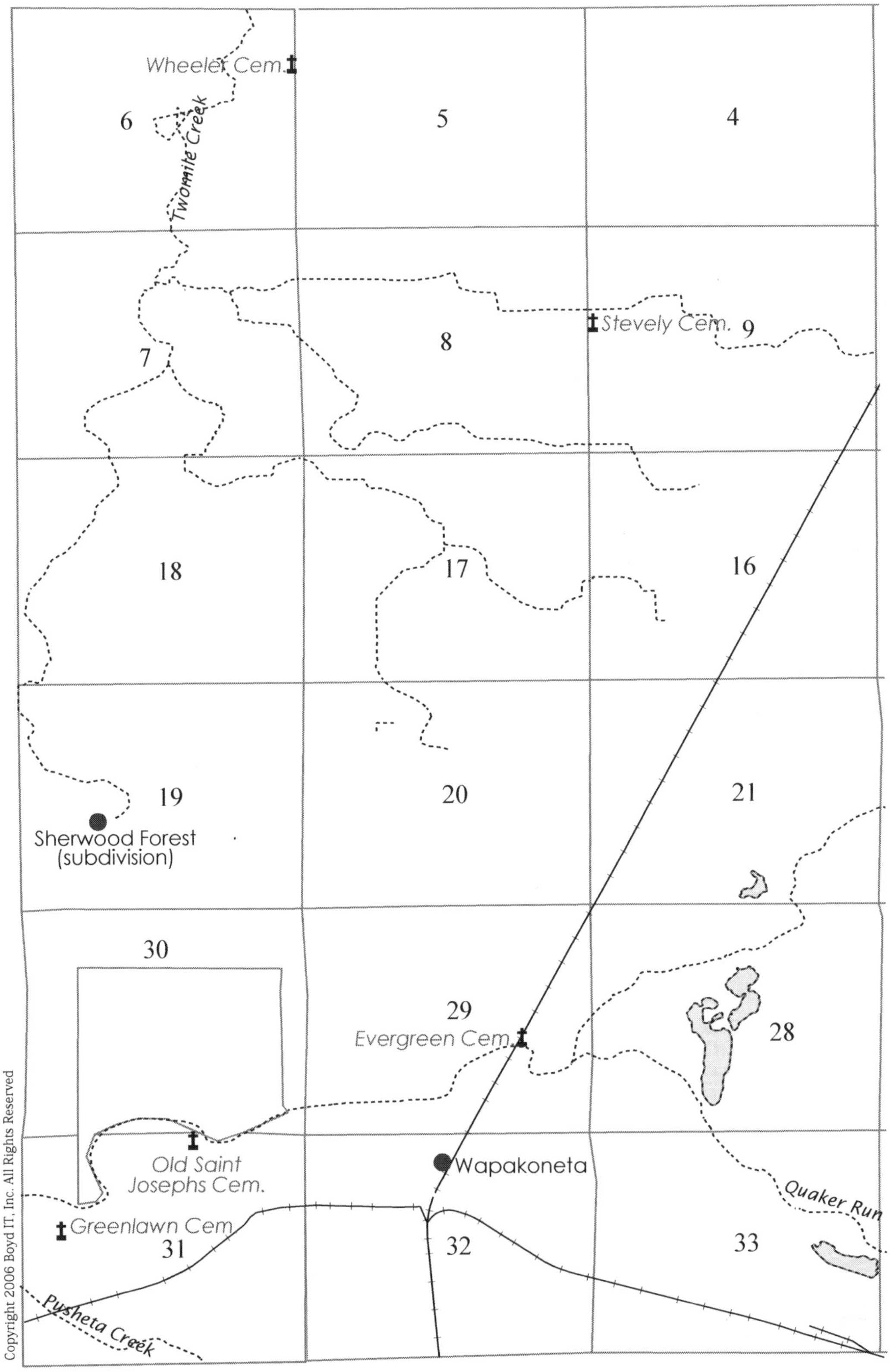

Wheeler Cem.

6

5

4

Twomile Creek

7

8

Stevely Cem. 9

18

17

16

19

Sherwood Forest
(subdivision)

20

21

30

29

Evergreen Cem.

28

Old Saint
Josephs Cem.

Wapakoneta

Greenlawn Cem.

31

32

33

Quaker Run

Pusheta Creek

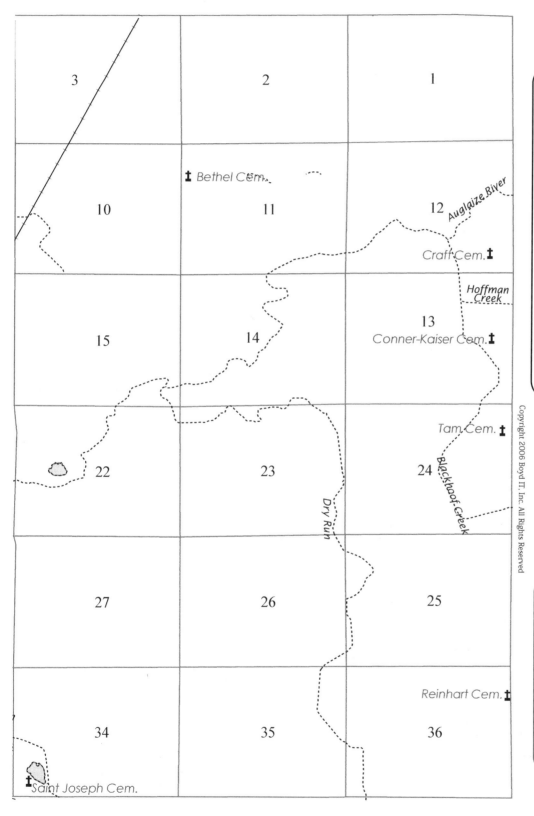

3

2

1

‡ *Bethel Cem.*

10

11

12 *Auglaize River*

Craft Cem. ‡

Hoffman Creek

13

15

14

Conner-Kaiser Cem. ‡

Tam Cem. ‡

22

23

24 *Blackhoof Creek*

Dry Run

27

26

25

Reinhart Cem. ‡

34

35

36

‡ *Saint Joseph Cem.*

Helpful Hints

1. This Map takes a different look at the same Congressional Township displayed in the preceding two maps. It presents features that can help you better envision the historical development of the area: a) Water-bodies (lakes & ponds), b) Water-courses (rivers, streams, etc.), c) Railroads, d) City/town center-points (where they were oftentimes located when first settled), and e) Cemeteries.

2. Using this "Historical" map in tandem with this Township's Patent Map and Road Map, may lead you to some interesting discoveries. You will often find roads, towns, cemeteries, and waterways are named after nearby landowners: sometimes those names will be the ones you are researching. See how many of these research gems you can find here in Auglaize County.

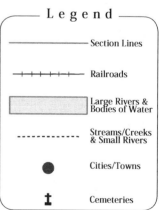

Legend

————————	Section Lines
‑+‑+‑+‑+‑+‑	Railroads
▭	Large Rivers & Bodies of Water
- - - - - - -	Streams/Creeks & Small Rivers
●	Cities/Towns
‡	Cemeteries

Scale: Section = 1 mile X 1 mile
(there are some exceptions)

Map Group 7: Index to Land Patents

Township 5-South Range 7-East (1st PM)

After you locate an individual in this Index, take note of the Section and Section Part then proceed to the Land Patent map on the pages immediately following. You should have no difficulty locating the corresponding parcel of land.

The "For More Info" Column will lead you to more information about the underlying Patents. See the Legend at right, and the "How to Use this Book" chapter, for more information.

ID	Individual in Patent	Sec.	Sec. Part	Date Issued	Other Counties	For More Info . . .
891	AFFOLTIR, John	16	NW	1844-09-10		A1 G1
994	ALLEN, Whiting	8	E½SW	1835-09-15		A1
995	" "	8	SE	1835-09-15		A1
996	" "	8	SENW	1835-09-15		A1
997	" "	8	SWNE	1835-09-15		A1
991	" "	33	E½NW	1835-10-16		A1
992	" "	33	NE	1835-10-16		A1
993	" "	34	W½NW	1835-10-16		A1
893	BAILEY, John	22	NWSW	1835-10-07		A1
894	" "	22	SWNW	1835-10-09		A1
892	" "	21	SESE	1835-12-24		A1
973	BAILEY, Richard	21	NESE	1835-10-07		A1
972	" "	21	NE	1835-10-09		A1
974	BAILY, Richard	22	SWSW	1837-03-16		A1 F
897	BALTZELL, John C	13	SWSE	1836-02-15		A1
964	BASIL, Nelson R	23	E½NE	1837-03-15		A1
966	" "	25	N½NE	1837-03-15		A1
965	" "	24	W½NW	1837-03-16		A1
934	BAYLIFF, Joshua	24	SENW	1837-03-15		A1
981	BERRY, Samuel	27	W½NW	1836-02-25		A1
817	BESSE, Alden	18	N½SE	1835-10-09		A1
998	BETHERS, William	19	NESW	1835-10-16		A1 V875
986	BIGGS, Silas	36	SE	1837-03-16		A1
828	BITLER, Daniel	32	NWSE	1835-10-09		A1 G15
826	" "	32	E½SE	1835-10-16		A1
827	" "	32	SWSE	1835-10-16		A1
982	BOWMAN, Samuel	25	NW	1835-10-09		A1
969	BRACKNEY, Reuben	34	W½SW	1837-03-18		A1 F
895	BRENTLINGER, John	5	N½NE	1835-10-07		A1
896	BRINTLINGER, John	3	SWNW	1837-03-20		A1 F
870	BROBST, Jacob	16	W½NE	1844-09-10		A1
926	BROWN, Joseph	13	E½NE	1837-03-15		A1
927	" "	13	N½SE	1837-03-15		A1
970	CARMONY, Rhoda	1	NESW	1835-09-15		A1
971	" "	1	W½SW	1835-09-15		A1
815	CARTER, Adcock	1	NESE	1836-02-15		A1
816	" "	1	W½SE	1836-02-15		A1
898	CARTER, John	8	NWNE	1835-10-09		A1
999	CARTER, William	5	E½SW	1835-10-09		A1
885	CASTEEL, Jefferson	28	SENE	1837-03-15		A1
851	COLEMAN, Henry	36	NWNW	1837-03-16		A1
850	" "	35	NENE	1837-03-18		A1
880	COLEMAN, James	22	NWNW	1835-10-07		A1
881	" "	24	SESE	1836-02-15		A1
989	COLEMAN, Thomas	33	NESW	1835-10-16		A1
1000	CONNER, William	21	NWSE	1837-03-15		A1

ID	Individual in Patent	Sec.	Sec. Part	Date Issued	Other Counties	For More Info . . .
809	COPELAND, Abner	23	E½SW	1837-03-15		A1
810	" "	23	W½SE	1837-03-16		A1
899	CORDER, John	23	SWSW	1835-10-08		A1
840	CRABB, Elliott	29	SWNW	1837-03-15		A1
940	CRETCHER, Mathew	20	SE	1837-03-15		A1
941	" "	20	SENE	1837-03-15		A1
942	" "	21	SESW	1837-03-15		A1
943	" "	21	SWSE	1837-03-15		A1
944	" "	21	W½SW	1837-03-15		A1
945	" "	28	NENE	1837-03-15		A1
946	" "	28	NW	1837-03-15		A1
947	" "	28	W½NE	1837-03-15		A1
948	" "	29	NE	1837-03-15		A1
938	" "	17	E½NE	1837-03-16		A1
939	" "	17	NESE	1837-03-16		A1
1001	DAVIS, William	5	NW	1835-10-07		A1
886	EDGE, Jesse	35	N½SW	1835-10-07		A1
887	" "	35	SESW	1836-02-15		A1
889	" "	35	SWSW	1836-02-25		A1
888	" "	35	SWSE	1852-06-01		A1
833	EDMISTON, David	6	NW	1835-10-07		A1
834	" "	6	SWNE	1835-10-07		A1
882	FINLAW, James	20	NENE	1837-03-15		A1
890	GOLDING, Jesse	18	W½SW	1835-12-24		A1
825	GRAHAM, Charles	3	NW	1835-10-16		A1
1002	GRAHAM, William	2	E½NE	1835-10-09		A1
891	HAGY, Samuel	16	NW	1844-09-10		A1 G1
836	HARROD, David	13	W½NE	1836-02-25		A1
835	" "	1	SESW	1837-08-21		A1
871	HARROD, Jacob	24	SW	1837-03-16		A1
872	" "	24	W½SE	1837-03-16		A1
873	" "	25	SE	1837-03-16		A1
935	HARROD, Levi	15	N½SW	1837-03-15		A1 F
936	" "	16	E½SE	1844-09-10		A1
954	HARROD, Michael	10	W½NW	1835-10-08		A1
955	" "	12	NW	1835-10-08		A1
957	" "	4	SW	1835-10-08		A1
958	" "	4	W½SE	1835-10-08		A1
959	" "	9	NE	1835-10-08		A1
956	" "	4	E½SE	1837-03-16		A1
837	HENRY, David	30	NWNE	1835-10-08		A1
990	HENRY, Thomas	16	E½NE	1844-09-10		A1
963	HESTER, Nancy	19	W½SW	1835-10-09		A1
874	HITTEL, Jacob	32	W½SW	1834-01-30		A1
900	HOFFMAN, John	17	S½SW	1835-10-09		A1
928	HOVER, Joseph	18	SWSE	1837-03-20		A1
929	" "	8	NENE	1837-03-20		A1
805	HOWELL, Aaron	17	NWSW	1835-10-16		A1
806	" "	17	W½NE	1836-02-15		A1
932	HOWELL, Joseph	6	W½SW	1835-10-09		A1
930	" "	18	SENW	1835-10-16		A1
931	" "	18	SWNE	1835-10-16		A1
987	HOWELL, Stephen	8	SENE	1836-02-15		A1
1004	HOWELL, William	7	NESE	1837-03-16		A1
1003	" "	33	SESW	1837-03-18		A1
975	JONES, Richard	8	NENW	1835-10-09		A1
819	JUSTICE, Allen	15	NW	1837-03-15		A1 F
818	" "	10	NWSW	1837-03-20		A1
847	KENT, Hannah	6	NESE	1835-10-08		A1
848	" "	6	SESW	1835-10-08		A1
849	" "	6	W½SE	1835-10-08		A1
1005	KENT, William J	6	SENE	1850-08-07		A1
807	KIRKBRIDE, Abel	6	SESE	1837-03-15		A1 G49
808	" "	8	W½SW	1837-03-15		A1 G49
845	KITE, George W	36	E½NW	1837-11-21		A1
875	LANDIS, Jacob	19	E½SW	1835-10-09		A1 V998
953	LANE, Micajah	33	SWSE	1837-03-16		A1
1010	LAYTON, William M	18	E½SW	1835-10-09		A1
867	LEMASTERS, Isaac	32	E½NW	1835-10-09		A1
868	" "	32	W½NE	1835-10-09		A1
979	LISLE, Robert	4	N½	1835-10-08		A1
980	" "	7	W½	1835-10-08		A1
852	LOONEY, Henry H	35	NWSE	1844-09-10		A1

ID	Individual in Patent	Sec.	Sec. Part	Date Issued	Other Counties	For More Info . . .
820	LUSK, Anna	23	NWNE	1837-03-15		A1
823	LUSK, Benjamin	25	NWSW	1835-10-07		A1
821	" "	16	E½SW	1844-09-10		A1
822	" "	16	W½SE	1844-09-10		A1
866	LUSK, Isaac H	24	NENW	1837-03-18		A1
1008	LUSK, William	23	E½NW	1835-10-09		A1
1006	" "	15	SWSW	1835-10-16		A1
1009	" "	36	NE	1837-03-20		A1
1007	" "	16	W½SW	1844-09-10		A1
902	MCCORMICK, John	1	SESE	1837-03-15		A1
841	MCLAUGHLIN, George F	17	SESE	1835-10-08		A1
907	MEDEARIS, John R	31	W½NW	1835-10-09		A1
967	MEDEARIS, Oliver	31	E½NW	1835-10-09		A1
830	MILLER, Daniel	17	S½NW	1835-09-15		A1
829	" "	17	NWNW	1836-02-15		A1
831	" "	33	NWSE	1836-02-15		A1
842	MILLER, George	32	E½NE	1835-10-07		A1
843	" "	33	NWNW	1835-10-07		A1
869	MILLER, Isaac	33	NESE	1837-11-21		A1
903	MILLER, John	29	SE	1835-10-16		A1
937	MIX, Levi	25	S½NE	1837-03-16		A1
853	MORRIS, Henry	12	NE	1835-10-09		A1
854	" "	19	NW	1835-10-09		A1
855	" "	19	SE	1835-10-09		A1
856	" "	20	SW	1835-10-09		A1
878	MORRIS, James A	35	SENE	1837-08-21		A1
879	" "	35	W½NE	1837-08-21		A1
904	MORRIS, John	30	SW	1835-10-09		A1
960	MORRIS, Moffit	36	SWNW	1837-08-21		A1
983	MORRIS, Samuel	17	W½SE	1835-10-09		A1
984	" "	20	E½NW	1835-10-09		A1
985	" "	20	W½NE	1835-10-09		A1
865	MUSSELMAN, Hiram	33	SWNW	1835-10-16		A1
839	MUSSER, Eliza A	13	SESE	1836-02-15		A1
883	NICKELL, James N	23	W½NW	1835-10-09		A1
905	OAR, John	27	W½SW	1837-03-15		A1 F
988	OLIPHANT, Susan	18	SESE	1836-02-15		A1
961	PORTER, Moses	29	E½NW	1835-10-07		A1
962	" "	29	NWNW	1835-10-07		A1
901	POWELL, John M	25	SWSW	1835-10-07		A1
906	PRICTCHARD, John	36	SW	1837-11-21		A1
824	RICHARDSON, Byrd	24	NE	1835-10-07		A1
1011	RICHARDSON, William	32	E½SW	1834-01-30		A1
828	" "	32	NWSE	1835-10-09		A1 G15
832	RIEMAN, Daniel	20	W½NW	1835-10-09		A1
908	ROGERS, John	29	SW	1835-10-09		A1
909	RUMAN, John	19	NE	1835-10-09		A1
876	SCHLOSSER, Jacob	30	SWNE	1835-10-08		A1
877	" "	32	W½NW	1835-10-08		A1
910	SCHOOLER, John	5	S½NE	1835-10-07		A1
911	" "	5	SE	1835-10-08		A1
933	SCHOOLER, Joseph	23	SWNE	1837-08-21		A1
1012	SHAW, William	7	W½SW	1835-09-15		A1
912	SHELBY, John	23	NWSW	1835-10-09		A1
811	SHOCKEY, Abraham	2	SENW	1835-10-09		A1
812	" "	2	W½NE	1835-10-09		A1
813	SKILLMAN, Abraham	28	S½	1835-10-09		A1
976	SKINNER, Robert J	31	E½SE	1834-01-30		A1
978	" "	31	W½SE	1834-01-30		A1
977	" "	31	SW	1835-10-16		A1
968	SLATER, Phebe	23	E½SE	1836-02-25		A1
857	SLOSS, Henry	24	NESE	1836-02-15		A1
913	SPEES, John	18	NENW	1835-10-16		A1
914	" "	18	NWNE	1835-10-16		A1
950	SPEES, Mathias	7	SESE	1835-10-07		A1
949	SPEES, Mathias E	17	NENW	1835-10-07		A1
951	SPEES, Matthias	18	E½NE	1835-10-16		A1
952	" "	6	NESW	1835-10-16		A1
838	STEVENS, Ebenezer D	18	W½NW	1835-10-08		A1
921	STILES, Jonathan	2	NENW	1835-10-16		A1
922	" "	2	W½NW	1835-10-16		A1
923	" "	3	W½SW	1835-10-16		A1
858	STODDARD, Henry	30	E½NE	1834-01-30		A1

ID	Individual in Patent	Sec.	Sec. Part	Date Issued	Other Counties	For More Info . . .
859	STODDARD, Henry (Cont'd)	30	E½NW	1834-01-30		A1
861	" "	30	W½NW	1834-01-30		A1
863	" "	31	NE	1834-01-30		A1
864	" "	33	W½SW	1834-01-30		A1
860	" "	30	E½SE	1834-03-28		A1
862	" "	30	W½SE	1834-03-28		A1
814	STUDEBAKER, Abraham	7	NE	1835-10-09		A1
844	SWISHER, George	21	W½NW	1835-10-16		A1
807	VANFLEET, Phelix W	6	SESE	1837-03-15		A1 G49
808	" "	8	W½SW	1837-03-15		A1 G49
915	VAUGHAN, John	10	SWSW	1835-10-08		A1
916	" "	9	SE	1835-10-08		A1
917	" "	9	W½	1835-10-08		A1
918	WAITE, John	21	E½NW	1835-12-24		A1
919	"	21	NESW	1835-12-24		A1
924	WALTON, Joseph B	5	SWSW	1837-11-21		A1
884	WATT, James	8	W½NW	1835-10-08		A1
925	WATTON, Joseph B	5	NWSW	1837-03-16		A1
846	WILLIAMS, George W	6	N½NE	1835-09-15		A1
920	ZEHNER, John	25	E½SW	1837-03-20		A1

Patent Map

T5-S R7-E
1st PM Meridian

Map Group 7

Township Statistics

Parcels Mapped	:	208
Number of Patents	:	182
Number of Individuals	:	124
Patentees Identified	:	123
Number of Surnames	:	94
Multi-Patentee Parcels	:	4
Oldest Patent Date	:	1/30/1834
Most Recent Patent	:	6/1/1852
Block/Lot Parcels	:	0
Parcels Re - Issued	:	0
Parcels that Overlap	:	2
Cities and Towns	:	2
Cemeteries	:	7

Map grid (Sections 4–9, 16–21, 28–33):

Section 6: EDMISTON David 1835; WILLIAMS George W 1835; EDMISTON David 1835; KENT William J 1850; HOWELL Joseph 1835; SPEES Matthias 1835; KENT Hannah 1835; KENT Hannah 1835; KENT Hannah 1835; KIRKBRIDE [49] Abel 1837

Section 5: DAVIS William 1835; WATTON Joseph B 1837; WALTON Joseph B 1837; CARTER William 1835

Section 4: BRENTLINGER John 1835; SCHOOLER John 1835; LISLE Robert 1835; HARROD Michael 1835; HARROD Michael 1835; HARROD Michael 1837; SCHOOLER John 1835; HARROD Michael 1835

Section 7: LISLE Robert 1835; STUDEBAKER Abraham 1835; SHAW William 1835; HOWELL William 1837; SPEES Mathias 1835

Section 8: WATT James 1835; JONES Richard 1835; CARTER John 1835; HOVER Joseph 1837; ALLEN Whiting 1835; ALLEN Whiting 1835; HOWELL Stephen 1836; KIRKBRIDE [49] Abel 1837; ALLEN Whiting 1835; ALLEN Whiting 1835

Section 9: HARROD Michael 1835; VAUGHAN John 1835; VAUGHAN John 1835

Section 18: STEVENS Ebenezer D 1835; SPEES John 1835; HOWELL Joseph 1835; GOLDING Jesse 1835; BESSE Alden 1835; LAYTON William M 1835; HOVER Joseph 1837; OLIPHANT Susan 1836

Section 17: SPEES John 1835; SPEES Matthias 1835; MILLER Daniel 1836; SPEES Mathias E 1835; MILLER Daniel 1835; HOWELL Aaron 1835; HOFFMAN John 1835; HOWELL Aaron 1836; MORRIS Samuel 1835

Section 16: CRETCHER Mathew 1837; AFFOLTIR [1] John 1844; BROBST Jacob 1844; HENRY Thomas 1844; CRETCHER Mathew 1837; LUSK William 1844; LUSK Benjamin 1844; MCLAUGHLIN George F 1835; LUSK Benjamin 1844; HARROD Levi 1844

Section 19: MORRIS Henry 1835; RUMAN John 1835; HESTER Nancy 1835; BETHERS William 1835; LANDIS Jacob 1835; MORRIS Henry 1835

Section 20: RIEMAN Daniel 1835; MORRIS Samuel 1835; MORRIS Samuel 1835; FINLAW James 1837; CRETCHER Mathew 1837; MORRIS Henry 1835; CRETCHER Mathew 1837

Section 21: SWISHER George 1835; BAILEY Richard 1835; WAITE John 1835; WAITE John 1835; CONNER William 1837; BAILEY Richard 1835; CRETCHER Mathew 1837; CRETCHER Mathew 1837; CRETCHER Mathew 1837; BAILEY John 1835

Section 30: STODDARD Henry 1834; HENRY David 1835; STODDARD Henry 1834; STODDARD Henry 1834; SCHLOSSER Jacob 1835; STODDARD Henry 1834; STODDARD Henry 1834; MORRIS John 1835; STODDARD Henry 1834

Section 29: PORTER Moses 1835; STODDARD Henry 1834; CRABB Elliott 1837; PORTER Moses 1835; ROGERS John 1835; MILLER John 1835

Section 28: CRETCHER Mathew 1837; CRETCHER Mathew 1837; CRETCHER Mathew 1837; CRETCHER Mathew 1837; CASTEEL Jefferson 1837; SKILLMAN Abraham 1835

Section 31: MEDEARIS John R 1835; MEDEARIS Oliver 1835; STODDARD Henry 1834; SKINNER Robert J 1835; SKINNER Robert J 1834; SKINNER Robert J 1834

Section 32: SCHLOSSER Jacob 1835; LEMASTERS Isaac 1835; LEMASTERS Isaac 1835; MILLER George 1835; HITTEL Jacob 1834; RICHARDSON William 1834; BITLER [15] Daniel 1835; BITLER Daniel 1835; BITLER Daniel 1835

Section 33: MILLER George 1835; MUSSELMAN Hiram 1835; ALLEN Whiting 1835; ALLEN Whiting 1835; STODDARD Henry 1834; COLEMAN Thomas 1835; MILLER Daniel 1836; MILLER Isaac 1837; HOWELL William 1837; LANE Micajah 1837

GRAHAM Charles 1835		STILES Jonathan 1835	STILES Jonathan 1835	SHOCKEY Abraham 1835			
BRINTLINGER John 1837			SHOCKEY Abraham 1835	GRAHAM William 1835		1	

3

2

CARMONY Rhoda 1835	CARMONY Rhoda 1835	CARTER Adcock 1836	CARTER Adcock 1836
	HARROD David 1837		MCCORMICK John 1837

STILES Jonathan 1835

HARROD Michael 1835				HARROD Michael 1835	MORRIS Henry 1835

JUSTICE Allen 1837

10

11

12

VAUGHAN John 1835

JUSTICE Allen 1837				HARROD David 1836	
					BROWN Joseph 1837

15

14

13

HARROD Levi 1837

BROWN Joseph 1837

LUSK William 1835				BALTZELL John C 1836	MUSSER Eliza A 1836

COLEMAN James 1835	NICKELL James N 1835		LUSK Anna 1837		BASIL Nelson R 1837	LUSK Isaac H 1837	RICHARDSON Byrd 1835	
BAILEY John 1835		LUSK William 1835	SCHOOLER Joseph 1837	BASIL Nelson R 1837		BAYLIFF Joshua 1837		

BAILEY John 1835	SHELBY John 1835	**23**	COPELAND Abner 1837		**24**	HARROD Jacob 1837	SLOSS Henry 1836
BAILY Richard 1837	CORDER John 1835	COPELAND Abner 1837		SLATER Phebe 1836	HARROD Jacob 1837		COLEMAN James 1836

22

BERRY Samuel 1836				BOWMAN Samuel 1835		BASIL Nelson R 1837	
						MIX Levi 1837	

27

26

25

OAR John 1837				LUSK Benjamin 1835		HARROD Jacob 1837	
				POWELL John M 1835	ZEHNER John 1837		

ALLEN Whiting 1835		MORRIS James A 1837	COLEMAN Henry 1837	COLEMAN Henry 1837		LUSK William 1837	
		35	MORRIS James A 1837	MORRIS Moffit 1837	KITE George W 1837		

34

BRACKNEY Reuben 1837	EDGE Jesse 1835	LOONEY Henry H 1844		**36**	
	EDGE Jesse 1836	EDGE Jesse 1836	EDGE Jesse 1852	PRICTCHARD John 1837	BIGGS Silas 1837

Copyright 2006 Boyd IT, Inc. All Rights Reserved

Helpful Hints

1. This Map's INDEX can be found on the preceding pages.

2. Refer to Map "C" to see where this Township lies within Auglaize County, Ohio.

3. Numbers within square brackets [ ] denote a multi-patentee land parcel (multi-owner). Refer to Appendix "C" for a full list of members in this group.

4. Areas that look to be crowded with Patentees usually indicate multiple sales of the same parcel (Re-issues) or Overlapping parcels. See this Township's Index for an explanation of these and other circumstances that might explain "odd" groupings of Patentees on this map.

Legend

———— Patent Boundary

━━━━ Section Boundary

░░░░ No Patents Found (or Outside County)

1., 2., 3., ... Lot Numbers (when beside a name)

[ ] Group Number (see Appendix "C")

Scale: Section = 1 mile X 1 mile (generally, with some exceptions)

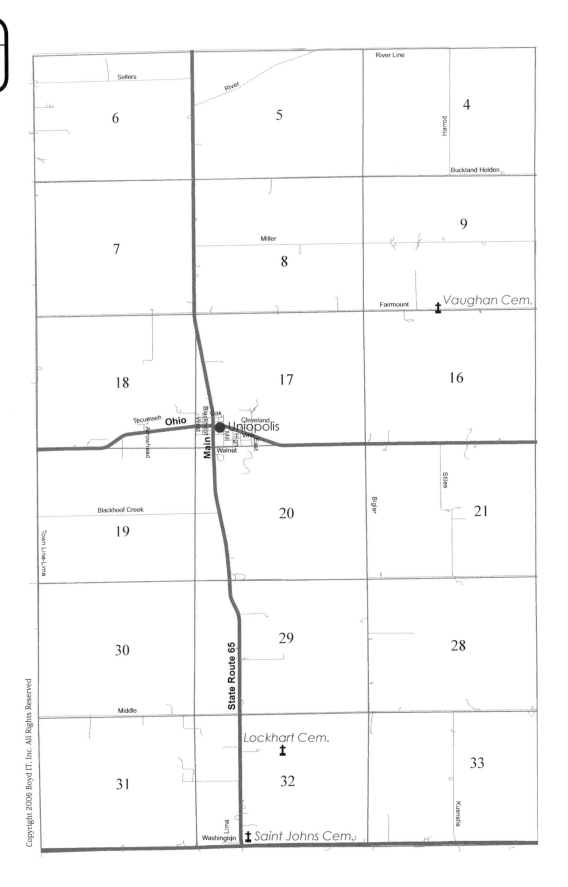

Road Map

T5-S R7-E
1st PM Meridian

Map Group 7

Cities & Towns
Rineharts (historical)
Uniopolis

Cemeteries
Fairmount Cemetery
Lockhart Cemetery
Mount Lookout Cemetery
Saint Johns Cemetery
Stiles Cemetery
Vaughan Cemetery
Wesley Chapel Cemetery

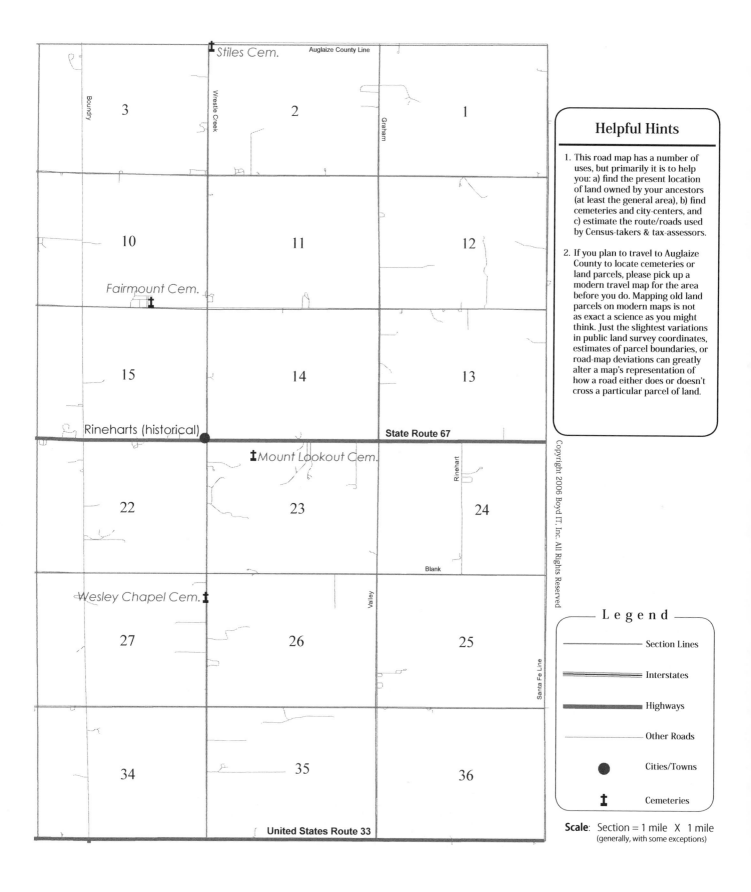

Helpful Hints

1. This road map has a number of uses, but primarily it is to help you: a) find the present location of land owned by your ancestors (at least the general area), b) find cemeteries and city-centers, and c) estimate the route/roads used by Census-takers & tax-assessors.

2. If you plan to travel to Auglaize County to locate cemeteries or land parcels, please pick up a modern travel map for the area before you do. Mapping old land parcels on modern maps is not as exact a science as you might think. Just the slightest variations in public land survey coordinates, estimates of parcel boundaries, or road-map deviations can greatly alter a map's representation of how a road either does or doesn't cross a particular parcel of land.

L e g e n d

————————	Section Lines
═══════════	Interstates
▬▬▬▬▬▬▬▬	Highways
————————	Other Roads
●	Cities/Towns
✝	Cemeteries

Scale: Section = 1 mile X 1 mile
(generally, with some exceptions)

Stiles Cem.
Auglaize County Line
Boundry
Wrestle Creek
Graham

3 | 2 | 1

10 | 11 | 12

Fairmount Cem.

15 | 14 | 13

Rineharts (historical)   State Route 67

Mount Lookout Cem.
Rinehart

22 | 23 | 24

Blank

Wesley Chapel Cem.
Valley

27 | 26 | 25

Santa Fe Line

34 | 35 | 36

United States Route 33

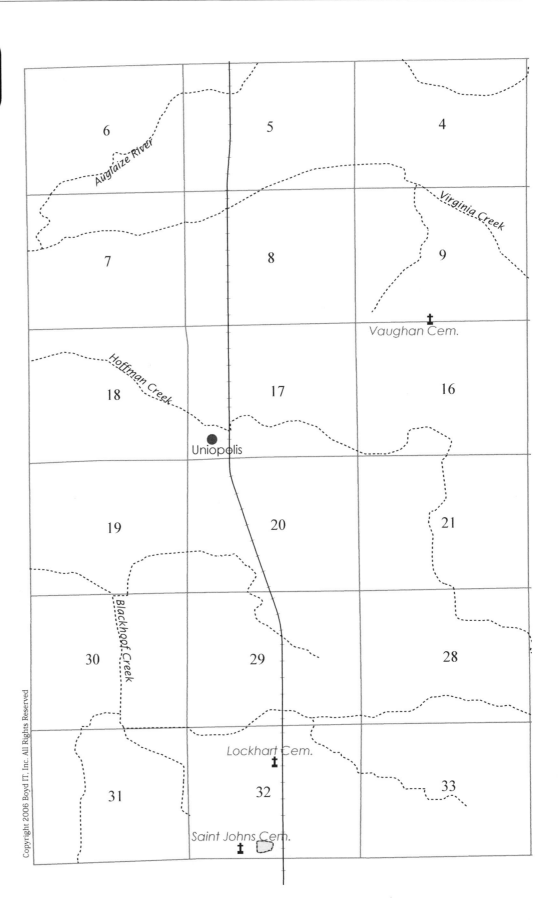

Historical Map

T5-S R7-E
1st PM Meridian

Map Group 7

Cities & Towns
Rineharts (historical)
Uniopolis

Cemeteries
Fairmount Cemetery
Lockhart Cemetery
Mount Lookout Cemetery
Saint Johns Cemetery
Stiles Cemetery
Vaughan Cemetery
Wesley Chapel Cemetery

Copyright 2006 Boyd IT, Inc. All Rights Reserved

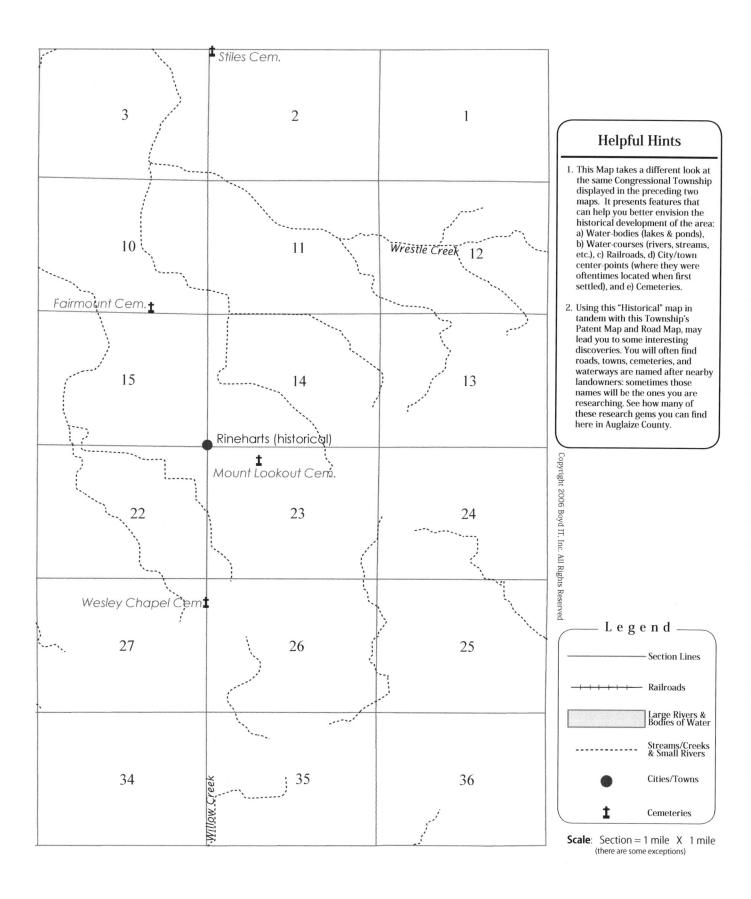

Stiles Cem.

3

2

1

10

11

Wrestle Creek   12

Fairmount Cem.

15

14

13

Rineharts (historical)

Mount Lookout Cem.

22

23

24

Wesley Chapel Cem.

27

26

25

34

Willow Creek   35

36

Helpful Hints

1. This Map takes a different look at the same Congressional Township displayed in the preceding two maps. It presents features that can help you better envision the historical development of the area: a) Water-bodies (lakes & ponds), b) Water-courses (rivers, streams, etc.), c) Railroads, d) City/town center-points (where they were oftentimes located when first settled), and e) Cemeteries.

2. Using this "Historical" map in tandem with this Township's Patent Map and Road Map, may lead you to some interesting discoveries. You will often find roads, towns, cemeteries, and waterways are named after nearby landowners: sometimes those names will be the ones you are researching. See how many of these research gems you can find here in Auglaize County.

Legend

────────	Section Lines
┼┼┼┼┼┼┼┼	Railroads
▭	Large Rivers & Bodies of Water
- - - - - -	Streams/Creeks & Small Rivers
●	Cities/Towns
✝	Cemeteries

Scale: Section = 1 mile X 1 mile
(there are some exceptions)

109

Map Group 8: Index to Land Patents

Township 5-South Range 8-East (1st PM)

After you locate an individual in this Index, take note of the Section and Section Part then proceed to the Land Patent map on the pages immediately following. You should have no difficulty locating the corresponding parcel of land.

The "For More Info" Column will lead you to more information about the underlying Patents. See the Legend at right, and the "How to Use this Book" chapter, for more information.

ID	Individual in Patent	Sec.	Sec. Part	Date Issued	Other Counties	For More Info . . .
1096	ABERNATHY, James	28	SW	1833-11-27		A1
1194	ARNOLD, Reuben B	14	SENE	1837-03-16		A1
1146	BALLARD, Joseph	11	E½SW	1837-03-16		A1
1147	" "	14	NWNW	1837-03-16		A1 V1182
1148	" "	14	SWNW	1837-03-16		A1 V1182
1175	BALLARD, Lyman	15	E½NE	1837-03-16		A1
1187	BALLARD, Nathan	14	SW	1837-03-16		A1 R1219
1238	BATES, Timothy G	25	S½NW	1844-09-10		A1 G12 V1214
1013	BERRY, Aaron D	12	NENW	1837-03-16		A1
1014	"	12	SENW	1837-03-16		A1
1080	BERRY, Henry B	1	N½SE	1837-03-16		A1
1112	BERRY, John	10	SE	1837-03-16		A1
1195	BERRY, Richard	12	E½SW	1835-10-09		A1
1046	BLACK, Daniel	35	E½NE	1831-07-01		A1
1045	" "	34	W½NE	1832-03-03		A1
1043	" "	27	NWSE	1836-02-15		A1
1047	" "	35	W½	1836-02-15		A1 F
1044	" "	27	SWNE	1837-03-16		A1
1113	BLACK, John	22	NENW	1837-03-16		A1
1214	BLACK, Samuel	25	SWNW	1837-03-15		A1 V1238
1245	BLACK, William	27	SWSE	1835-09-15		A1
1244	" "	27	SESE	1835-10-16		A1
1246	" "	2	SESW	1836-02-25		A1 G16
1243	" "	27	NESE	1837-03-16		A1
1251	BOND, William W	12	E½SE	1835-10-09		A1
1054	BOWDLE, David L	11	NENE	1837-03-16		A1
1055	" "	12	NWNW	1837-03-16		A1
1083	BOWDLE, Henry W	11	SESE	1835-10-08		A1
1111	BOWDLE, Jessee L	24	N½SW	1837-03-15		A1
1169	BOWDLE, Joseph W	13	SE	1831-08-01		A1
1170	" "	24	NE	1831-08-01		A1
1221	BOWDLE, Samuel P	1	W½SW	1837-03-16		A1
1149	BROWN, Joseph	30	NESE	1837-03-16		A1
1209	BUFENBARGER, Sampson	32	SE	1835-10-08		A1
1212	BUFFENBARGER, Sampson	33	W½SE	1835-10-09		A1
1210	" "	28	E½SE	1836-02-15		A1
1211	" "	28	SENE	1836-02-15		A1
1232	BUFFENBARGER, Simonton	27	SWSW	1836-02-15		A1
1241	BUFFENBARGER, Washington	34	SW	1833-11-27		A1
1240	" "	33	SENE	1835-10-16		A1 R1095
1213	BUFFINBARGER, Sampson	28	SWSE	1836-02-15		A1
1215	BUFFINBARGER, Samuel	33	W½NE	1836-02-15		A1
1233	BUFFINBARGER, Simonton	34	NW	1835-10-09		A1
1114	BURGET, John	27	NWSW	1835-10-16		A1
1115	" "	27	SENW	1836-02-15		A1
1024	CALDWELL, Andrew	8	SWNW	1835-09-15		A1

ID	Individual in Patent	Sec.	Sec. Part	Date Issued	Other Counties	For More Info . . .
1235	CALL, Thomas	14	NENE	1835-10-09		A1
1199	CAMPBELL, Richard	17	E½NW	1837-03-16		A1
1200	" "	17	NWSE	1837-03-16		A1
1216	CAVINDER, Samuel	14	NENW	1835-09-15		A1 V1182
1186	COATS, Nancy	4	E½SE	1837-03-18		A1 R1072
1097	COLEMAN, James	19	NENW	1837-08-21		A1
1064	CORSON, Eli E	33	E½SE	1835-10-09		A1
1065	" "	33	NENE	1835-10-16		A1
1118	COVER, John	10	NW	1836-02-15		A1
1184	COVER, Michael	4	NW	1836-02-15		A1
1119	COX, John	10	SW	1837-03-16		A1
1247	COX, William	11	S½NE	1835-10-07		A1
1098	CRAMER, James	29	NWSE	1854-06-15		A1
1136	CRAMER, John W	27	NWNW	1836-02-15		A1
1137	" "	28	NENE	1836-02-15		A1
1138	" "	28	W½NE	1836-02-15		A1
1201	CRAMER, Richard	21	W½SE	1836-02-15		A1
1202	" "	27	SWNW	1836-02-15		A1
1099	CRAWFORD, James	29	W½NW	1837-03-15		A1
1018	DAVIDSON, Amaziah	2	NESW	1837-03-20		A1
1120	DAVIDSON, John	3	SENE	1837-03-16		A1
1084	DAVISON, Isaac	5	NE	1835-09-15		A1
1019	DAVISSON, Amaziah	2	SWSW	1836-02-25		A1 G29
1019	DAVISSON, Arthur C	2	SWSW	1836-02-25		A1 G29
1019	DAVISSON, David	2	SWSW	1836-02-25		A1 G29
1031	DAWSON, Aran	15	NW	1837-03-16		A1
1153	DAWSON, Joseph	17	SW	1837-03-16		A1
1154	" "	17	SWNW	1837-03-16		A1
1155	" "	7	SE	1837-03-16		A1
1156	" "	8	NE	1837-03-16		A1
1157	" "	8	SW	1837-03-16		A1
1158	" "	8	W½SE	1837-03-16		A1
1151	" "	10	E½NE	1837-03-18		A1 V1162
1152	" "	10	SWNE	1837-03-18		A1 V1162
1035	DAY, Bazel	33	SENW	1835-10-16		A1
1036	DAY, Bazzle	33	N½NW	1833-11-27		A1
1248	DIXON, William	22	SESE	1849-08-10		A1
1218	DONNEL, Samuel	23	NW	1835-10-08		A1
1217	" "	15	E½SW	1837-03-15		A1
1048	ELSWORTH, Daniel	17	E½SE	1835-10-08		A1
1049	" "	17	SWSE	1835-10-16		A1
1150	ELSWORTH, Joseph C	29	E½NW	1835-09-15		A1
1132	FERRAL, John O	3	W½NE	1835-10-16		A1
1203	GANT, Robert	4	NE	1833-11-27		A1
1121	GILROY, John	29	SW	1835-12-24		A1
1122	" "	32	W½NW	1837-03-15		A1
1123	HARBERT, John	3	NENE	1837-03-16		A1
1066	HARROD, Elijah	19	SW	1837-03-16		A1
1085	HARROD, Jacob	19	SE	1837-03-16		A1
1086	" "	30	NE	1837-03-16		A1
1087	" "	30	SW	1837-03-16		A1 F
1181	HARROD, Martha	19	W½NW	1837-03-16		A1 F
1193	HARROD, Rachel	7	NE	1835-10-16		A1 V1109
1063	HATHAWAY, Eleazar	22	SWNE	1838-09-04		A1
1238	HELFENSTEIN, William L	25	S½NW	1844-09-10		A1 G12 V1214
1242	HENDERSHOT, Westly	1	E½NW	1837-03-16		A1
1236	HENRY, Thomas	8	N½NW	1835-10-16		A1
1160	HIPPLE, Joseph	31	NWNW	1845-06-01		A1 F
1108	HOFFMAN, Jesse	7	E½NW	1835-10-16		A1
1109	" "	7	SWNE	1835-10-16		A1 V1193
1050	HOLLY, Daniel	18	NWSW	1836-02-15		A1
1051	" "	18	SE	1836-02-15		A1
1052	" "	18	SWSW	1836-02-15		A1
1179	HOLLY, Manning	17	NWNW	1836-02-15		A1
1180	" "	18	NENE	1836-02-15		A1
1076	HORN, Hardman	19	SENW	1848-06-01		A1 F
1075	HURLEY, Gilbert	15	SWSW	1836-02-15		A1
1074	" "	15	NWSW	1837-03-15		A1
1116	HURLEY, John C	15	NESE	1837-03-16		A1
1117	" "	15	SESE	1837-03-20		A1
1027	INSKEEP, Anna M	15	W½NE	1837-03-20		A1
1028	" "	2	N½SE	1837-03-20		A1
1029	INSKEEP, Anne M	14	SENW	1835-09-15		A1 V1182

ID	Individual in Patent	Sec.	Sec. Part	Date Issued	Other Counties	For More Info . . .
1030	INSKEEP, Anne M (Cont'd)	14	SWNE	1835-09-15		A1
1020	JOY, Amos	1	NWNW	1836-02-15		A1
1021	" "	2	NENE	1836-02-15		A1
1249	KEAM, William	11	N½SE	1835-10-16		A1
1125	KENT, John	24	NW	1832-11-05		A1
1124	" "	13	SW	1834-01-30		A1
1126	KERNS, John	23	SW	1834-01-30		A1
1127	" "	23	SWNE	1834-01-30		A1
1128	" "	26	NW	1834-01-30		A1
1182	KING, Mary	14	NW	1837-03-18		A1 V1029, 1216, 1147
1219	KING, Samuel	14	SW	1837-03-18		A1 R1187
1053	KIRKPATRICK, David	12	NWNE	1837-03-16		A1
1129	KIRKPATRICK, John	1	S½SE	1837-03-16		A1
1130	" "	12	E½NE	1837-03-16		A1
1161	KLINE, Joseph	32	E½SW	1837-03-16		A1
1100	KRAMER, James	29	SWSE	1845-06-01		A1
1101	" "	32	NWNE	1845-06-01		A1
1145	LEVINGSTON, Johnston R	12	NWSW	1837-03-16		A1
1162	LEWIS, Joseph	10	NE	1834-01-30		A1 V1062, 1151, 1152
1131	LINDLEY, John	19	NENE	1837-03-16		A1
1015	MADDEN, Alexander	22	NENE	1840-10-10		A1
1041	MADDEN, Benjamin	2	NWSW	1836-02-15		A1
1039	" "	1	E½SW	1837-03-16		A1
1040	" "	1	SWNW	1837-03-20		A1
1192	MADDEN, Perry G	1	NE	1837-03-16		A1
1250	MADDEN, William	2	NW	1836-02-15		A1
1102	MAHEN, James	13	E½NW	1835-10-09		A1
1103	" "	13	NWNW	1835-10-09		A1
1032	MAHIN, Asa B	12	SWNE	1837-03-16		A1
1034	MAHIN, Asa R	12	W½SE	1835-09-15		A1
1033	" "	12	SWSW	1836-02-15		A1
1061	MAHIN, Edward K	22	NESE	1837-03-20		A1
1106	MAHIN, James	14	NWNE	1835-09-15		A1
1104	" "	11	SWSE	1835-10-09		A1
1105	" "	13	SWNW	1837-03-16		A1
1062	MALAIM, Edward K	10	NWNE	1837-03-15		A1 V1162
1072	MASTERS, George	4	E½SE	1837-03-15		A1 R1186
1026	MCCOY, Andrew	24	S½SW	1837-03-16		A1
1067	MCCOY, Elisha	25	N½NW	1837-03-16		A1
1057	MCGEEHAN, Duncan	5	W½	1835-09-15		A1
1058	" "	5	W½SE	1835-09-15		A1
1071	MCLAUGHLIN, George F	13	E½NE	1833-11-27		A1
1088	MCPHERON, Jacob	8	SENW	1837-03-16		A1
1204	MEANS, Robert L	30	S½SE	1837-03-16		A1
1205	" "	31	SENE	1845-06-01		A1
1059	MILES, Ebenezer	18	E½SW	1837-11-21		A1
1164	MILLER, Joseph	4	SESW	1832-11-05		A1
1165	" "	4	SWSW	1832-11-05		A1
1166	" "	9	NE	1832-11-05		A1
1163	" "	4	N½SW	1835-10-16		A1
1089	MIX, Jacob	31	W½SW	1837-11-21		A1 F
1174	MIX, Levi	30	S½SW	1837-03-16		A1
1171	MOFFITT, Lawrence	15	W½SE	1837-03-16		A1
1220	MORECRAFT, Samuel	34	SE	1831-07-01		A1
1228	MORECRAFT, Simeon	33	N½SW	1834-01-30		A1
1231	" "	33	SWSW	1835-09-15		A1
1229	" "	33	SESW	1835-10-09		A1
1226	" "	28	NWSE	1836-02-15		A1
1230	" "	33	SWNW	1836-02-15		A1
1225	" "	27	NENW	1837-03-16		A1
1227	" "	29	E½SE	1837-03-16		A1
1042	MORRIS, Benjamin	21	NWSW	1837-03-18		A1
1038	MORRIS, Benjamin F	21	S½SW	1837-03-18		A1
1037	" "	21	NESW	1845-06-01		A1
1197	MORRIS, Richard C	28	S½NW	1835-10-16		A1
1196	" "	28	N½NW	1836-02-15		A1
1198	" "	29	S½NE	1850-07-01		A1
1167	MORROW, Joseph	24	SE	1837-03-15		A1
1090	MYERS, Jacob	19	W½NE	1837-03-18		A1
1139	NASON, John W	22	SENW	1837-03-18		A1
1234	NEAL, St Leger	2	S½SE	1837-03-16		A1
1176	NORTH, Lyman	31	NENW	1837-03-16		A1
1177	" "	31	W½NE	1837-03-16		A1

ID	Individual in Patent	Sec.	Sec. Part	Date Issued	Other Counties	For More Info . . .
1068	OSBORNE, Eliza	11	NENW	1842-01-25		A1 G58
1069	" "	11	NWNE	1842-01-25		A1 G58
1068	OSBORNE, Michael	11	NENW	1842-01-25		A1 G58
1069	" "	11	NWNE	1842-01-25		A1 G58
1068	OSBORNE, Penelope	11	NENW	1842-01-25		A1 G58
1069	" "	11	NWNE	1842-01-25		A1 G58
1068	OSBORNE, William	11	NENW	1842-01-25		A1 G58
1069	" "	11	NWNE	1842-01-25		A1 G58
1246	PETTY, George	2	SESW	1836-02-25		A1 G16
1237	PIERCE, Thomas	19	SENE	1837-03-18		A1
1178	PRATT, Lyman	11	W½NW	1837-03-15		A1
1081	REABURN, Henry	36		1836-02-15		A1 F
1110	REES, Jesse	11	SENW	1835-09-15		A1
1159	RHODES, Joseph H	3	SE	1835-10-16		A1
1133	RIDLEY, John	18	SENE	1837-03-16		A1
1134	" "	18	W½NE	1837-03-16		A1
1073	ROBINSON, George	29	NENE	1838-09-04		A1
1253	ROBINSON, Winslow	26	NE	1844-09-10		A1
1254	" "	26	S½	1844-09-10		A1
1255	" "	27	E½NE	1844-09-10		A1
1256	" "	27	NWNE	1844-09-10		A1
1257	" "	35	E½NW	1844-09-10		A1
1258	" "	35	NE	1844-09-10		A1 F
1185	ROSS, Moses	13	W½NE	1833-11-27		A1
1135	SCHOOLER, John	18	N½NW	1837-03-16		A1
1168	SCHOOLER, Joseph	18	S½NW	1836-02-15		A1
1082	SHAW, Henry	22	NWNW	1836-02-15		A1
1070	SHIGLEY, Frederick	12	SWNW	1835-10-16		A1
1107	SMITH, James	4	W½SE	1837-03-15		A1
1239	SMITH, Warren B	22	SENE	1849-02-01		A1
1207	SPROUL, Robert	9	NW	1832-11-05		A1
1208	" "	9	S½	1832-11-05		A1
1206	" "	8	E½SE	1837-03-15		A1
1025	STARKEY, Andrew J	21	SWNW	1840-10-10		A1
1183	STEWART, Mathew	22	SW	1837-03-16		A1
1017	TAMPLETON, Alexander	25	SE	1835-10-08		A1
1016	" "	25	NE	1836-02-15		A1
1060	THAYER, Ebenezer	17	NE	1835-09-15		A1
1140	THOMAS, John W	31	E½SW	1838-09-04		A1
1141	" "	31	S½NW	1838-09-04		A1 F
1142	" "	31	SE	1838-09-04		A1
1190	TOLMAN, Osee	32	NENE	1837-03-20		A1
1223	TOLMAN, Silas	32	E½NW	1837-03-16		A1
1224	" "	32	SWNE	1837-03-16		A1
1056	TURNER, David	32	SENE	1836-02-15		A1
1173	TURNER, Lee	2	W½NE	1836-02-25		A1
1172	" "	2	SENE	1837-03-18		A1
1077	WELLS, Harris	21	E½NW	1836-02-15		A1
1078	" "	21	NE	1836-02-15		A1
1079	" "	21	NWNW	1837-03-16		A1
1252	WHETSTONE, William	29	NWNE	1850-07-01		A1
1068	WILCOX, Phineas B	11	NENW	1842-01-25		A1 G58
1069	" "	11	NWNE	1842-01-25		A1 G58
1091	WILLIAMS, Jacob	14	E½SE	1833-11-27		A1
1094	" "	23	N½NE	1833-11-27		A1
1092	" "	14	NWSE	1835-09-15		A1
1093	" "	14	SWSE	1837-03-16		A1
1095	" "	33	SENE	1837-03-16		A1 R1240
1222	WILLIAMS, Samuel	11	W½SW	1837-03-16		A1
1022	WITHAM, Amos	27	NESW	1835-09-15		A1
1023	" "	27	SESW	1835-10-16		A1
1191	WITHAM, Otis R	21	E½SE	1835-10-16		A1
1188	WOODBURY, Nathan	22	NWNE	1837-03-16		A1
1189	" "	22	W½SE	1849-02-01		A1
1143	ZEHNER, John	30	N½NW	1837-03-20		A1
1144	" "	30	NWSE	1837-03-20		A1

Patent Map

T5-S R8-E
1st PM Meridian

Map Group 8

Township Statistics

Parcels Mapped	:	246
Number of Patents	:	226
Number of Individuals	:	163
Patentees Identified	:	156
Number of Surnames	:	108
Multi-Patentee Parcels	:	5
Oldest Patent Date	:	7/1/1831
Most Recent Patent	:	6/15/1854
Block/Lot Parcels	:	0
Parcels Re - Issued	:	3
Parcels that Overlap	:	13
Cities and Towns	:	2
Cemeteries	:	7

6

MCGEEHAN
Duncan
1835

DAVISON
Isaac
1835

5

MCGEEHAN
Duncan
1835

COVER
Michael
1836

4

GANT
Robert
1833

MILLER
Joseph
1835

SMITH
James
1837

MASTERS
George
1837

MILLER
Joseph
1832

MILLER
Joseph
1832

COATS
Nancy
1837

HOFFMAN
Jesse
1835

HARROD
Rachel
1835

HOFFMAN
Jesse
1835

HENRY
Thomas
1835

CALDWELL
Andrew
1835

MCPHERON
Jacob
1837

DAWSON
Joseph
1837

SPROUL
Robert
1832

9

MILLER
Joseph
1832

7

DAWSON
Joseph
1837

8

DAWSON
Joseph
1837

DAWSON
Joseph
1837

SPROUL
Robert
1837

SPROUL
Robert
1832

SCHOOLER
John
1837

RIDLEY
John
1837

HOLLY
Manning
1836

HOLLY
Manning
1836

SCHOOLER
Joseph
1836

18

RIDLEY
John
1837

DAWSON
Joseph
1837

CAMPBELL
Richard
1837

THAYER
Ebenezer
1835

16

HOLLY
Daniel
1836

HOLLY
Daniel
1836

17

CAMPBELL
Richard
1837

HOLLY
Daniel
1836

MILES
Ebenezer
1837

HOLLY
Daniel
1836

DAWSON
Joseph
1837

ELSWORTH
Daniel
1835

ELSWORTH
Daniel
1835

HARROD
Martha
1837

COLEMAN
James
1837

MYERS
Jacob
1837

LINDLEY
John
1837

WELLS
Harris
1837

WELLS
Harris
1836

WELLS
Harris
1836

HORN
Hardman
1848

19

PIERCE
Thomas
1837

STARKEY
Andrew J
1840

21

HARROD
Elijah
1837

HARROD
Jacob
1837

20

MORRIS
Benjamin
1837

MORRIS
Benjamin F
1845

CRAMER
Richard
1836

MORRIS
Benjamin F
1837

WITHAM
Otis R
1835

ZEHNER
John
1837

HARROD
Jacob
1837

CRAWFORD
James
1837

WHETSTONE
William
1850

ROBINSON
George
1838

MORRIS
Richard C
1836

CRAMER
John W
1836

CRAMER
John W
1836

ELSWORTH
Joseph C
1835

MORRIS
Richard C
1850

MORRIS
Richard C
1835

BUFFENBARGER
Sampson
1836

30

ZEHNER
John
1837

BROWN
Joseph
1837

29

CRAMER
James
1854

MORECRAFT
Simeon
1836

28

MORECRAFT
Simeon
1836

HARROD
Jacob
1837

GILROY
John
1835

MORECRAFT
Simeon
1837

ABERNATHY
James
1833

BUFFENBARGER
Sampson
1836

MIX
Levi
1837

MEANS
Robert L
1837

KRAMER
James
1845

BUFFINBARGER
Sampson
1836

HIPPLE
Joseph
1845

NORTH
Lyman
1837

NORTH
Lyman
1837

GILROY
John
1837

KRAMER
James
1845

TOLMAN
Osee
1837

DAY
Bazzle
1833

BUFFINBARGER
Samuel
1836

CORSON
Eli E
1835

THOMAS
John W
1838

31

MEANS
Robert L
1845

TOLMAN
Silas
1837

TOLMAN
Silas
1837

TURNER
David
1836

MORECRAFT
Simeon
1836

DAY
Bazel
1835

33

BUFFENBARGER
Washington
1835

WILLIAMS
Jacob
1837

MIX
Jacob
1837

THOMAS
John W
1838

32

KLINE
Joseph
1837

BUFENBARGER
Sampson
1835

MORECRAFT
Simeon
1834

BUFFENBARGER
Sampson
1835

THOMAS
John W
1838

MORECRAFT
Simeon
1835

MORECRAFT
Simeon
1835

CORSON
Eli E
1835

Map showing land patent parcels for Township 5-S Range 8-E (1st PM), Map Group 8, Auglaize County, Ohio.

Section 3

Section 2
- FERRAL John O 1835
- HARBERT John 1837
- DAVIDSON John 1837
- MADDEN William 1836
- TURNER Lee 1836
- JOY Amos 1836
- JOY Amos 1836
- HENDERSHOT Westly 1837
- MADDEN Perry G 1837
- MADDEN Benjamin 1837
- TURNER Lee 1837

Section 1
- RHODES Joseph H 1835
- MADDEN Benjamin 1836
- DAVIDSON Amaziah 1837
- INSKEEP Anna M 1837
- BOWDLE Samuel P 1837
- BERRY Henry B 1837
- DAVISSON [29] Amaziah 1836
- BLACK [16] William 1836
- NEAL St Leger 1837
- MADDEN Benjamin 1837
- KIRKPATRICK John 1837

Section 10
- COVER John 1836
- MALAIM Edward K 1837
- DAWSON Joseph 1837
- LEWIS Joseph 1834
- DAWSON Joseph 1837
- COX John 1837
- BERRY John 1837

Section 11
- PRATT Lyman 1837
- OSBORNE [58] Eliza 1842
- OSBORNE [58] Eliza 1842
- BOWDLE David L 1837
- REES Jesse 1835
- COX William 1835
- WILLIAMS Samuel 1837
- KEAM William 1837
- BALLARD Joseph 1837
- MAHIN James 1835
- BOWDLE Henry W 1835

Section 12
- BOWDLE David L 1837
- BERRY Aaron D 1837
- KIRKPATRICK David 1837
- KIRKPATRICK John 1837
- SHIGLEY Frederick 1835
- BERRY Aaron D 1837
- MAHIN Asa B 1837
- LEVINGSTON Johnston R 1837
- MAHIN Asa R 1835
- MAHIN Asa R 1836
- BERRY Richard 1835
- BOND William W 1835

Section 15
- DAWSON Aran 1837
- INSKEEP Anna M 1837
- BALLARD Lyman 1837
- HURLEY Gilbert 1837
- MOFFITT Lawrence 1837
- HURLEY John C 1837
- HURLEY Gilbert 1836
- DONNEL Samuel 1837
- HURLEY John C 1837

Section 14
- BALLARD Joseph 1837
- CAVINDER Samuel 1835
- MAHIN James 1835
- CALL Thomas 1835
- KING Mary 1837
- BALLARD Joseph 1837
- INSKEEP Anne M 1835
- INSKEEP Anne M 1835
- ARNOLD Reuben B 1837
- BALLARD Nathan 1837
- WILLIAMS Jacob 1835
- KING Samuel 1837
- WILLIAMS Jacob 1837
- WILLIAMS Jacob 1833

Section 13
- MAHIN James 1835
- MAHIN James 1837
- MAHEN James 1835
- ROSS Moses 1833
- MCLAUGHLIN George F 1833
- KENT John 1834
- BOWDLE Joseph W 1831

Section 22
- SHAW Henry 1836
- BLACK John 1837
- WOODBURY Nathan 1837
- MADDEN Alexander 1840
- NASON John W 1837
- HATHAWAY Eleazar 1838
- SMITH Warren B 1849
- WOODBURY Nathan 1849
- MAHIN Edward K 1837
- DIXON William 1849
- STEWART Mathew 1837

Section 23
- DONNEL Samuel 1835
- KERNS John 1834
- KERNS John 1834

Section 24
- WILLIAMS Jacob 1833
- KENT John 1832
- BOWDLE Joseph W 1831
- BOWDLE Jessee L 1837
- MCCOY Andrew 1837
- MORROW Joseph 1837

Section 27
- CRAMER John W 1836
- MORECRAFT Simeon 1837
- ROBINSON Winslow 1844
- CRAMER Richard 1836
- BURGET John 1836
- BLACK Daniel 1836
- ROBINSON Winslow 1844
- BURGET John 1835
- WITHAM Amos 1835
- BLACK Daniel 1836
- BLACK William 1837
- BUFFENBARGER Simonton 1836
- WITHAM Amos 1835
- BLACK William 1835
- BLACK William 1835

Section 26
- KERNS John 1834
- ROBINSON Winslow 1844
- ROBINSON Winslow 1844

Section 25
- MCCOY Elisha 1837
- BLACK Samuel 1837
- BATES [12] Timothy G 1844
- TAMPLETON Alexander 1836
- TAMPLETON Alexander 1835

Section 34
- BLACK Daniel 1832
- BUFFINBARGER Simonton 1835
- BUFFENBARGER Washington 1833
- MORECRAFT Samuel 1831

Section 35
- BLACK Daniel 1836
- ROBINSON Winslow 1844
- ROBINSON Winslow 1844
- BLACK Daniel 1831

Section 36
- REABURN Henry 1836

Helpful Hints

1. This Map's INDEX can be found on the preceding pages.

2. Refer to Map "C" to see where this Township lies within Auglaize County, Ohio.

3. Numbers within square brackets [ ] denote a multi-patentee land parcel (multi-owner). Refer to Appendix "C" for a full list of members in this group.

4. Areas that look to be crowded with Patentees usually indicate multiple sales of the same parcel (Re-issues) or Overlapping parcels. See this Township's Index for an explanation of these and other circumstances that might explain "odd" groupings of Patentees on this map.

Legend

- Patent Boundary
- Section Boundary
- No Patents Found (or Outside County)
- 1., 2., 3., ... Lot Numbers (when beside a name)
- [ ] Group Number (see Appendix "C")

Scale: Section = 1 mile X 1 mile (generally, with some exceptions)

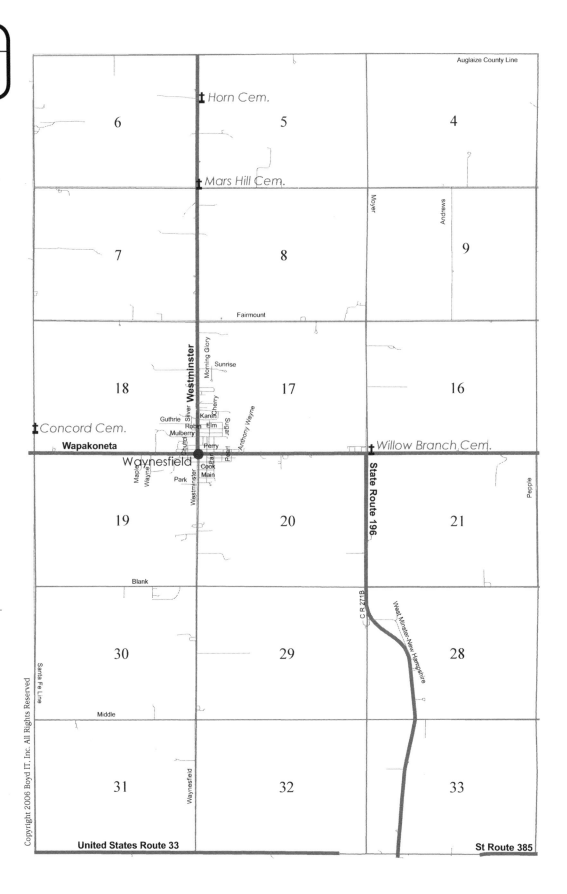

Road Map

T5-S R8-E
1st PM Meridian

Map Group 8

Cities & Towns
Waynesfield
Holden

Cemeteries
Berry Cemetery
Concord Cemetery
Hopewell Cemetery
Horn Cemetery
Mars Hill Cemetery
Walnut Hill Cemetery
Willow Branch Cemetery

Auglaize County Line

‡ Horn Cem.

6   5   4

‡ Mars Hill Cem.

Moyer

Andrews

7   8   9

Fairmount

Morning Glory

Westminster

Sunrise

18   17   16

Guthrie   Silver   Karen
Robin Elm
Mulberry   Sugar   Anthony Wayne
Cherry
Church
Pearl

‡ Concord Cem.

Wapakoneta   ‡ Willow Branch Cem.

Waynesfield

Perry
Cook
Maple   Main
Wayne
Park
Westminster

State Route 196

Pepple

19   20   21

Blank

C R 271B

West Minster-New Hampshire

Santa Fe Line

30   29   28

Middle

Waynesfield

31   32   33

United States Route 33   **St Route 385**

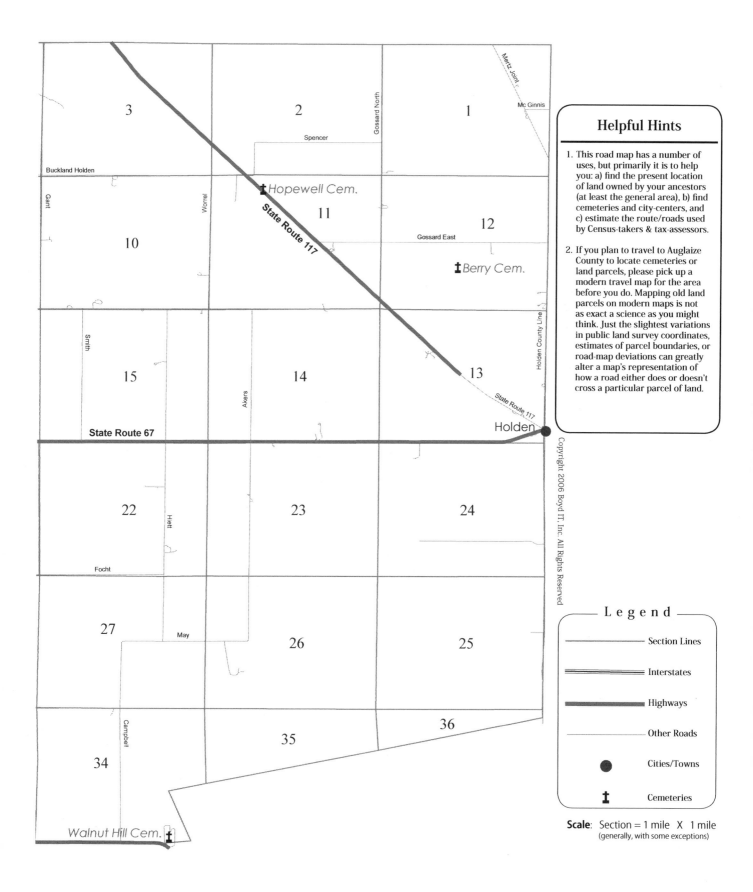

3

2

1

Mertz Joint

Mc Ginnis

Gossard North

Spencer

Buckland Holden

Gant

Worrel

✝ Hopewell Cem.

11

State Route 117

10

Gossard East

12

✝ Berry Cem.

Holden County Line

Smith

15

Akers

14

13

State Route 117

State Route 67

Holden

22

Hiett

23

24

Focht

27

May

26

25

Campbell

34

35

36

Walnut Hill Cem. ✝

Helpful Hints

1. This road map has a number of uses, but primarily it is to help you: a) find the present location of land owned by your ancestors (at least the general area), b) find cemeteries and city-centers, and c) estimate the route/roads used by Census-takers & tax-assessors.

2. If you plan to travel to Auglaize County to locate cemeteries or land parcels, please pick up a modern travel map for the area before you do. Mapping old land parcels on modern maps is not as exact a science as you might think. Just the slightest variations in public land survey coordinates, estimates of parcel boundaries, or road-map deviations can greatly alter a map's representation of how a road either does or doesn't cross a particular parcel of land.

Legend

—————— Section Lines

══════ Interstates

━━━━━━ Highways

—————— Other Roads

● Cities/Towns

✝ Cemeteries

Scale: Section = 1 mile X 1 mile
(generally, with some exceptions)

Historical Map

T5-S R8-E
1st PM Meridian

Map Group 8

Cities & Towns
Waynesfield
Holden

Cemeteries
Berry Cemetery
Concord Cemetery
Hopewell Cemetery
Horn Cemetery
Mars Hill Cemetery
Walnut Hill Cemetery
Willow Branch Cemetery

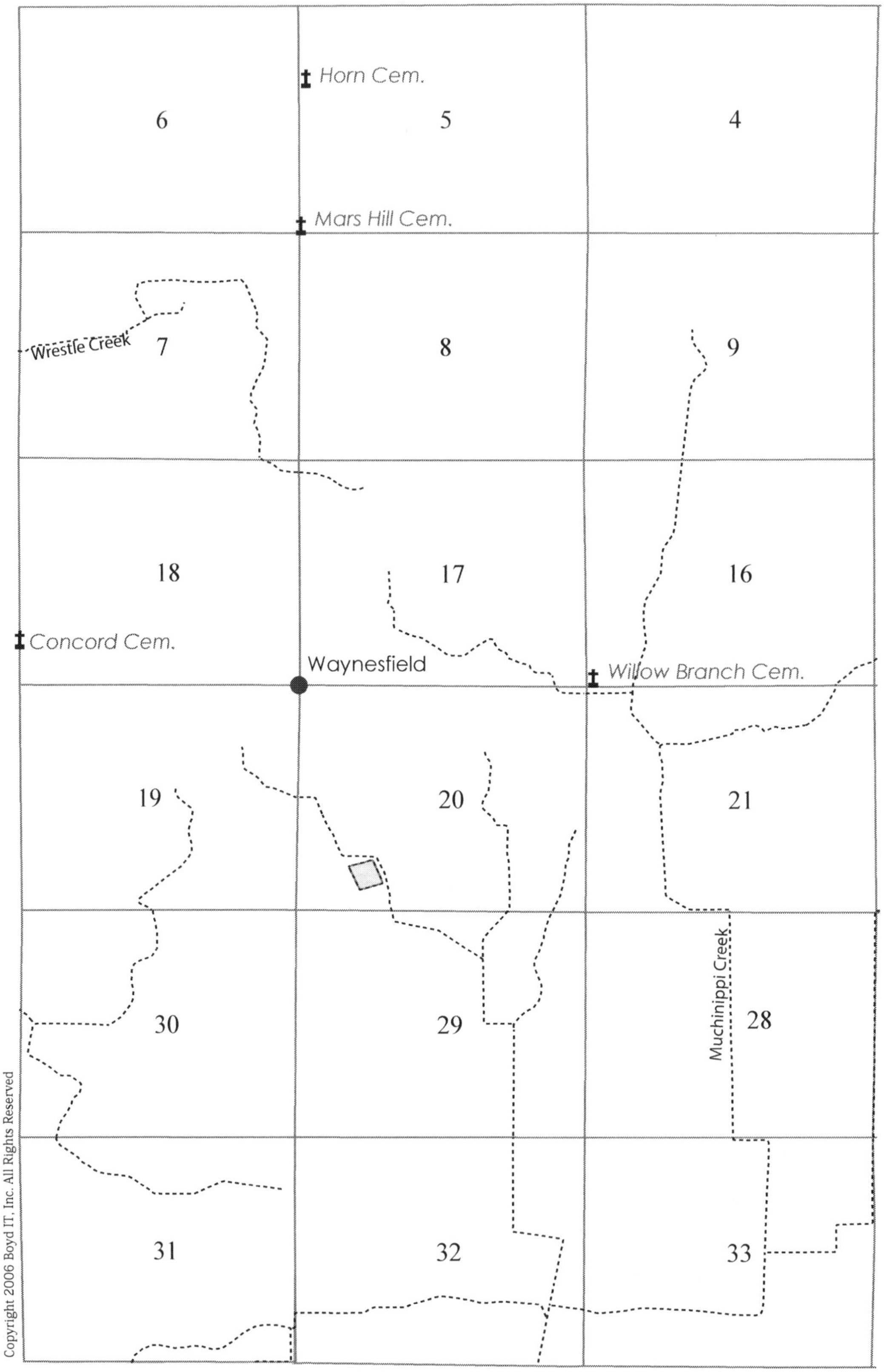

† Horn Cem.

6

5

4

† Mars Hill Cem.

Wrestle Creek

7

8

9

18

17

16

† Concord Cem.

● Waynesfield

† Willow Branch Cem.

19

20

21

Muchinippi Creek

30

29

28

31

32

33

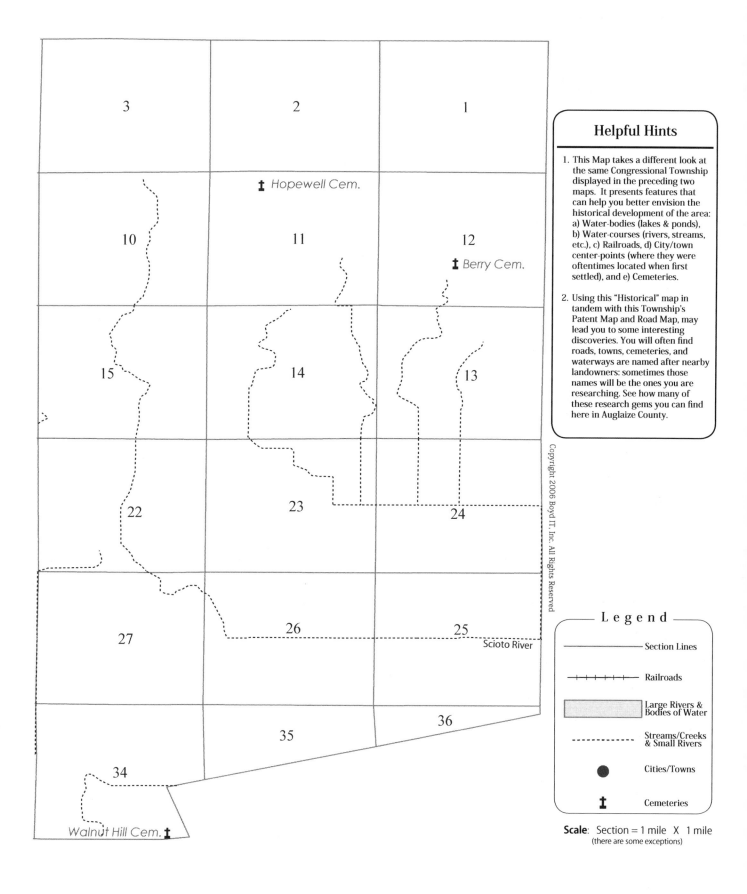

3

2

1

✝ *Hopewell Cem.*

10

11

12

✝ *Berry Cem.*

15

14

13

22

23

24

27

26

25

Scioto River

34

35

36

Walnut Hill Cem. ✝

Helpful Hints

1. This Map takes a different look at the same Congressional Township displayed in the preceding two maps. It presents features that can help you better envision the historical development of the area: a) Water-bodies (lakes & ponds), b) Water-courses (rivers, streams, etc.), c) Railroads, d) City/town center-points (where they were oftentimes located when first settled), and e) Cemeteries.

2. Using this "Historical" map in tandem with this Township's Patent Map and Road Map, may lead you to some interesting discoveries. You will often find roads, towns, cemeteries, and waterways are named after nearby landowners: sometimes those names will be the ones you are researching. See how many of these research gems you can find here in Auglaize County.

L e g e n d

———————— Section Lines

+–+–+–+–+– Railroads

�юLarge Rivers & Bodies of Water

- - - - - - Streams/Creeks & Small Rivers

● Cities/Towns

✝ Cemeteries

Scale: Section = 1 mile X 1 mile
(there are some exceptions)

Road Map
Supplemental Map
East of Map Group 8

Supplemental Map for
Area just East of Map Group 8

<u>Cities & Towns</u>
None

This Small Area lies within
Auglaize County, but is not
part of the same Public Land
Survey under which the rest of
the county is mapped.

See Map "C" on p. 21 to gain
a better idea of just where this
land lies.

This area of land was part of
the Virginia Military District
(VMD).

For a brief but useful
explanation of the VMD, go to
http://en.wikipedia.org
and search for:
Virginia Military District.

<u>Cemeteries</u>
None

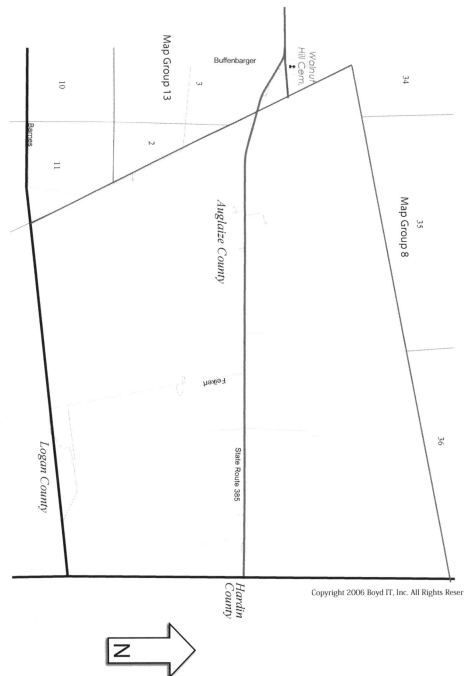

Map Group 13

Buffenbarger

Walnut
Hill Cem.

10

3

34

Barnes

2

11

Auglaize County

Map Group 8

35

Felkert

36

Logan County

State Route 385

Hardin County

N

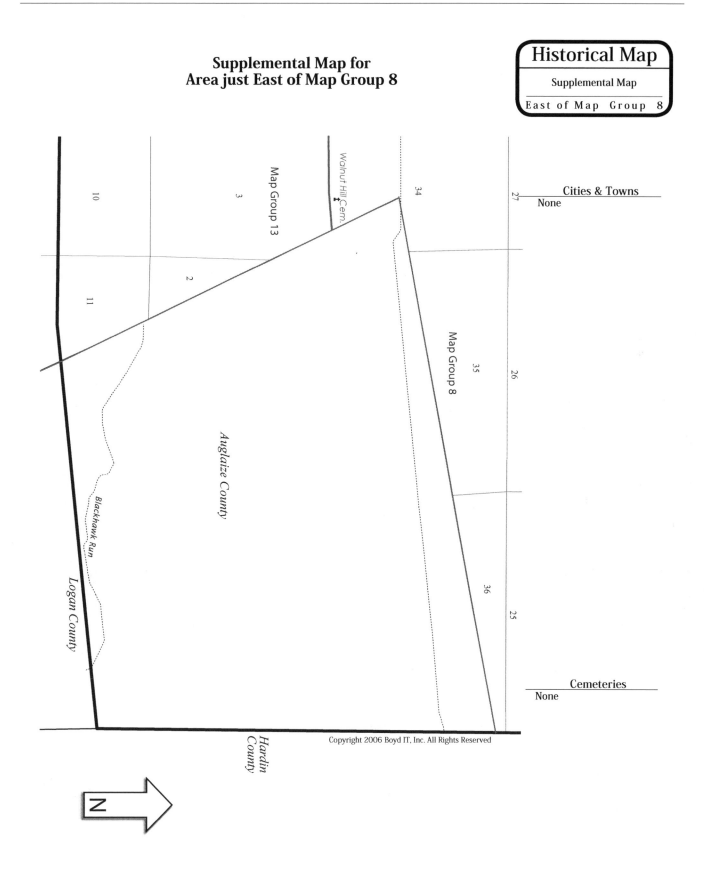

**Supplemental Map for
Area just East of Map Group 8**

Cities & Towns
None

Cemeteries
None

Map Group 9: Index to Land Patents

Township 6-South Range 4-East (1st PM)

After you locate an individual in this Index, take note of the Section and Section Part then proceed to the Land Patent map on the pages immediately following. You should have no difficulty locating the corresponding parcel of land.

The "For More Info" Column will lead you to more information about the underlying Patents. See the Legend at right, and the "How to Use this Book" chapter, for more information.

```
                          LEGEND
              "For More Info . . . " column
  A = Authority (Legislative Act, See Appendix "A")
  B = Block or Lot (location in Section unknown)
  C = Cancelled Patent
  F = Fractional Section
  G = Group  (Multi-Patentee Patent, see Appendix "C")
  V = Overlaps another Parcel
  R = Re-Issued (Parcel patented more than once)

  (A & G items require you to look in the Appendixes referred
  to above. All other Letter-designations followed by a number
  require you to locate line-items in this index that possess
  the ID number found after the letter).
```

ID	Individual in Patent	Sec.	Sec. Part	Date Issued	Other Counties	For More Info . . .
1297	ARMSTRONG, David	9	E½SE	1821-08-01		A1
1298	" "	9	W½SE	1821-09-06		A1
1437	ARMSTRONG, Thomas	9	W½SW	1831-07-01		A1
1261	BADGLEY, Aaron C	1	SENW	1848-06-01		A1 F
1260	" "	1	NENW	1848-08-01		A1 F
1426	BARRINGTON, Richard	11	E½NE	1824-08-09		A1
1429	BARRINGTON, Richard R	11	W½NE	1831-11-01		A1
1427	" "	1	SWNE	1846-10-01		A1
1428	" "	11	N½SE	1848-08-01		A1
1294	BASINK, Coonrod	35	NENW	1848-06-01		A1
1285	BENNER, Christian	2	SE	1822-08-06		A1
1286	" "	2	W½SW	1822-08-06		A1
1284	" "	2	E½SW	1824-05-03		A1
1288	" "	4	E½NE	1825-09-03		A1
1287	" "	3	NE	1828-01-03		A1 F
1289	" "	4	W½NE	1828-01-03		A1
1405	BENNER, Joshua	12	NW	1822-08-06		A1
1299	BERRY, David	12	W½SE	1825-09-03		A1
1300	" "	24	E½NW	1825-09-03		A1
1420	BLISS, Oramel H	11	S½SW	1846-10-01		A1
1338	BOLKINS, James	28	E½SE	1821-09-06		A1
1266	BORTON, Andrew J	29	NENE	1852-06-01		A1
1359	BOSCHE, John F	27	W½SE	1846-10-01		A1
1353	" "	15	E½NE	1848-06-01		A1
1354	" "	15	NESE	1848-06-01		A1
1356	" "	23	NESW	1848-06-01		A1
1357	" "	27	SENE	1848-06-01		A1
1358	" "	27	W½NE	1848-06-01		A1
1362	" "	31	NWSE	1848-06-01		A1
1363	" "	31	S½SE	1848-06-01		A1
1365	" "	31	SW	1848-06-01		A1 F
1367	" "	35	SENW	1848-06-01		A1
1361	" "	31	NENW	1850-07-01		A1
1364	" "	31	SENW	1850-07-01		A1
1366	" "	31	W½NW	1850-07-01		A1
1355	" "	19	E½SE	1854-12-15		A1
1360	" "	29	NW	1854-12-15		A1
1335	BOTHIN, Jackson	25	SENW	1848-06-01		A1
1336	BOTKIN, Jackson	25	SWNW	1848-06-01		A1
1339	BOTKIN, James	27	E½SW	1833-11-27		A1 V1334
1455	BOTKIN, William	27	W½SW	1831-07-01		A1
1453	" "	25	NWNE	1848-06-01		A1
1454	" "	27	NENE	1848-06-01		A1
1434	BUNN, Samuel	4	SW	1822-04-08		A1
1267	BURTON, Andrew J	25	SESW	1848-06-01		A1
1440	CARPER, Thomas J	17	SESE	1852-06-01		A1

ID	Individual in Patent	Sec.	Sec. Part	Date Issued	Other Counties	For More Info . . .
1419	CARTER, Nancy	13	W½NE	1827-04-15		A1
1296	COLGAN, Daniel	20	NWNE	1834-07-01		A1 G28
1265	COLLINS, Andrew	8	E½SE	1833-11-27		A1
1264	" "	17	NENE	1835-10-08		A1
1312	CROSS, Elliot	27	E½SE	1832-03-03		A1
1412	DOENYES, Ludwig	33	S½NW	1849-02-01		A1
1422	DOUTE, Picket	10	SEE½	1826-05-10		A1 F
1402	DOUTEE, Joseph	22	W½NW	1827-01-30		A1
1423	DOUTEE, Picket	11	W½NW	1827-01-30		A1
1424	" "	15	W½NW	1827-01-30		A1
1438	DOUTEY, Thomas	23	NWSW	1848-06-01		A1
1313	DOUTY, Esquire W	23	S½SW	1848-06-01		A1
1263	DOWTY, Amos	21	SENE	1835-10-16		A1
1326	FLEDDERIOHAN, Herman H	25	SENE	1848-06-01		A1
1327	" "	25	SESE	1848-06-01		A1
1328	FLEDDERJOHN, Herman H	25	NENE	1850-07-01		A1
1439	FLOWERS, Thomas	15	SWSW	1834-01-30		A1
1314	FOSTER, Franklin E	5	E½NW	1846-11-05		A1 F
1316	FRANKLIN, George F	17	N½SW	1866-06-27		A1 G39
1317	" "	17	SWSW	1866-06-27		A1 G39
1319	FRIEDLINE, Henry	21	NWNW	1850-07-01		A1
1315	GAULHOUST, Gearhart F	19	S½NW	1853-09-01		A1 F
1431	GORDON, Robert B	11	SWSE	1848-06-01		A1
1430	" "	1	SENE	1849-08-10		A1
1448	GORDON, Wakeman H	21	NENE	1848-06-01		A1
1332	HALL, Isabella	35	E½SE	1832-11-05		A1 V1350
1333	" "	36	W½SW	1832-11-05		A1
1377	HALLER, John	20	NESE	1834-01-30		A1
1378	" "	21	W½	1834-01-30		A1 F
1296	HALLER, William	20	NWNE	1834-07-01		A1 G28
1397	HANEY, Jonas	1	SE	1833-11-27		A1
1379	HAWTHORN, John	15	W½NE	1822-04-08		A1
1380	HAWTHORNE, John	15	E½NW	1824-05-03		A1
1341	HAY, James D	21	E½NW	1832-11-05		A1
1456	HAY, William	21	W½NE	1832-11-05		A1
1321	HELM, Henry M	12	E½SW	1833-11-27		A1
1320	" "	11	N½SW	1835-10-16		A1
1381	HELM, John	5	E½SW	1831-07-01		A1
1411	HEUSCH, Lewis H	19	S½NE	1853-06-01		A1
1269	HINKLE, Asa	22	E½SW	1822-04-08		A1
1270	" "	22	W½SE	1822-04-08		A1
1271	" "	22	W½SW	1822-04-08		A1
1302	HINKLE, David M	15	SESE	1848-06-01		A1
1421	HINKLE, Peter	29	W½NE	1852-06-01		A1
1349	HOBERG, Johan D	31	NESE	1851-02-01		A1
1330	HOLDRIDGE, Hiram H	19	NWNW	1864-12-20		A1
1316	" "	17	N½SW	1866-06-27		A1 G39
1317	" "	17	SWSW	1866-06-27		A1 G39
1382	HOOK, John	13	SWNW	1848-06-01		A1
1451	HOUSTON, William A	10	NE	1821-08-01		A1 G46 V1386
1452	" "	10	NW	1821-08-01		A1 G46 F
1457	HUDSON, William	13	SWSE	1846-10-01		A1
1306	HUNT, Duran T	19	SESW	1852-06-01		A1 F
1307	" "	19	W½SE	1852-06-01		A1
1383	INGLERIGHT, John	27	W½NW	1827-04-15		A1
1324	KINNING, Herman F	33	NWNW	1850-07-01		A1
1384	KOCH, John	34	E½NW	1833-11-27		A1
1325	KUNNEG, Herman F	33	NENW	1848-06-01		A1
1417	LAREW, Moses	22	W½NE	1822-04-08		A1
1301	LINTCH, David	25	N½NW	1835-10-16		A1 G53
1301	LINTCH, Joseph	25	N½NW	1835-10-16		A1 G53
1407	LINTCH, Lemuel	25	NESW	1848-06-01		A1
1408	" "	25	NWSE	1848-06-01		A1 V1342
1409	" "	25	SWNE	1849-08-10		A1
1400	LONGWORTH, Jonathan	13	E½NE	1825-09-03		A1
1401	" "	13	NESE	1848-06-01		A1
1442	LONGWORTH, Thomas	13	SESE	1848-06-01		A1
1441	" "	13	NENW	1848-08-01		A1
1459	LUTTERBECK, William	25	NESE	1848-06-01		A1
1370	MAENS, John H	33	SESW	1835-10-08		A1
1371	" "	33	SWSW	1835-10-16		A1
1345	MAJORS, James	9	E½SW	1828-01-03		A1
1337	MARSHALL, James A	17	NESE	1852-06-01		A1

ID	Individual in Patent	Sec.	Sec. Part	Date Issued	Other Counties	For More Info . . .
1385	MCCORCLE, John	10	E½SW	1821-08-01		A1
1386	" "	10	SWNE	1821-08-01		A1 V1451
1387	" "	10	W½SE	1821-08-01		A1
1388	" "	3	NWS½	1821-08-01		A1 F
1308	MESSER, Edward	35	W½NW	1833-11-27		A1
1368	MILLER, John F	13	SWSW	1848-06-01		A1
1416	MILLIGAN, Michael	19	NWNE	1853-09-01		A1
1303	MITCHELL, David	5	SE	1821-09-06		A1
1372	MOHRMAN, John H	34	E½SE	1833-11-27		A1
1373	" "	34	E½SW	1833-11-27		A1
1374	" "	34	W½SE	1833-11-27		A1
1375	" "	34	W½SW	1833-11-27		A1
1398	MONEYSMITH, Jonas	1	NENE	1848-08-01		A1 F
1399	" "	1	NWNE	1848-08-01		A1 F
1323	MORGAN, Henry W	17	SWSE	1852-06-01		A1
1449	MULLER, Wilhelm M	34	W½NW	1833-11-27		A1
1273	MURRAY, Barney	14	W½NW	1835-10-16		A1
1451	MURRY, Charles	10	NE	1821-08-01		A1 G46 V1386
1452	" "	10	NW	1821-08-01		A1 G46 F
1276	" "	10	S½NW	1821-08-01		A1
1277	" "	3	SES½	1821-08-01		A1 F
1278	" "	3	SWS½	1821-08-01		A1 F
1272	NEEDLES, Avery	13	NWNW	1848-06-01		A1
1322	NIEHING, Henry	33	NWSW	1851-02-01		A1
1403	NIEWATZ, Joseph	17	E½NW	1875-10-01		A2
1340	NORTON, James C	5	SWNW	1846-11-05		A1 F
1304	OPDYCKE, David	33	E½SE	1832-11-05		A1
1305	" "	33	SWSE	1835-10-08		A1
1262	OPDYKE, Albert	28	E½NE	1829-04-02		A1
1458	ROSS, William L	1	NWNW	1850-07-01		A1
1460	RUSSELL, William P	17	W½NW	1875-10-01		A2
1450	SCHWENKE, Wilhelm	29	S½SE	1852-06-01		A1
1346	SCOTT, James	3	NES½	1821-09-06		A1 F
1406	SCOTT, Labirt	19	NENW	1856-04-15		A1 F
1443	SCOTT, Thomas	10	W½SW	1821-09-06		A1
1444	" "	3	NWN½	1821-09-06		A1 F
1445	" "	3	SEN½	1821-09-06		A1 F
1446	" "	3	SWN½	1821-09-06		A1 F
1447	" "	9	N½	1821-09-06		A1
1334	SHEPHERD, Isaiah	27	SESW	1846-10-01		A1 V1339
1344	SIMES, James L	30	W½SW	1831-08-01		A1
1259	SMITH, Aaron A	21	SWNW	1852-06-01		A1
1268	SMITH, Asa H	29	SENE	1852-06-01		A1
1279	SMITH, Charles	21	E½SE	1824-08-09		A1
1282	" "	33	E½NE	1824-08-09		A1
1280	" "	21	NESW	1835-10-16		A1
1281	" "	21	NWSE	1835-10-16		A1
1292	SMITH, Christian	35	NWSE	1848-06-01		A1
1311	SMITH, Elizabeth	33	W½NE	1833-11-27		A1
1318	SMITH, Henry A	15	NWSW	1835-10-16		A1
1404	SMITH, Joseph S	1	SWNW	1849-02-01		A1
1414	SMITH, Marmaduke W	21	SESW	1848-06-01		A1
1415	" "	21	SWSE	1848-06-01		A1
1435	STATLER, Samuel	1	SW	1834-01-30		A1
1436	" "	2	SWNW	1835-10-08		A1
1290	STAUTHITE, Christian H	33	NESW	1835-10-09		A1
1291	" "	33	NWSE	1835-10-09		A1
1432	STEEN, Robert	15	E½SW	1822-04-08		A1
1433	" "	15	W½SE	1822-04-08		A1
1391	STOCKER, John W	17	SWNE	1850-07-01		A1
1392	STOKER, John W	17	NWNE	1849-02-01		A1
1395	" "	17	SESW	1849-08-10		A1
1394	" "	17	SENE	1850-07-01		A1
1393	" "	17	NWSE	1852-06-01		A1
1331	STOUT, Ira	35	NE	1835-10-08		A1
1342	STOUT, James F	25	W½SE	1835-10-08		A1 V1329, 1408
1343	" "	26	SESE	1835-10-08		A1
1389	STRASBURG, John	34	W½NE	1833-11-27		A1
1352	STRASBURG, John D	35	W½SW	1833-11-27		A1
1351	" "	35	NESW	1848-07-01		A1
1390	STUBBS, John	20	E½NE	1835-10-08		A1 C F
1418	STURGEON, Moses	4	SE	1825-09-03		A1
1369	TONGAMAN, John G	35	SWSE	1835-10-09		A1

ID	Individual in Patent	Sec.	Sec. Part	Date Issued	Other Counties	For More Info . . .
1295	VINSON, Cuthbert	4	SWNW	1835-10-08		A1
1413	VINSON, Malachi	4	SENW	1835-10-08		A1
1293	VOEGE, Claus	5	W½SW	1875-10-01		A2
1309	WATERS, Elias	24	SW	1832-11-05		A1
1310	" "	27	NENW	1832-11-05		A1
1283	WATKIN, Charles	11	E½NW	1831-11-01		A1
1329	WIERWILLE, Herman H	25	SWSE	1848-06-01		A1 V1342
1376	WILDENBREW, John H	26	S½SW	1833-11-27		A1
1274	WILKINS, Belithe	13	SESW	1846-10-01		A1
1275	WILKINS, Billitha	13	NESW	1846-10-01		A1 G71
1348	WILKINS, James	13	NWSE	1835-10-16		A1
1347	" "	11	SESE	1848-08-01		A1
1410	WILKINS, Leven	13	SENW	1846-10-01		A1
1275	WILKINS, Reuben	13	NESW	1846-10-01		A1 G71
1425	" "	13	NWSW	1848-06-01		A1
1396	WILLIAMS, John	34	SENE	1833-11-27		A1
1350	WUPPENHARST, John C	35	SESE	1835-10-09		A1 V1332

Patent Map

T6-S R4-E
1st PM Meridian

Map Group 9

Township Statistics

Parcels Mapped	:	202
Number of Patents	:	194
Number of Individuals	:	133
Patentees Identified	:	131
Number of Surnames	:	102
Multi-Patentee Parcels	:	7
Oldest Patent Date	:	8/1/1821
Most Recent Patent	:	10/1/1875
Block/Lot Parcels	:	7
Parcels Re - Issued	:	0
Parcels that Overlap	:	9
Cities and Towns	:	8
Cemeteries	:	6

6

NORTON
James C
1846

FOSTER
Franklin E
1846

5

BENNER
Christian
1828

BENNER
Christian
1825

VINSON
Cuthbert
1835

VINSON
Malachi
1835

VOEGE
Claus
1875

HELM
John
1831

MITCHELL
David
1821

4

BUNN
Samuel
1822

STURGEON
Moses
1825

7

8

SCOTT
Thomas
1821

9

ARMSTRONG
Thomas
1831

ARMSTRONG
David
1821

ARMSTRONG
David
1821

COLLINS
Andrew
1833

MAJORS
James
1828

18

RUSSELL
William P
1875

NIEWATZ
Joseph
1875

17

STOKER
John W
1849

COLLINS
Andrew
1835

STOCKER
John W
1850

STOKER
John W
1850

FRANKLIN [39]
George F
1866

STOKER
John W
1852

MARSHALL
James A
1852

16

FRANKLIN [39]
George F
1866

STOKER
John W
1849

MORGAN
Henry W
1852

CARPER
Thomas J
1852

HOLDRIDGE
Hiram H
1864

SCOTT
Labirt
1856

MILLIGAN
Michael
1853

COLGAN [28]
Daniel
1834

FRIEDLINE
Henry
1850

HAY
William
1832

GORDON
Wakeman H
1848

GAULHOUST
Gearhart F
1853

19

HEUSCH
Lewis H
1853

20

STUBBS
John
1835

SMITH
Aaron A
1852

HAY
James D
1832

21

DOWTY
Amos
1835

HALLER
John
1834

HUNT
Duran T
1852

HALLER
John
1834

SMITH
Charles
1835

SMITH
Charles
1835

HUNT
Duran T
1852

BOSCHE
John F
1854

SMITH
Marmaduke W
1848

SMITH
Marmaduke W
1848

SMITH
Charles
1824

30

BOSCHE
John F
1854

HINKLE
Peter
1852

BORTON
Andrew J
1852

28

OPDYKE
Albert
1829

SMITH
Asa H
1852

29

SIMES
James L
1831

SCHWENKE
Wilhelm
1852

BOLKINS
James
1821

BOSCHE
John F
1850

BOSCHE
John F
1850

31

KINNING
Herman F
1850

KUNNEG
Herman F
1848

SMITH
Elizabeth
1833

BOSCHE
John F
1850

DOENYES
Ludwig
1849

33

SMITH
Charles
1824

BOSCHE
John F
1848

HOBERG
Johan D
1851

32

NIEHING
Henry
1851

STAUTHITE
Christian H
1835

STAUTHITE
Christian H
1835

BOSCHE
John F
1848

BOSCHE
John F
1848

MAENS
John H
1835

MAENS
John H
1835

OPDYCKE
David
1835

OPDYCKE
David
1832

SCOTT Thomas 1821		BENNER Christian 1828	STATLER Samuel 1835	2	ROSS William L 1850	BADGLEY Aaron C 1848	MONEYSMITH Jonas 1848 MONEYSMITH Jonas 1848
SCOTT Thomas 1821		SCOTT Thomas 1821	BENNER Christian 1822		SMITH Joseph S 1849	BADGLEY Aaron C 1848	BARRINGTON Richard R 1846 GORDON Robert B 1849

SCOTT Thomas 1821
BENNER Christian 1828
SCOTT Thomas 1821
STATLER Samuel 1835

2

ROSS William L 1850
BADGLEY Aaron C 1848
MONEYSMITH Jonas 1848
MONEYSMITH Jonas 1848

SCOTT Thomas 1821
SCOTT Thomas 1821
BENNER Christian 1822
SMITH Joseph S 1849
BADGLEY Aaron C 1848
BARRINGTON Richard R 1846
GORDON Robert B 1849

MCCORCLE John 1821
SCOTT James 1821
3

BENNER Christian 1824

1

STATLER Samuel 1834
HANEY Jonas 1833

MURRY Charles 1821
MURRY Charles 1821

HOUSTON [46] William A 1821
HOUSTON [46] William A 1821
DOUTEE Picket 1827
BARRINGTON Richard R 1831

BENNER Joshua 1822

MURRY Charles 1821
MCCORCLE John 1821
WATKIN Charles 1831
11
BARRINGTON Richard 1824

12

SCOTT Thomas 1821
10
MCCORCLE John 1821
DOUTE Picket 1826
HELM Henry M 1835
BARRINGTON Richard R 1848

BERRY David 1825

MCCORCLE John 1821
BLISS Oramel H 1848
GORDON Robert B 1848
WILKINS James 1848
HELM Henry M 1833

DOUTEE Picket 1827
HAWTHORN John 1822
MURRAY Barney 1835
NEEDLES Avery 1848
LONGWORTH Thomas 1848
CARTER Nancy 1827

HAWTHORNE John 1824
15
BOSCHE John F 1848
LONGWORTH Jonathan 1825

14

HOOK John 1848
WILKINS Leven 1846
13

SMITH Henry A 1835
STEEN Robert 1822
BOSCHE John F 1848
WILKINS Reuben 1848
WILKINS [71] Billitha 1846
WILKINS James 1835
LONGWORTH Jonathan 1848

FLOWERS Thomas 1834
STEEN Robert 1822
HINKLE David M 1848
MILLER John F 1848
WILKINS Belithe 1846
HUDSON William 1846
LONGWORTH Thomas 1848

DOUTEE Joseph 1827
LAREW Moses 1822

22

23

BERRY David 1825
24

HINKLE Asa 1822
HINKLE Asa 1822
DOUTEY Thomas 1848
BOSCHE John F 1848

HINKLE Asa 1822
DOUTY Esquire W 1848
WATERS Elias 1832

INGLERIGHT John 1827
WATERS Elias 1832
27
BOSCHE John F 1848
BOTKIN William 1848

LINTCH [53] David 1835
BOTKIN William 1848
FLEDDERJOHN Herman H 1850

BOSCHE John F 1848
26
BOTKIN Jackson 1848
BOTHIN Jackson 1848
LINTCH Lemuel 1849
FLEDDERIOHAN Herman H 1848

BOTKIN William 1831
BOSCHE John F 1846
LINTCH Lemuel 1848
LINTCH Lemuel 1848
LUTTERBECK William 1848

SHEPHERD Isaiah 1846
BOTKIN James 1833
CROSS Elliot 1832
WILDENBREW John H 1833
STOUT James F 1835
STOUT James F 1835
BURTON Andrew J 1848
WIERWILLE Herman H 1848
FLEDDERIOHAN Herman H 1848

MULLER Wilhelm M 1833
STRASBURG John 1833
MESSER Edward 1833
BASINK Coonrod 1848

KOCH John 1833
34
WILLIAMS John 1833
BOSCHE John F 1848
STOUT Ira 1835
35

36

MOHRMAN John H 1833
MOHRMAN John H 1833
STRASBURG John D 1848
SMITH Christian 1848
HALL Isabella 1832

MOHRMAN John H 1833
MOHRMAN John H 1833
STRASBURG John D 1833
TONGAMAN John G 1835
WUPPENHARST John C 1835
HALL 1835
Isabella 1832

Helpful Hints

1. This Map's INDEX can be found on the preceding pages.

2. Refer to Map "C" to see where this Township lies within Auglaize County, Ohio.

3. Numbers within square brackets [ ] denote a multi-patentee land parcel (multi-owner). Refer to Appendix "C" for a full list of members in this group.

4. Areas that look to be crowded with Patentees usually indicate multiple sales of the same parcel (Re-issues) or Overlapping parcels. See this Township's Index for an explanation of these and other circumstances that might explain "odd" groupings of Patentees on this map.

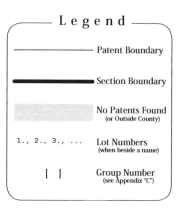

Legend

— Patent Boundary

━ Section Boundary

▒ No Patents Found (or Outside County)

1., 2., 3., ... Lot Numbers (when beside a name)

[ ] Group Number (see Appendix "C")

Scale: Section = 1 mile X 1 mile (generally, with some exceptions)

Road Map

T6-S R4-E
1st PM Meridian

Map Group 9

Cities & Towns
Breezewood
Bulkhead
Harmons Landing
Saint Marys
Sandy Beach
South Shore Acres
Southmoor Shores
Villa Nova

Cemeteries
Benner Cemetery
Elm Grove Cemetery
Gethsemane Cemetery
Lutheran Cemetery
Old Catholic Cemetery
Old Saint Marys Cemetery

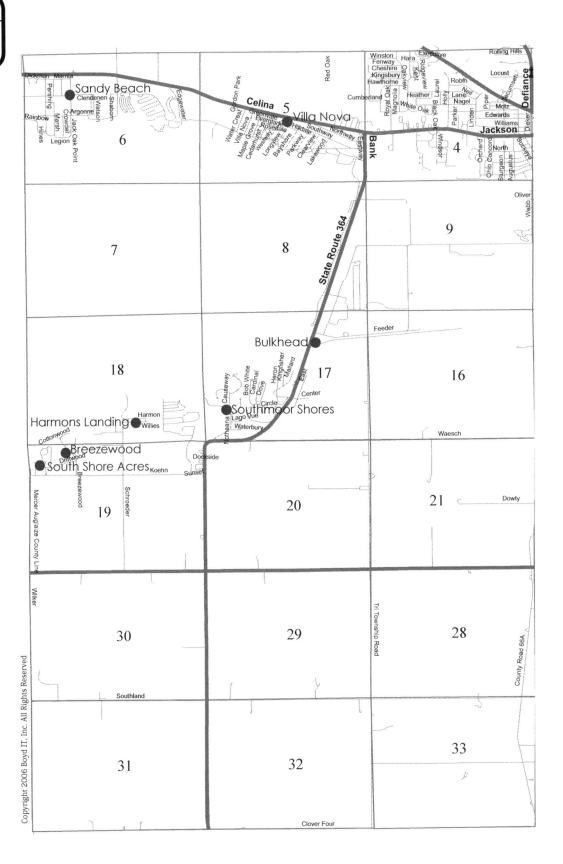

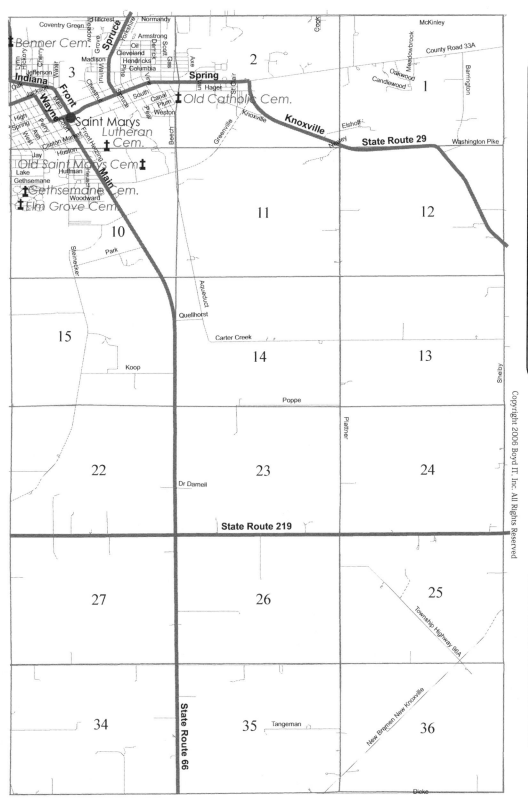

Helpful Hints

1. This road map has a number of uses, but primarily it is to help you: a) find the present location of land owned by your ancestors (at least the general area), b) find cemeteries and city-centers, and c) estimate the route/roads used by Census-takers & tax-assessors.

2. If you plan to travel to Auglaize County to locate cemeteries or land parcels, please pick up a modern travel map for the area before you do. Mapping old land parcels on modern maps is not as exact a science as you might think. Just the slightest variations in public land survey coordinates, estimates of parcel boundaries, or road-map deviations can greatly alter a map's representation of how a road either does or doesn't cross a particular parcel of land.

Legend

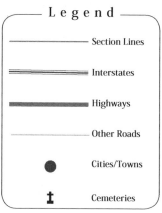

——————— Section Lines

═══════ Interstates

▬▬▬▬▬ Highways

——————— Other Roads

● Cities/Towns

✝ Cemeteries

Scale: Section = 1 mile X 1 mile
(generally, with some exceptions)

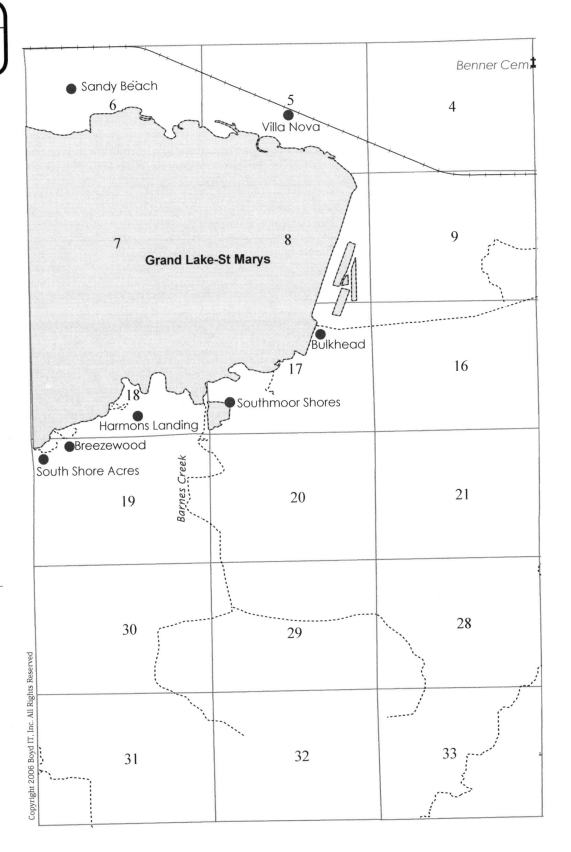

Historical Map

T6-S R4-E
1st PM Meridian

Map Group 9

Cities & Towns
Breezewood
Bulkhead
Harmons Landing
Saint Marys
Sandy Beach
South Shore Acres
Southmoor Shores
Villa Nova

Cemeteries
Benner Cemetery
Elm Grove Cemetery
Gethsemane Cemetery
Lutheran Cemetery
Old Catholic Cemetery
Old Saint Marys Cemetery

Benner Cem.

Sandy Beach

6

5

Villa Nova

4

7

Grand Lake-St Marys

8

9

Bulkhead

17

16

18

Southmoor Shores

Harmons Landing

Breezewood

South Shore Acres

19

Barnes Creek

20

21

30

29

28

31

32

33

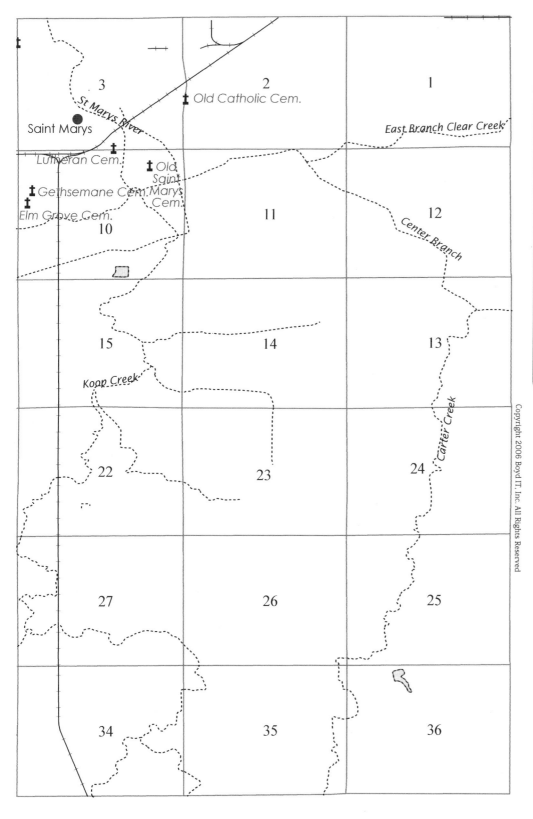

3

2

1

St Marys River

☩ *Old Catholic Cem.*

● Saint Marys

East Branch Clear Creek

☩ *Lutheran Cem.*

☩ *Old Saint Marys Cem.*

☩ *Gethsemane Cem.*

☩ *Elm Grove Cem.*

10

11

12

Center Branch

15

14

13

Kopp Creek

22

23

24

Carter Creek

27

26

25

34

35

36

Helpful Hints

1. This Map takes a different look at the same Congressional Township displayed in the preceding two maps. It presents features that can help you better envision the historical development of the area: a) Water-bodies (lakes & ponds), b) Water-courses (rivers, streams, etc.), c) Railroads, d) City/town center-points (where they were oftentimes located when first settled), and e) Cemeteries.

2. Using this "Historical" map in tandem with this Township's Patent Map and Road Map, may lead you to some interesting discoveries. You will often find roads, towns, cemeteries, and waterways are named after nearby landowners: sometimes those names will be the ones you are researching. See how many of these research gems you can find here in Auglaize County.

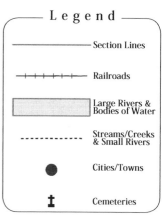

L e g e n d

———— Section Lines

+‑+‑+‑+‑+‑+ Railroads

▭ Large Rivers & Bodies of Water

‑ ‑ ‑ ‑ Streams/Creeks & Small Rivers

● Cities/Towns

☩ Cemeteries

Scale: Section = 1 mile X 1 mile
(there are some exceptions)

Map Group 10: Index to Land Patents

Township 6-South Range 5-East (1st PM)

After you locate an individual in this Index, take note of the Section and Section Part then proceed to the Land Patent map on the pages immediately following. You should have no difficulty locating the corresponding parcel of land.

The "For More Info" Column will lead you to more information about the underlying Patents. See the Legend at right, and the "How to Use this Book" chapter, for more information.

```
                          LEGEND
                "For More Info . . . " column
  A = Authority (Legislative Act, See Appendix "A")
  B = Block or Lot (location in Section unknown)
  C = Cancelled Patent
  F = Fractional Section
  G = Group  (Multi-Patentee Patent, see Appendix "C")
  V = Overlaps another Parcel
  R = Re-Issued (Parcel patented more than once)

  (A & G items require you to look in the Appendixes referred
  to above. All other Letter-designations followed by a number
  require you to locate line-items in this index that possess
  the ID number found after the letter).
```

ID	Individual in Patent	Sec.	Sec. Part	Date Issued	Other Counties	For More Info . . .
1467	ALEXANDER, Arba	13	SENE	1837-03-20		A1
1555	ARNET, Jacob	8	SE	1835-10-08		A1
1576	ARNET, John	9	SW	1835-10-08		A1
1575	" "	22	NWNW	1835-10-16		A1
1621	ASPINALL, Robert	14	E½SE	1837-03-16		A1
1641	ASPINALL, Thomas	14	NE	1837-03-16		A1
1650	AUFDERHAR, William H	17	SENE	1846-11-05		A1
1646	AUFDERHARK, William	17	NENE	1849-02-01		A1
1472	AUFFORTH, Bernard H	23	NESW	1837-11-21		A1
1613	AUGKINBAUGH, Peter	20	NWSW	1835-10-07		A1 G5
1614	" "	30	E½SE	1835-10-07		A1 G5
1615	" "	30	SENE	1835-10-07		A1 G5
1613	BARNETT, Joseph	20	NWSW	1835-10-07		A1 G5
1614	" "	30	E½SE	1835-10-07		A1 G5
1615	" "	30	SENE	1835-10-07		A1 G5
1620	BARRINGTON, Richard R	7	W½NW	1848-08-01		A1 F
1577	BATES, John	22	NESE	1841-09-06		A1
1578	" "	22	S½NE	1841-09-06		A1 F
1579	" "	22	W½SE	1841-09-06		A1
1625	BLAKELY, Samuel	4	SWNW	1835-10-16		A1
1626	BLEAKLY, Samuel	4	NWSW	1835-10-09		A1
1666	BOARDMAN, William Z	7	E½NE	1851-02-01		A1
1667	" "	7	NESE	1851-02-01		A1
1596	BOLANDER, Jonathan	10	E½SW	1837-03-20		A1
1583	BOSCHE, John F	17	NENW	1846-10-01		A1
1584	"	17	NWNE	1846-10-01		A1
1624	BRACKSEACK, Rodolph	29	NWSW	1846-10-01		A1
1505	BRAMBLET, George	2	SWSE	1837-11-21		A1
1607	BRANHAM, Mary	1	NENW	1835-10-08		A1
1622	BRANNAN, Robert	22	NWNE	1837-03-20		A1 F
1623	BRANNUM, Robert	22	NENE	1838-09-04		A1 F
1500	BROCK, Francis	1	N½NE	1835-10-08		A1
1655	BROWN, William J	19	SESE	1835-10-07		A1
1656	" "	20	SWSW	1835-10-07		A1
1496	BUCK, Enoch	18	NENE	1835-10-09		A1
1580	BUCK, John	17	NWNW	1835-10-09		A1
1581	CAMPBELL, John	23	W½SE	1833-11-27		A1
1606	CAMPBELL, Malcom	15	SWSW	1835-10-09		A1
1645	CAREY, Thomas M	20	E½SW	1835-10-07		A1 G26
1511	CECIL, Gordan	10	E½	1837-03-18		A1
1512	" "	11	NENW	1837-03-18		A1
1513	" "	11	SW	1837-03-18		A1
1514	" "	11	W½NE	1837-03-18		A1
1515	" "	11	W½NW	1837-03-18		A1
1516	" "	26	SW	1837-03-18		A1
1517	" "	3	SE	1837-03-18		A1

ID	Individual in Patent	Sec.	Sec. Part	Date Issued	Other Counties	For More Info . . .
1484	CHATTERTON, David	14	W½SE	1837-03-16		A1
1610	CLEVELAND, Morgan H	5	SESW	1835-10-16		A1
1553	COLE, Hollister S	22	NENW	1837-03-20		A1
1638	COLE, Spencer	15	E½SW	1844-08-01		A1
1571	CONGER, Joel	20	NENE	1835-10-16		A1
1598	CONGER, Joseph	20	SENW	1835-10-16		A1
1599	" "	20	SWNE	1835-10-16		A1
1506	COPSEY, George	2	SESW	1837-03-15		A1
1647	COPSEY, William	10	W½NW	1837-03-20		A1
1510	COTTERL, Gersham	24	E½SE	1837-03-20		A1
1556	COVERSTONE, Jacob	15	W½NE	1838-09-04		A1
1645	CUMMINGS, Joseph	20	E½SW	1835-10-07		A1 G26
1483	CURTIS, Daniel M	11	SE	1837-03-16		A1
1507	DIEGEL, George	17	NESW	1848-06-01		A1
1508	" "	17	SESW	1850-07-01		A1
1582	ELLIOTT, John	15	NENE	1850-07-01		A1
1542	ELSHOF, Herman	29	SWSW	1848-06-01		A1
1463	ESCHMEIRE, Adolph	19	NESW	1851-02-01		A1 F
1464	" "	19	NWSE	1851-02-01		A1
1585	FARNSLER, John	8	NENE	1835-10-09		A1
1586	" "	8	W½NE	1835-10-09		A1
1587	" "	9	NWNW	1835-10-09		A1
1554	FISHER, Ignaz	2	NENW	1845-06-01		A1 F
1462	FLADERIOHAN, Adam	19	SWSE	1848-06-01		A1
1543	FLEDDERIOHAN, Herman H	19	SWSW	1848-06-01		A1 F
1520	FLEDDERJOHAN, Harmon H	21	W½NW	1852-06-01		A1
1643	FLOWERS, Thomas	15	NWSE	1837-11-21		A1
1475	FORNEY, Christian	10	E½NW	1837-03-20		A1
1588	FORNEY, John	10	W½SW	1837-03-20		A1 F
1611	FRAME, Nathan	12	E½	1835-10-09		A1
1524	FRISCHE, Henry	12	SW	1837-03-15		A1
1525	" "	7	E½NW	1852-06-01		A1 F
1526	" "	7	W½NE	1852-06-01		A1
1572	FULLER, Joel	15	E½NW	1837-03-20		A1
1573	" "	15	NWSW	1837-03-20		A1 F
1574	" "	15	SWNW	1837-03-20		A1 F
1482	GEARHEART, Daniel	3	S½NW	1837-03-18		A1 F
1589	GEARHEART, John	2	N½SE	1837-03-18		A1 F
1590	" "	2	S½NE	1837-03-18		A1 F
1627	GEARHEART, Samuel	2	N½SW	1837-03-18		A1
1628	" "	2	S½NW	1837-03-18		A1 F
1591	GRABLE, John	17	SENW	1835-10-16		A1
1528	GREEN, Henry	3	SWNE	1835-09-15		A1
1527	" "	3	E½SW	1837-03-20		A1
1648	GREEN, William	3	N½NW	1837-03-20		A1
1649	" "	3	NWNE	1837-03-20		A1 F
1529	GUDORF, Henry	22	SESE	1835-09-15		A1
1569	HAINES, Job	30	W½NE	1835-10-07		A1
1570	" "	30	W½SE	1835-10-07		A1
1597	HANKINS, Jonathan	23	E½NW	1835-10-08		A1
1466	HARVEY, Ambrose	2	N½NE	1835-10-08		A1 F
1604	HERMAN, Lauren D	1	E½SE	1835-10-09		A1
1473	HERMES, Bernard	23	SESW	1837-11-21		A1
1617	HERZING, Philip	15	NWNW	1838-09-04		A1
1557	HITTEL, Jacob	23	E½NE	1840-10-10		A1 F
1558	" "	24	W½NW	1840-10-10		A1 F
1544	HOGE, Herman H	29	SWNW	1848-06-01		A1
1652	HOLLINGSWORTH, William	5	E½NE	1852-06-01		A1 F
1565	HUDSON, Jesse	18	E½NW	1835-10-16		A1
1566	" "	18	NWNE	1835-10-16		A1
1567	" "	18	SWNW	1835-10-16		A1
1653	HUDSON, William	17	SWNW	1849-02-01		A1
1654	" "	7	SWSE	1852-06-01		A1
1489	HUTSON, Dennis	7	SESW	1848-08-01		A1 F
1657	JACKSON, William	25	NWNW	1838-09-04		A1
1468	JULIAN, Benjamin	2	SWSW	1837-03-20		A1
1469	JULIEN, Benjamin	11	SENW	1835-10-16		A1
1518	KALLMEIER, Harman H	29	NESE	1846-10-01		A1
1545	KALLMEIER, Herman H	29	SESE	1848-06-01		A1
1546	KATTERHEINRICH, Herman H	29	NENE	1848-06-01		A1 R1465
1550	KATTERHEINRICH, Herman W	19	SESW	1848-06-01		A1 F
1530	KATTERHENRICH, Henry	29	SENE	1846-10-01		A1
1659	KATTMAN, William	29	SWNE	1846-10-01		A1

ID	Individual in Patent	Sec.	Sec. Part	Date Issued	Other Counties	For More Info . . .
1658	KATTMAN, William (Cont'd)	29	SENW	1848-06-01		A1
1651	KOOK, William H	29	NENW	1848-07-01		A1
1540	KOTTERHEINRICH, Henry W	29	NWNE	1848-06-01		A1
1532	KRUSI, Henry	21	SESW	1846-10-01		A1
1533	" "	21	SWSW	1848-06-01		A1
1531	" "	21	N½SW	1851-06-02		A1
1534	KUCK, Henry	29	W½SE	1846-10-01		A1
1501	LEATHERS, Frederick	15	S½SE	1837-11-21		A1
1608	LEATHERS, Mary	23	SWNW	1837-03-20		A1 F
1609	" "	23	W½SW	1837-03-20		A1
1481	LONGWITH, Cyrus	7	NWSE	1850-07-01		A1
1630	LONGWITH, Samuel	7	NESW	1851-06-02		A1 F
1644	LONGWORTH, Thomas	7	NWSW	1849-02-01		A1
1492	LUCAS, Ebenezer	5	SE	1832-11-05		A1
1502	LUCAS, Frederick P	4	NESW	1835-10-09		A1
1503	" "	4	NWSE	1835-10-09		A1
1535	LUTTERBECK, Henry	7	SESE	1846-10-01		A1
1551	LUTTERBIEN, Herman W	19	NWSW	1850-07-01		A1 F
1561	LUTTRELL, James	4	NESE	1835-10-16		A1
1602	MACKLIN, Juliann	17	SE	1835-10-07		A1 G55
1603	" "	20	NWNE	1835-10-07		A1 G55
1631	MATHERS, Samuel	29	NWNW	1835-10-07		A1
1632	" "	30	NENE	1835-10-07		A1
1592	MCCLELLAN, John	1	W½NW	1835-10-09		A1
1629	MCCULLOUGH, Samuel H	23	E½SE	1832-03-03		A1
1499	MCKINNEY, Ephraim	25	E½SW	1832-11-05		A1
1465	MCVEIGH, Alfred	29	NENE	1856-04-15		A1 C R1546
1519	MECKSTOTT, Harman	29	NESW	1846-10-01		A1
1552	MECKSTROTT, Herman W	29	SESW	1848-06-01		A1
1616	MELLINGER, Peter D	23	W½NE	1835-10-16		A1 F
1461	MEYERS, Aaron	17	SWNE	1835-10-16		A1
1474	MILLER, Christ	13	E½NW	1837-03-18		A1
1536	MILLER, Henry	5	SWSW	1848-08-01		A1
1593	MILLER, John	23	W½N½	1838-09-04		A1 G57 F
1509	MULLER, Gerrard	11	E½NE	1837-03-15		A1
1537	MULLER, Henry	12	W½NW	1837-03-15		A1
1470	NOGGLE, Benjamin	2	SESE	1837-03-16		A1
1547	NURMEIER, Herman H	19	NENW	1848-08-01		A1 F
1523	NUSMEIER, Henry A	19	SWNW	1850-07-01		A1 F
1548	NUSMEIRE, Herman H	19	NWNW	1850-07-01		A1 F
1605	ORTH, Ludwig	15	NESE	1840-10-10		A1
1600	PATTON, Joseph	1	SW	1835-10-09		A1
1601	" "	1	W½SE	1835-10-09		A1
1633	PENCE, Samuel	5	E½NW	1835-10-16		A1
1634	" "	5	NWNW	1835-10-16		A1
1635	" "	5	W½NE	1835-10-16		A1
1660	PENCE, William	9	SE	1835-10-08		A1
1471	POWELL, Benjamin	3	SENE	1837-03-20		A1 F
1494	RITTER, Elvira	24	N½NE	1835-10-07		A1
1495	" "	24	S½NE	1835-10-07		A1
1568	ROBERTS, Jessee	13	SW	1837-03-20		A1
1619	ROBERTS, Rebecca	26	SE	1837-03-20		A1
1637	ROBERTS, Sarah	26	NE	1837-03-20		A1
1661	RYAN, William	13	SE	1835-10-09		A1
1669	RYAN, Zachariah	13	SWNE	1835-10-07		A1
1668	" "	13	N½NE	1835-10-16		A1
1602	SAUM, Solomon	17	SE	1835-10-07		A1 G55
1603	" "	20	NWNE	1835-10-07		A1 G55
1538	SCHRER, Henry	17	NWSW	1848-08-01		A1
1549	SCHRER, Herman H	17	SWSW	1849-08-10		A1
1662	SCHRER, William	19	NWNE	1852-06-01		A1
1562	SHERIDEN, James	19	SWNE	1851-02-01		A1
1642	SHINN, Thomas E	13	W½NW	1837-03-20		A1
1563	SHIRDEN, James	19	SENW	1849-08-10		A1 F
1504	SNELLER, Frederick	21	E½NW	1852-06-01		A1
1663	SPRAY, William	25	E½NW	1832-03-03		A1
1636	STATLER, Samuel	6	W½SW	1834-01-30		A1
1618	STILLNAG, Philip	15	SENE	1840-10-10		A1
1478	STROH, Conrad	12	E½NW	1838-09-04		A1 G66
1479	" "	14	W½NW	1838-09-04		A1 G66
1480	" "	14	W½SW	1838-09-04		A1 G66
1478	STROH, John	12	E½NW	1838-09-04		A1 G66
1479	" "	14	W½NW	1838-09-04		A1 G66

ID	Individual in Patent	Sec.	Sec. Part	Date Issued	Other Counties	For More Info . . .
1480	STROH, John (Cont'd)	14	W½SW	1838-09-04		A1 G66
1476	TOBIAS, Christian	6	E½SW	1835-10-09		A1
1477	" "	6	SE	1835-10-09		A1
1497	TUCKER, Enoch M	5	NWSW	1835-10-08		A1
1498	" "	5	SWNW	1835-10-08		A1
1493	VANCE, Elizabeth	21	E½NE	1835-09-15		A1
1490	VANDERVEER, Dominicus	24	NENW	1837-03-20		A1 F
1491	" "	24	W½SE	1837-03-20		A1
1664	VANDERVEER, William	25	SWNW	1837-03-20		A1
1665	" "	25	W½SW	1837-03-20		A1
1521	VENNEMANN, Heinrich	19	NESE	1848-06-01		A1
1522	" "	19	SENE	1848-06-01		A1
1539	VENNEMANN, Henry	19	NENE	1851-06-02		A1
1559	WELLER, Jacob	8	SENE	1835-10-08		A1
1560	" "	9	SWNW	1835-10-08		A1
1478	WELLMAN, Henry	12	E½NW	1838-09-04		A1 G66
1479	" "	14	W½NW	1838-09-04		A1 G66
1480	" "	14	W½SW	1838-09-04		A1 G66
1541	" "	21	W½NE	1852-06-01		A1
1594	WILEY, John	14	E½NW	1837-03-16		A1
1595	" "	14	E½SW	1837-03-16		A1
1593	WILKINS, James	23	W½N½	1838-09-04		A1 G57 F
1564	" "	7	SWSW	1848-06-01		A1 F
1488	WOODRUFF, David	5	NESW	1835-10-09		A1
1485	" "	2	NWNW	1837-03-16		A1 F
1486	" "	3	NENE	1837-03-16		A1 F
1487	" "	3	W½SW	1837-03-20		A1 F
1612	YORK, Nehemiah	21	SE	1835-10-09		A1
1639	YOUNG, Susan	1	S½NE	1835-10-09		A1
1640	" "	1	SENW	1835-10-09		A1

Patent Map

T6-S R5-E
1st PM Meridian

Map Group 10

Township Statistics

Parcels Mapped	:	209
Number of Patents	:	187
Number of Individuals	:	156
Patentees Identified	:	152
Number of Surnames	:	127
Multi-Patentee Parcels	:	10
Oldest Patent Date	:	3/3/1832
Most Recent Patent	:	4/15/1856
Block/Lot Parcels	:	0
Parcels Re - Issued	:	1
Parcels that Overlap	:	0
Cities and Towns	:	1
Cemeteries	:	7

Section 6

Section 5: PENCE Samuel 1835; PENCE Samuel 1835; HOLLINGSWORTH William 1852; TUCKER Enoch M 1835; PENCE Samuel 1835; TUCKER Enoch M 1835; WOODRUFF David 1835; LUCAS Ebenezer 1832; MILLER Henry 1848; CLEVELAND Morgan H 1835

Section 4: BLAKELY Samuel 1835; BLEAKLY Samuel 1835; LUCAS Frederick P 1835; LUCAS Frederick P 1835; LUTTRELL James 1835

Section 7: STATLER Samuel 1834; TOBIAS Christian 1835; TOBIAS Christian 1835; BARRINGTON Richard R 1848; FRISCHE Henry 1852; BOARDMAN William Z 1851; FRISCHE Henry 1852; LONGWORTH Thomas 1849; LONGWITH Samuel 1851; LONGWITH Cyrus 1850; BOARDMAN William Z 1851; WILKINS James 1848; HUTSON Dennis 1848; HUDSON William 1852; LUTTERBECK Henry 1846

Section 8: FARNSLER John 1835; FARNSLER John 1835; FARNSLER John 1835; WELLER Jacob 1835; ARNET Jacob 1835

Section 9: WELLER Jacob 1835; ARNET John 1835; PENCE William 1835

Section 18: HUDSON Jesse 1835; BUCK Enoch 1835; HUDSON Jesse 1835; HUDSON Jesse 1835

Section 17: BUCK John 1835; BOSCHE John F 1846; BOSCHE John F 1846; AUFDERHARK William 1849; HUDSON William 1849; GRABLE John 1835; MEYERS Aaron 1835; AUFDERHARM William H 1846; SCHRER Henry 1848; DIEGEL George 1848; MACKLIN [55] Juliann 1835; SCHRER Herman H 1849; DIEGEL George 1850

Section 16

Section 19: NUSMEIRE Herman H 1850; NURMEIER Herman H 1848; SCHRER William 1852; VENNEMANN Henry 1851; NUSMEIER Henry A 1850; SHIRDEN James 1849; SHERIDEN James 1851; VENNEMANN Heinrich 1848; LUTTERBIEN Herman W 1850; ESCHMEIRE Adolph 1851; ESCHMEIRE Adolph 1851; VENNEMANN Heinrich 1848; FLEDDERIOHAN Herman H 1848; KATTERHEINRICH Herman W 1848; FLADERIOHAN Adam 1848; BROWN William J 1835

Section 20: MACKLIN [55] Juliann 1835; CONGER Joel 1835; CONGER Joseph 1835; CONGER Joseph 1835; AUGKINBAUGH [5] Peter 1835; CAREY [26] Thomas M 1835; BROWN William J 1835

Section 21: FLEDDERJOHAN Harmon H 1852; WELLMAN Henry 1852; SNELLER Frederick 1852; VANCE Elizabeth 1835; KRUSI Henry 1851; KRUSI Henry 1848; KRUSI Henry 1846; YORK Nehemiah 1835

Section 30

Section 29: HAINES Job 1835; MATHERS Samuel 1835; MATHERS Samuel 1835; KOOK William H 1848; KOTTERHEINRICH Henry W 1848; KATTERHEINRICH Herman H 1848; MCVEIGH Alfred 1856; AUGKINBAUGH [5] Peter 1835; HOGE Herman H 1848; KATTMAN William 1848; KATTMAN William 1846; KATTERHENRICH Henry 1846; BRACKSEACK Rodolph 1846; MECKSTOTT Harman 1846; KUCK Henry 1846; KALLMEIER Harman H 1846; HAINES Job 1835; AUGKINBAUGH [5] Peter 1835; ELSHOF Herman 1848; MECKSTROTT Herman W 1848; KALLMEIER Herman H 1848

Section 28

Section 31

Section 32

Section 33

GREEN William 1837	GREEN William 1837	WOODRUFF David 1837	WOODRUFF David 1837	FISHER Ignaz 1845	HARVEY Ambrose 1835	MCCLELLAN John 1835	BRANHAM Mary 1835	BROCK Francis 1835

GEARHEART Daniel 1837 · GREEN Henry 1835 · POWELL Benjamin 1837 · GEARHEART Samuel 1837 · **2** GEARHEART John 1837 · YOUNG Susan 1835 · YOUNG Susan 1835

WOODRUFF David 1837 · GREEN Henry 1837 · **3** · CECIL Gordan 1837 · GEARHEART Samuel 1837 · GEARHEART John 1837 · PATTON Joseph 1835 · **1** · PATTON Joseph 1835 · HERMAN Lauren D 1835

JULIAN Benjamin 1837 · COPSEY George 1837 · BRAMBLET George 1837 · NOGGLE Benjamin 1837

COPSEY William 1837 · FORNEY Christian 1837 · CECIL Gordan 1837 · CECIL Gordan 1837 · CECIL Gordan 1837 · CECIL Gordan 1837 · MULLER Henry 1837 · STROH [66] Conrad 1838

FORNEY John 1837 · **10** · JULIEN Benjamin 1835 · **11** · MULLER Gerrard 1837 · FRAME Nathan 1835 · **12**

BOLANDER Jonathan 1837 · CECIL Gordan 1837 · CURTIS Daniel M 1837 · FRISCHE Henry 1837

HERZING Philip 1838 · COVERSTONE Jacob 1838 · ELLIOTT John 1850 · STROH [66] Conrad 1838 · ASPINALL Thomas 1837 · SHINN Thomas E 1837 · RYAN Zachariah 1835

FULLER Joel 1837 · FULLER Joel 1837 · **15** · STILLNAG Philip 1840 · WILEY John 1837 · MILLER Christ 1837 · RYAN Zachariah 1835 · ALEXANDER Arba 1837

FULLER Joel 1837 · FLOWERS Thomas 1837 · ORTH Ludwig 1840 · STROH [66] Conrad 1838 · **14** · CHATTERTON David 1837 · ROBERTS Jessee 1837 · **13** · RYAN William 1835

CAMPBELL Malcom 1835 · COLE Spencer 1844 · LEATHERS Frederick 1837 · WILEY John 1837 · ASPINALL Robert 1837

ARNET John 1835 · COLE Hollister S 1837 · BRANNAN Robert 1837 · BRANNUM Robert 1838 · MELLINGER Peter D 1835 · HITTEL Jacob 1840 · VANDERVEER Dominicus 1837 · RITTER Elvira 1835

22 · BATES John 1841 · MILLER [57] John 1838 · LEATHERS Mary 1837 · HANKINS Jonathan 1835 · **23** · HITTEL Jacob 1840 · **24** · RITTER Elvira 1835

BATES John 1841 · BATES John 1841 · LEATHERS Mary 1837 · AUFFORTH Bernard H 1837 · CAMPBELL John 1833 · MCCULLOUGH Samuel H 1832 · VANDERVEER Dominicus 1837 · COTTERL Gersham 1837

GUDORF Henry 1835 · HERMES Bernard 1837

JACKSON William 1838 · ROBERTS Sarah 1837 · SPRAY William 1832

27 · **26** · VANDERVEER William 1837 · **25**

VANDERVEER William 1837

Auglaize County · CECIL Gordan 1837 · ROBERTS Rebecca 1837 · MCKINNEY Ephraim 1832

Shelby County

34 · **35** · **36**

Helpful Hints

1. This Map's INDEX can be found on the preceding pages.

2. Refer to Map "C" to see where this Township lies within Auglaize County, Ohio.

3. Numbers within square brackets [ ] denote a multi-patentee land parcel (multi-owner). Refer to Appendix "C" for a full list of members in this group.

4. Areas that look to be crowded with Patentees usually indicate multiple sales of the same parcel (Re-issues) or Overlapping parcels. See this Township's Index for an explanation of these and other circumstances that might explain "odd" groupings of Patentees on this map.

Legend

————	Patent Boundary
————	Section Boundary
▨	No Patents Found (or Outside County)
1., 2., 3., ...	Lot Numbers (when beside a name)
[ ]	Group Number (see Appendix "C")

Scale: Section = 1 mile X 1 mile (generally, with some exceptions)

Road Map

T6-S R5-E
1st PM Meridian

Map Group 10

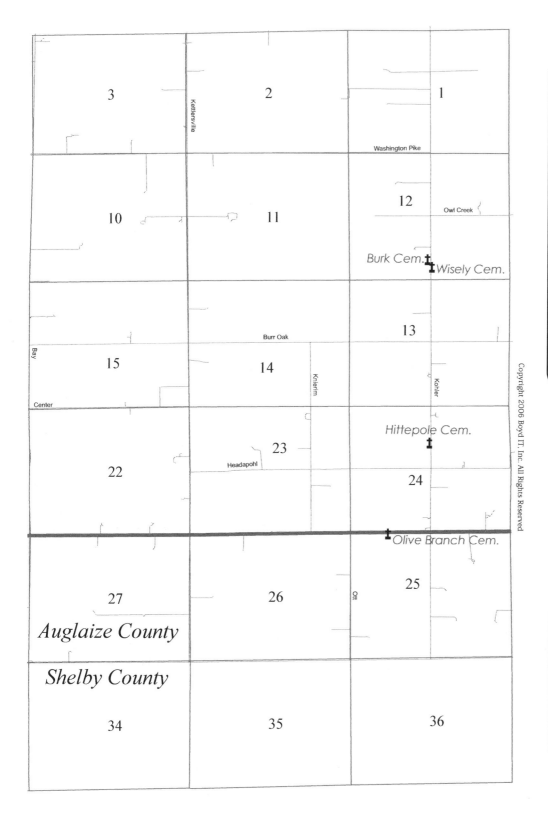

Kettersville

Washington Pike

3

2

1

12

Owl Creek

10

11

Burk Cem. Wisely Cem.

13

Burr Oak

15

14

Knierm

Kohler

Bay

Center

Hittepole Cem.

22

23

Headapohl

24

Olive Branch Cem.

27

26

25

Ott

Auglaize County

Shelby County

34

35

36

Helpful Hints

1. This road map has a number of uses, but primarily it is to help you: a) find the present location of land owned by your ancestors (at least the general area), b) find cemeteries and city-centers, and c) estimate the route/roads used by Census-takers & tax-assessors.

2. If you plan to travel to Auglaize County to locate cemeteries or land parcels, please pick up a modern travel map for the area before you do. Mapping old land parcels on modern maps is not as exact a science as you might think. Just the slightest variations in public land survey coordinates, estimates of parcel boundaries, or road-map deviations can greatly alter a map's representation of how a road either does or doesn't cross a particular parcel of land.

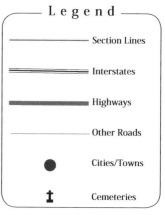

Legend

———————— Section Lines

════════ Interstates

━━━━━━━━ Highways

———————— Other Roads

● Cities/Towns

‡ Cemeteries

Scale: Section = 1 mile X 1 mile
(generally, with some exceptions)

Historical Map

T6-S R5-E
1st PM Meridian

Map Group 10

Cities & Towns
New Knoxville

Cemeteries
Arnett Cemetery
Burk Cemetery
Hittepole Cemetery
Olive Branch Cemetery
Pilger Ruhe Cemetery
Protestant Evangelical Cemetery
Wisely Cemetery

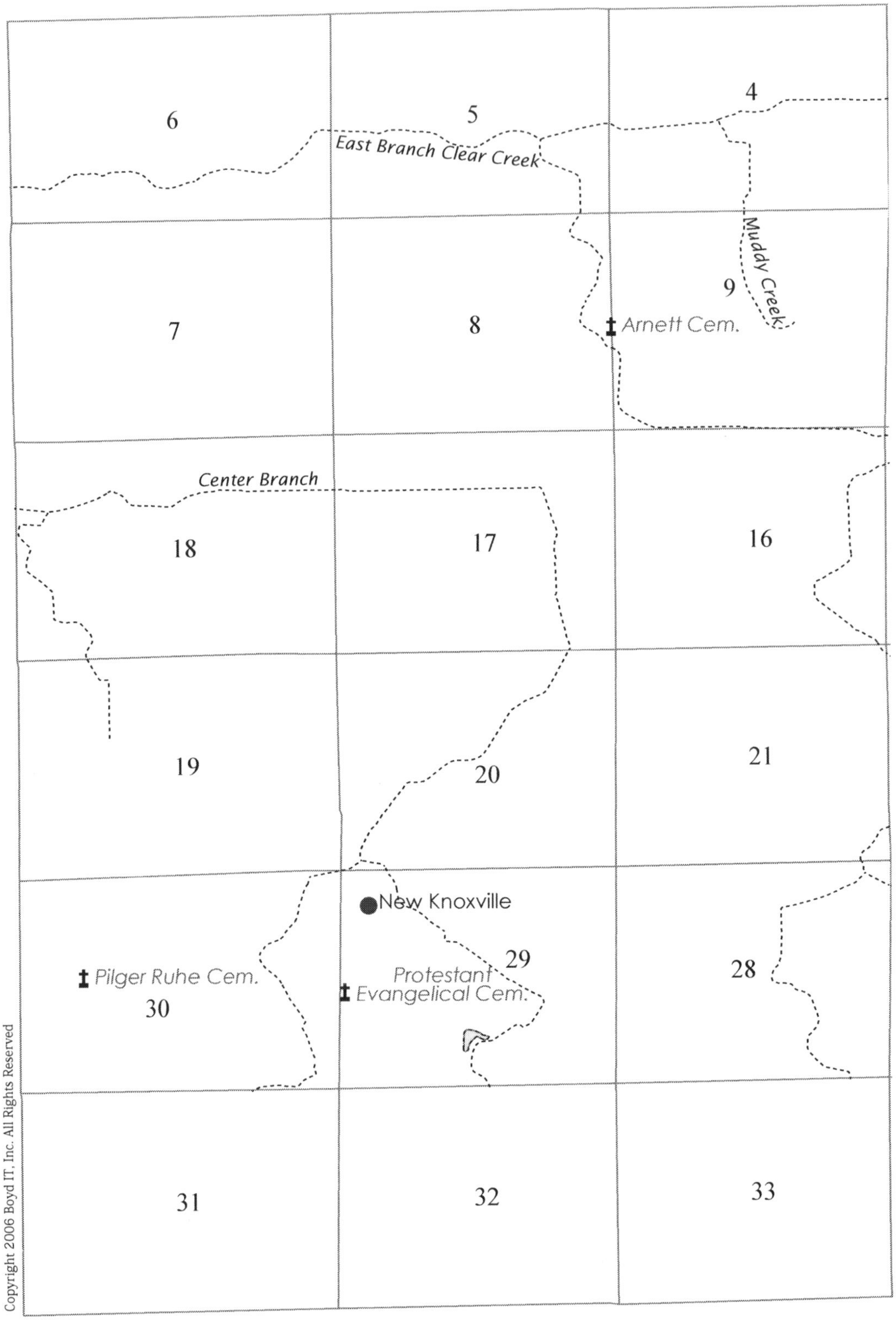

6	5	4
7	8	9
18	17	16
19	20	21
30	29	28
31	32	33

East Branch Clear Creek

Muddy Creek

✝ Arnett Cem.

Center Branch

● New Knoxville

✝ Pilger Ruhe Cem.

✝ Protestant Evangelical Cem.

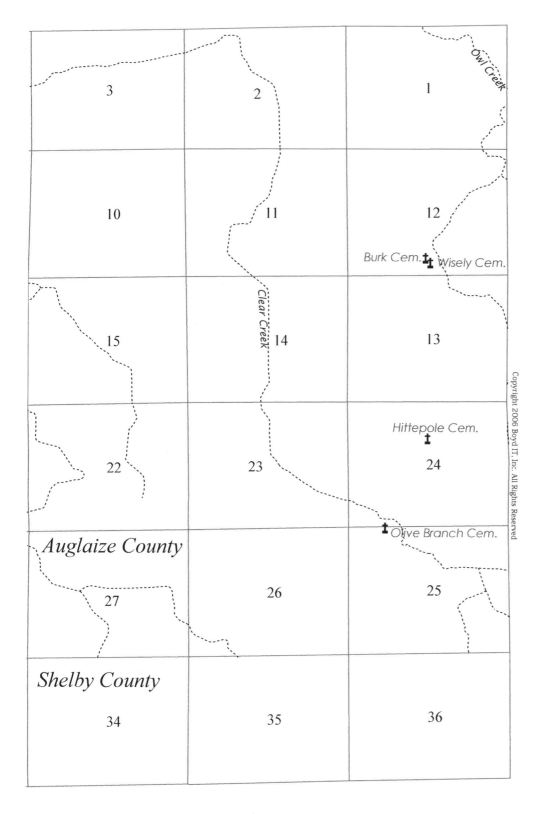

3

2

1

Owl Creek

10

11

12

Burk Cem. 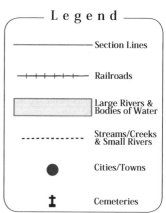 *Wisely Cem.*

Clear Creek 14

15

13

Hittepole Cem.

22

23

24

Olive Branch Cem.

Auglaize County

27

26

25

Shelby County

34

35

36

Helpful Hints

1. This Map takes a different look at the same Congressional Township displayed in the preceding two maps. It presents features that can help you better envision the historical development of the area: a) Water-bodies (lakes & ponds), b) Water-courses (rivers, streams, etc.), c) Railroads, d) City/town center-points (where they were oftentimes located when first settled), and e) Cemeteries.

2. Using this "Historical" map in tandem with this Township's Patent Map and Road Map, may lead you to some interesting discoveries. You will often find roads, towns, cemeteries, and waterways are named after nearby landowners: sometimes those names will be the ones you are researching. See how many of these research gems you can find here in Auglaize County.

L e g e n d

————————	Section Lines
+++++++++	Railroads
▭	Large Rivers & Bodies of Water
– – – – –	Streams/Creeks & Small Rivers
●	Cities/Towns
✝	Cemeteries

Scale: Section = 1 mile X 1 mile
(there are some exceptions)

Map Group 11: Index to Land Patents

Township 6-South Range 6-East (1st PM)

After you locate an individual in this Index, take note of the Section and Section Part then proceed to the Land Patent map on the pages immediately following. You should have no difficulty locating the corresponding parcel of land.

The "For More Info" Column will lead you to more information about the underlying Patents. See the Legend at right, and the "How to Use this Book" chapter, for more information.

```
                        LEGEND
              "For More Info . . . " column

A = Authority (Legislative Act, See Appendix "A")
B = Block or Lot (location in Section unknown)
C = Cancelled Patent
F = Fractional Section
G = Group  (Multi-Patentee Patent, see Appendix "C")
V = Overlaps another Parcel
R = Re-Issued (Parcel patented more than once)

(A & G items require you to look in the Appendixes referred
to above. All other Letter-designations followed by a number
require you to locate line-items in this index that possess
the ID number found after the letter).
```

ID	Individual in Patent	Sec.	Sec. Part	Date Issued	Other Counties	For More Info . . .
1703	ABBEY, Charles H	9	E½SE	1834-01-30		A1
1705	ABBEY, Charles W	9	W½SE	1835-10-08		A1
1729	ALBR, Henry	4	NENE	1835-10-08		A1 G2
1820	ALBRANT, Mena	4	NWSW	1840-10-10		A1
1809	ARTENBRACK, Leon H	1	SWSW	1835-10-07		A1
1673	BACH, Adam	9	NENE	1836-02-25		A1 G10
1674	BACK, Adam	4	S½SE	1835-10-09		A1
1866	BECHTEL, William	11	NWNW	1835-10-08		A1
1810	BEIENSDORFER, Leonard	29	E½SW	1835-09-15		A1
1721	BICK, Ezzard	10	W½NW	1836-02-15		A1
1829	BINK, Paul	16	SESE	1845-06-01		A1
1830	" "	16	SWSW	1845-06-01		A1
1758	BLUEST, John	15	SW	1835-10-09		A1
1722	BOB, Felix	22	NWNE	1835-10-07		A1
1695	BOBB, Betsy	4	NESE	1835-10-16		A1
1759	BOBB, John	4	N½SE	1835-10-08		A1
1825	BOBB, Nicholas	4	E½NW	1835-10-16		A1
1824	BOWERS, Nathaniel	17	SESE	1835-10-09		A1
1844	BOWERS, Samuel	29	NWSW	1836-02-15		A1
1702	BRESAR, Charles	6	NWNW	1835-10-09		A1
1837	BROWN, Phillip	13	SW	1835-10-08		A1
1860	BURKET, Valtin	9	NWNE	1837-03-20		A1
1795	BUSH, Joseph	12	SE	1835-10-07		A1
1796	" "	12	SENE	1835-10-07		A1
1867	BUTTERWORTH, William	5	W½NE	1835-10-08		A1
1731	CALBE, Henry	2	E½SW	1835-10-07		A1
1839	CANON, Richard M	17	SENW	1835-10-08		A1
1840	" "	17	SWNE	1835-10-08		A1
1789	CAREY, John W	9	E½SW	1835-10-08		A1 G24
1790	" "	9	NWSW	1835-10-08		A1 G24
1785	CASTLE, John T	28	SESE	1835-10-16		A1
1858	CHILDERS, Thomas	1	SESE	1835-10-08		A1
1868	CRAFT, William	1	NESE	1835-10-07		A1
1869	" "	1	S½NE	1835-10-07		A1
1870	" "	1	W½SE	1835-10-07		A1
1797	CUMMINGS, Joseph	4	W½NW	1835-10-09		A1
1798	" "	5	E½NE	1835-10-09		A1
1789	DEEMS, John	9	E½SW	1835-10-08		A1 G24
1790	" "	9	NWSW	1835-10-08		A1 G24
1806	DELANY, Justis	11	E½NW	1835-10-08		A1
1807	" "	11	SWNW	1835-10-08		A1
1832	DICK, Peter	28	W½NE	1835-10-07		A1 G30
1684	DRESHU, Andrew	23	N½NE	1835-09-15		A1
1754	ELLIOTT, James	8	E½NW	1835-10-08		A1 G35
1745	" "	18	SENW	1837-03-16		A1
1743	" "	18	NENW	1837-03-18		A1 F

ID	Individual in Patent	Sec.	Sec. Part	Date Issued	Other Counties	For More Info . . .
1744	ELLIOTT, James (Cont'd)	18	NWSE	1837-03-18		A1
1746	" "	19	NWNE	1837-03-18		A1 F
1747	" "	7	NENW	1840-10-10		A1
1748	" "	7	NESW	1840-10-10		A1
1750	" "	7	NWSE	1840-10-10		A1
1751	" "	7	SENW	1840-10-10		A1
1753	" "	7	SWNE	1840-10-10		A1
1752	" "	7	SESW	1840-11-10		A1 F
1749	" "	7	NWNE	1844-08-01		A1
1859	FAIRFIELD, Thomas	6	W½NE	1835-10-08		A1
1821	FARIS, Michael	29	N½NW	1835-10-07		A1 G37
1737	FISHER, Hignaz	9	NENW	1844-08-01		A1
1766	FOLKAMPF, John H	6	E½NW	1835-10-08		A1
1762	FONTS, John	14	NWNW	1835-10-08		A1
1822	FORIS, Michael	29	SWNW	1836-02-15		A1
1763	FRANTS, John	17	S½SW	1835-10-16		A1
1764	FREAS, John	22	S½NE	1835-10-09		A1 G40 F
1811	GEISLER, Leonart	4	SWSW	1837-03-16		A1
1812	" "	9	NWNW	1837-03-16		A1
1821	HAMER, Joseph	29	N½NW	1835-10-07		A1 G37
1845	HAMILTON, Samuel H	2	W½SE	1835-10-08		A1
1813	HARMEL, Lewis	16	SENE	1844-09-10		A1 G44
1767	HARSHMAN, John	13	NW	1835-10-08		A1
1682	HARVEY, Ambrose	1	NWSW	1835-10-16		A1
1689	HARVEY, Asa	11	NWNE	1836-02-15		A1
1718	HARVEY, Elizabeth	2	NESE	1835-10-16		A1
1725	HEADEPOHL, Frederick	4	SESW	1835-10-07		A1
1871	HEINE, William	6	S½SW	1835-10-07		A1
1799	HEMMERT, Joseph	29	SENW	1835-09-15		A1
1732	HERMAN, Henry H	7	W½NW	1835-10-09		A1
1715	HEROFF, David	2	NE	1835-10-08		A1
1768	HEROFF, John	2	W½SW	1835-10-08		A1
1872	HEROFF, William	12	N½NW	1835-10-08		A1
1765	HERTIG, John G	26	SE	1832-11-05		A1
1706	HEYSLER, Christian	11	SESE	1835-10-08		A1
1707	" "	11	W½SE	1835-10-08		A1
1694	HOLSINGER, Bernard	30	SENE	1837-03-16		A1
1729	HORTAS, Conrad	4	NENE	1835-10-08		A1 G2
1733	HOTTES, Henry	4	SENE	1835-10-07		A1
1709	HOUCK, Christopher	11	NENE	1835-10-07		A1
1846	HOWELL, Samuel	3	NE	1835-10-08		A1
1681	HUTZLER, Albert	5	S½SE	1837-03-16		A1
1757	JACKSON, Jesse	6	SWNW	1840-10-10		A1 F
1738	JUDY, Jacob	3	W½	1835-10-08		A1
1734	KADIEBERT, Henry	6	NESW	1835-10-08		A1
1675	KEENER, Adam	10	S½SW	1835-10-08		A1 G47
1676	KEEVER, Adam	10	N½SW	1835-10-09		A1 G48
1720	KENTNER, Emanuel	3	E½SE	1834-01-30		A1
1727	KENTNER, George	3	W½SE	1834-01-30		A1
1675	KERR, Nicholas	10	S½SW	1835-10-08		A1 G47
1723	KLIPFEL, Francis	16	NWSW	1844-09-10		A1
1813	" "	16	SENE	1844-09-10		A1 G44
1800	KLIPFEL, Joseph	28	NENE	1835-09-15		A1
1815	KLOPF, Martin	22	N½NW	1835-10-09		A1 G51
1816	" "	22	S½NW	1835-10-09		A1 G51
1826	KNARR, Nicholas	16	NESE	1844-09-10		A1
1677	KNECHT, Adam	16	E½NW	1844-09-10		A1
1678	" "	16	W½NE	1844-09-10		A1
1679	" "	16	W½NW	1844-09-10		A1
1673	KOCH, John	9	NENE	1836-02-25		A1 G10
1814	KUHN, Lorenz	26	W½NW	1835-12-24		A1
1817	LEBEL, Matthias	1	N½NE	1835-10-07		A1
1818	" "	12	S½NW	1835-10-07		A1
1819	" "	12	SWNE	1835-10-07		A1
1772	LENOX, John	8	W½SW	1834-01-30		A1
1726	LONG, George D	8	E½SE	1835-10-08		A1
1801	LYONS, Joseph	18	E½SE	1835-10-09		A1 G54
1847	MARSHALL, Samuel	17	NENW	1835-10-08		A1
1848	" "	17	NWNW	1835-10-08		A1
1849	" "	8	E½SW	1835-10-08		A1
1813	MATHER, Andrew	16	SENE	1844-09-10		A1 G44
1842	MCCULLOUGH, Robert	19	NENW	1835-10-08		A1 F
1843	" "	7	W½SW	1837-11-21		A1 F

ID	Individual in Patent	Sec.	Sec. Part	Date Issued	Other Counties	For More Info . . .
1698	MCMILLIN, Bushrod T	9	SWSW	1837-03-16		A1 G56
1697	MCNAMUR, Bryant	17	NESE	1835-10-09		A1
1773	MELLINGER, John	22	NEN½	1835-10-08		A1 F
1774	" "	23	NWN½	1835-10-08		A1 F
1670	MILLER, Abraham	18	NE	1835-10-07		A1
1671	" "	18	SW	1835-10-07		A1
1775	MILLER, John	27	E½NW	1835-09-15		A1
1776	" "	27	NE	1835-09-15		A1
1764	" "	22	S½NE	1835-10-09		A1 G40 F
1777	MITZ, John	27	W½NW	1835-09-15		A1
1802	MONGER, Joseph	27	SE	1835-09-15		A1
1815	MONTER, Andreas	22	N½NW	1835-10-09		A1 G51
1816	" "	22	S½NW	1835-10-09		A1 G51
1803	MYERS, Joseph	14	SWNW	1835-10-08		A1
1804	" "	23	NENW	1835-10-09		A1 F
1850	MYERS, Samuel	14	E½NW	1835-10-08		A1
1835	NAGLE, Philip	5	E½SW	1837-08-21		A1
1836	" "	5	N½SE	1837-08-21		A1
1853	NAUMBURGER, Sophia D	7	SWSE	1840-10-10		A1
1676	NERR, Nicholas	10	N½SW	1835-10-09		A1 G48
1730	NIETERT, Henry C	6	W½SE	1835-10-08		A1
1700	NIPPGEN, Casper	24	E½NE	1837-03-15		A1 F
1808	PEACHE, Kasper	6	NWSW	1835-10-09		A1
1704	POWELL, Charles	30	E½SE	1835-09-15		A1
1755	POWELL, James	30	W½SE	1835-10-08		A1
1841	REED, Richard	15	NESE	1835-10-08		A1
1832	RISBARGER, Michael	28	W½NE	1835-10-07		A1 G30
1675	ROLLINS, Mihew	10	S½SW	1835-10-08		A1 G47
1685	ROSS, Andrew	13	S½NE	1835-10-16		A1
1778	ROTH, John	13	E½SE	1835-09-15		A1
1780	" "	24	W½NW	1835-09-15		A1 C
1779	" "	24	W½NE	1884-03-10		A1 F
1781	ROUCH, John	10	SE	1835-10-08		A1
1782	SAMMETINGER, John	16	NENE	1844-09-10		A1
1833	SCHAUL, Peter	29	SWSW	1836-02-15		A1
1712	SCHEMMEL, Conrad	19	NENE	1835-10-09		A1 F
1713	" "	20	4	1835-10-09		A1
1714	" "	21	4	1835-10-09		A1
1783	SCHURE, John	11	NESE	1835-10-07		A1
1688	SEITER, Anthony	14	W½SE	1835-10-09		A1
1728	SEITER, Gerwasy	14	SW	1835-10-08		A1 G61
1728	SEITER, Michael	14	SW	1835-10-08		A1 G61
1831	SEIVERT, Paul	28	SENE	1835-09-15		A1
1724	SHAEFFER, Francis	4	W½NE	1835-10-08		A1
1769	SHERMER, John L	15	NWSE	1835-10-09		A1
1770	" "	15	SENW	1835-10-09		A1
1771	" "	15	SWSE	1835-10-09		A1
1698	SHULL, Henry	9	SWSW	1837-03-16		A1 G56
1699	SIDES, Carl L	17	N½SW	1835-10-16		A1
1823	SIFORT, Michael	27	E½SW	1835-09-15		A1
1784	SNAVELY, John	12	N½NE	1835-10-16		A1
1680	SNIDER, Adam	15	NE	1835-10-08		A1
1739	SNIDER, Jacob	9	SENE	1836-02-15		A1
1673	SNYDER, Adam	9	NENE	1836-02-25		A1 G10
1740	SNYDER, Jacob	10	E½NW	1836-02-15		A1
1692	SPRAY, Benjamin	30	SW	1824-05-03		A1
1693	" "	30	W½NW	1832-11-05		A1
1756	SPRAY, James	19	NW	1835-10-08		A1 F
1690	SPURRIER, Beal	15	W½NW	1835-10-08		A1
1691	SPURRIER, Beals	9	SWNE	1837-03-16		A1
1716	STEVENS, Ebenezer D	2	NW	1835-10-08		A1
1873	STOCKDALE, William	30	E½NW	1835-10-09		A1
1874	" "	30	N½NE	1835-10-09		A1
1735	STODDARD, Henry	7	E½SE	1834-01-30		A1
1696	SUTER, Blaize	13	NWSE	1835-09-15		A1
1875	SWEARINGEN, William	18	SWSE	1835-10-07		A1
1801	" "	18	E½SE	1835-10-09		A1 G54
1793	TAYLOR, Jonathan	19	NE	1822-04-08		A1 F
1794	" "	19	SE	1822-04-08		A1
1672	TOBIAS, Abraham	14	E½SE	1835-10-08		A1
1708	TOBIAS, Christian	1	E½SW	1835-10-09		A1
1741	TOBIAS, Jacob	14	E½NE	1835-10-08		A1
1786	TOBIAS, John	14	W½NE	1835-10-08		A1

ID	Individual in Patent	Sec.	Sec. Part	Date Issued	Other Counties	For More Info . . .
1834	TOBIAS, Peter	12	SW	1835-10-08		A1
1686	TODD, Andrew	18	W½NW	1837-08-21		A1 F
1876	TREBEIN, William	16	E½SW	1844-09-10		A1
1877	" "	16	W½SE	1844-09-10		A1
1760	VAN ANTWERP, JOHN D	17	SWNW	1835-10-08		A1
1761	" "	8	W½SE	1835-10-08		A1
1787	VAN BLARACOM, JOHN	15	NENW	1835-10-08		A1
1788	"	17	W½SE	1835-10-16		A1
1838	VAN BLARACOM, PHILLIP	15	SESE	1835-10-08		A1
1736	VAN BLARICOM, HENRY	9	SWNW	1835-10-08		A1 G67
1854	VAN HORNE, THOMAS B	5	W½SW	1834-01-30		A1
1855	" "	6	E½SE	1834-01-30		A1
1856	" "	7	E½NE	1834-01-30		A1
1857	" "	8	W½NW	1834-01-30		A1
1754	" "	8	E½NW	1835-10-08		A1 G35
1736	" "	9	SWNW	1835-10-08		A1 G67
1862	VAN HORNE, WILLIAM A	5	W½NW	1835-10-08		A1
1863	" "	6	E½NE	1835-10-08		A1
1864	" "	8	NE	1835-10-08		A1
1861	" "	5	E½NW	1835-10-09		A1
1865	" "	9	SENW	1835-10-16		A1
1878	VERTH, William	30	SWNE	1837-03-16		A1
1683	VOLL, Andreas	22	S½	1835-10-09		A1
1742	VOORHIS, Jacob	11	SW	1835-10-08		A1
1711	WAGGONER, Christopher	13	NENE	1835-10-07		A1
1710	" "	10	NE	1835-10-08		A1
1851	WAYMIRE, Solomon	26	E½NW	1832-03-03		A1
1852	" "	26	NE	1832-03-03		A1
1827	WAYNER, Nicholas	28	NWSE	1835-09-15		A1 V1828
1828	" "	28	W½SE	1835-09-15		A1 V1827
1687	WERST, Andrew	1	NW	1835-10-09		A1
1701	WILHELM, Catherine	24	N½NW	1835-09-15		A1 G70
1701	WILHELM, George	24	N½NW	1835-09-15		A1 G70
1701	WILHELM, Roliburn	24	N½NW	1835-09-15		A1 G70
1717	WILLIAMS, Edward	13	NWNE	1835-10-16		A1
1805	WIMERT, Joseph	2	SESE	1835-10-07		A1
1719	WISE, Elizabeth	13	SWSE	1835-10-07		A1
1791	ZANGLEIN, John	17	E½NE	1835-10-07		A1
1792	" "	17	NWNE	1835-10-07		A1

Patent Map

T6-S R6-E
1st PM Meridian

Map Group 11

Township Statistics

Parcels Mapped	:	209
Number of Patents	:	192
Number of Individuals	:	167
Patentees Identified	:	153
Number of Surnames	:	140
Multi-Patentee Parcels	:	18
Oldest Patent Date	:	4/8/1822
Most Recent Patent	:	3/10/1884
Block/Lot Parcels	:	3
Parcels Re - Issued	:	0
Parcels that Overlap	:	2
Cities and Towns	:	1
Cemeteries	:	8

Map grid

Section 6
- BRESAR Charles 1835
- JACKSON Jesse 1840
- FOLKAMPF John H 1835
- FAIRFIELD Thomas 1835
- HORNE William A Van 1835
- PEACHE Kasper 1835
- KADIEBERT Henry 1835
- NIETERT Henry C 1835
- HEINE William 1835
- HORNE Thomas B Van 1834

Section 5
- HORNE William A Van 1835
- HORNE William A Van 1835
- BUTTERWORTH William 1835
- CUMMINGS Joseph 1835
- HORNE Thomas B Van 1834
- NAGLE Philip 1837
- NAGLE Philip 1837
- HUTZLER Albert 1837

Section 4
- CUMMINGS Joseph 1835
- SHAEFFER Francis 1835
- ALBR [2] Henry 1835
- BOBB Nicholas 1835
- 4
- HOTTES Henry 1835
- CUMMINGS Joseph 1835
- ALBRANT Mena 1840
- BOBB Betsy 1835
- BOBB John 1835
- GEISLER Leonart 1837
- HEADEPOHL Frederick 1835
- BACK Adam 1835

Section 7
- HERMAN Henry H 1835
- ELLIOTT James 1840
- ELLIOTT James 1844
- ELLIOTT James 1840
- ELLIOTT James 1840
- HORNE Thomas B Van 1834
- 7
- MCCULLOUGH Robert 1837
- ELLIOTT James 1840
- ELLIOTT James 1840
- ELLIOTT James 1840
- NAUMBURGER Sophia D 1840
- STODDARD Henry 1834

Section 8
- HORNE Thomas B Van 1834
- HORNE William A Van 1835
- ELLIOTT [35] James 1835
- LENOX John 1834
- 8
- ANTWERP John D Van 1835
- MARSHALL Samuel 1835
- LONG George D 1835

Section 9
- GEISLER Leonart 1837
- FISHER Hignaz 1844
- BURKET Valtin 1837
- BACH [10] Adam 1836
- BLARICOM [67] Henry Van 1835
- HORNE William A Van 1835
- SPURRIER Beals 1837
- SNIDER Jacob 1836
- CAREY [24] John W 1835
- 9
- ABBEY Charles W 1835
- MCMILLIN [56] Bushrod T 1837
- CAREY [24] John W 1835
- ABBEY Charles H 1834

Section 18
- TODD Andrew 1837
- ELLIOTT James 1837
- MILLER Abraham 1835
- ELLIOTT James 1837
- 18
- ELLIOTT James 1837
- ELLIOTT James 1837
- LYONS [54] Joseph 1835
- SWEARINGEN William 1835
- MILLER Abraham 1835

Section 17
- MARSHALL Samuel 1835
- MARSHALL Samuel 1835
- ZANGLEIN John 1835
- ANTWERP John D Van 1835
- CANON Richard M 1835
- CANON Richard M 1835
- ZANGLEIN John 1835
- SIDES Carl L 1835
- 17
- BLARACOM John Van 1835
- MCNAMUR Bryant 1835
- FRANTS John 1835
- BOWERS Nathaniel 1835

Section 16
- KNECHT Adam 1844
- KNECHT Adam 1844
- SAMMETINGER John 1844
- KNECHT Adam 1844
- HARMEL [44] Lewis 1844
- KLIPFEL Francis 1844
- 16
- TREBEIN William 1844
- KNARR Nicholas 1844
- BINK Paul 1845
- TREBEIN William 1844
- BINK Paul 1845

Section 19
- MCCULLOUGH Robert 1835
- ELLIOTT James 1837
- SCHEMMEL Conrad 1835
- SPRAY James 1835
- TAYLOR Jonathan 1822
- 19
- TAYLOR Jonathan 1822

Section 20
- Lots-Sec. 20
- 4 SCHEMMEL, Conrad 1835
- 20

Section 21
- Lots-Sec. 21
- 4 SCHEMMEL, Conrad 1835
- 21

Section 30
- SPRAY Benjamin 1832
- STOCKDALE William 1835
- STOCKDALE William 1835
- VERTH William 1837
- HOLSINGER Bernard 1837
- POWELL James 1835
- 30
- SPRAY Benjamin 1824
- POWELL Charles 1835

Section 29
- FARIS [37] Michael 1835
- FORIS Michael 1836
- HEMMERT Joseph 1835
- 29
- BOWERS Samuel 1836
- SCHAUL Peter 1836
- BEIENSDORFER Leonard 1835

Section 28
- 28
- DICK [30] Peter 1835
- KLIPFEL Joseph 1835
- SEIVERT Paul 1835
- WAYNER Nicholas 1835
- WAYNER Nicholas 1835
- CASTLE John T 1835

Section 31
- 31

Section 32
- 32

Section 33
- 33

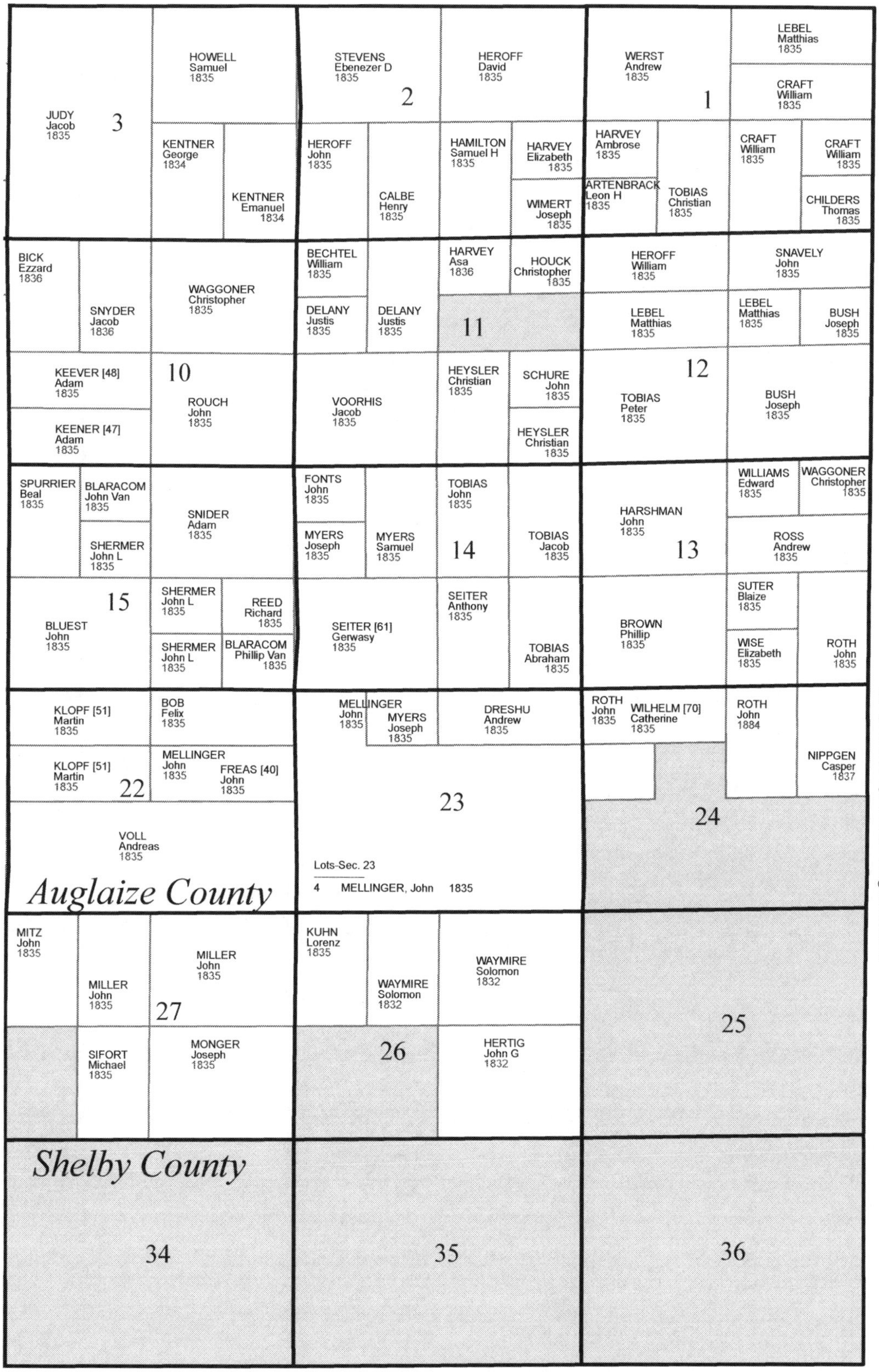

				LEBEL Matthias 1835
JUDY Jacob 1835 **3**	HOWELL Samuel 1835	STEVENS Ebenezer D 1835 **2**	HEROFF David 1835	WERST Andrew 1835 **1**	CRAFT William 1835

Map layout (sections and patentees):

Section 3
- JUDY Jacob 1835
- HOWELL Samuel 1835
- KENTNER George 1834
- KENTNER Emanuel 1834

Section 2
- STEVENS Ebenezer D 1835
- HEROFF John 1835
- CALBE Henry 1835
- HAMILTON Samuel H 1835

Section 1
- HEROFF David 1835
- WERST Andrew 1835
- HARVEY Elizabeth 1835
- WIMERT Joseph 1835
- HARVEY Ambrose 1835
- ARTENBRACK Leon H 1835
- TOBIAS Christian 1835
- LEBEL Matthias 1835
- CRAFT William 1835
- CRAFT William 1835
- CRAFT William 1835
- CHILDERS Thomas 1835

Section 10
- BICK Ezzard 1836
- SNYDER Jacob 1836
- WAGGONER Christopher 1835
- KEEVER [48] Adam 1835
- ROUCH John 1835
- KEENER [47] Adam 1835

Section 11
- BECHTEL William 1835
- HARVEY Asa 1836
- HOUCK Christopher 1835
- DELANY Justis 1835
- DELANY Justis 1835
- HEYSLER Christian 1835
- SCHURE John 1835
- VOORHIS Jacob 1835
- HEYSLER Christian 1835

Section 12
- HEROFF William 1835
- SNAVELY John 1835
- LEBEL Matthias 1835
- LEBEL Matthias 1835
- BUSH Joseph 1835
- TOBIAS Peter 1835
- BUSH Joseph 1835

Section 15
- SPURRIER Beal 1835
- BLARACOM John Van 1835
- SHERMER John L 1835
- SNIDER Adam 1835
- SHERMER John L 1835
- REED Richard 1835
- BLUEST John 1835
- SHERMER John L 1835
- BLARACOM Phillip Van 1835

Section 14
- FONTS John 1835
- TOBIAS John 1835
- MYERS Joseph 1835
- MYERS Samuel 1835
- TOBIAS Jacob 1835
- SEITER Anthony 1835
- SEITER [61] Genwasy 1835
- TOBIAS Abraham 1835

Section 13
- HARSHMAN John 1835
- WILLIAMS Edward 1835
- WAGGONER Christopher 1835
- ROSS Andrew 1835
- SUTER Blaize 1835
- BROWN Phillip 1835
- WISE Elizabeth 1835
- ROTH John 1835

Section 22
- KLOPF [51] Martin 1835
- BOB Felix 1835
- KLOPF [51] Martin 1835
- MELLINGER John 1835
- FREAS [40] John 1835
- VOLL Andreas 1835

Section 23
- MELLINGER John 1835
- MYERS Joseph 1835
- DRESHU Andrew 1835

Lots-Sec. 23
4   MELLINGER, John   1835

Section 24
- ROTH John 1835
- WILHELM [70] Catherine 1835
- ROTH John 1884
- NIPPGEN Casper 1837

Auglaize County

Section 27
- MITZ John 1835
- MILLER John 1835
- MILLER John 1835
- SIFORT Michael 1835
- MONGER Joseph 1835

Section 26
- KUHN Lorenz 1835
- WAYMIRE Solomon 1832
- WAYMIRE Solomon 1832
- HERTIG John G 1832

Section 25

Shelby County

Section 34

Section 35

Section 36

Helpful Hints

1. This Map's INDEX can be found on the preceding pages.

2. Refer to Map "C" to see where this Township lies within Auglaize County, Ohio.

3. Numbers within square brackets [ ] denote a multi-patentee land parcel (multi-owner). Refer to Appendix "C" for a full list of members in this group.

4. Areas that look to be crowded with Patentees usually indicate multiple sales of the same parcel (Re-issues) or Overlapping parcels. See this Township's Index for an explanation of these and other circumstances that might explain "odd" groupings of Patentees on this map.

Legend

— Patent Boundary

— Section Boundary

▦ No Patents Found (or Outside County)

1., 2., 3., . . .   Lot Numbers (when beside a name)

[ ]   Group Number (see Appendix "C")

Scale: Section = 1 mile X 1 mile (generally, with some exceptions)

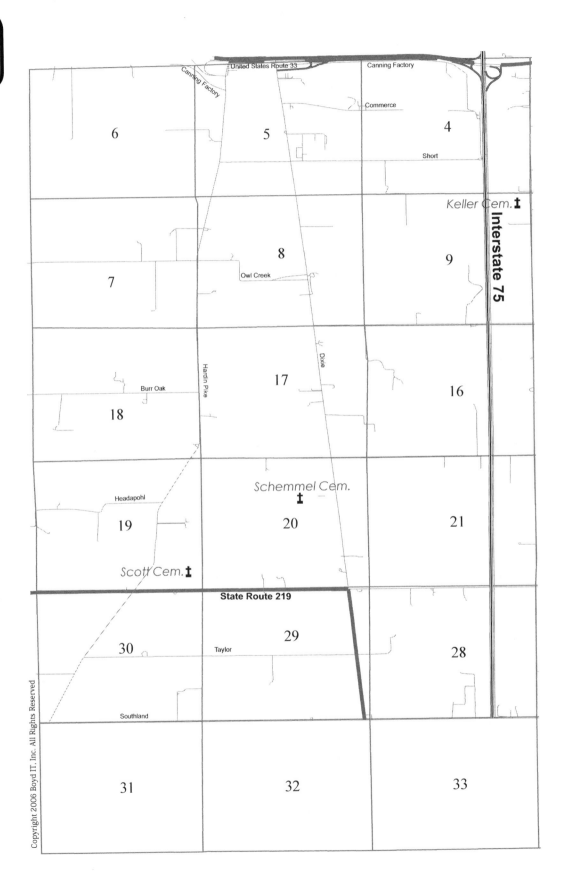

Road Map

T6-S   R6-E
1st PM Meridian

Map Group 11

Cities & Towns
Fryburg

Cemeteries
Haruff Cemetery
Keller Cemetery
Old Saint Johns Cemetery
Rupert Cemetery
Saint Johns Cemetery
Saint Johns Cemetery
Schemmel Cemetery
Scott Cemetery

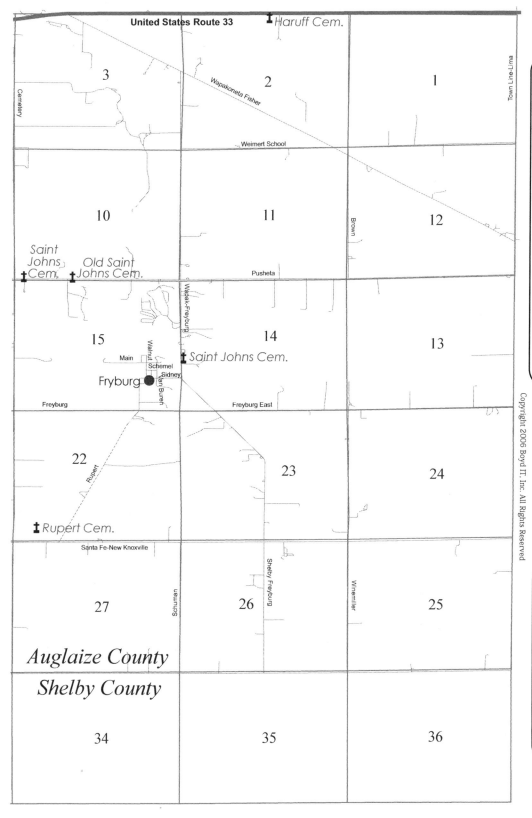

United States Route 33

Haruff Cem.

3

2

1

Wapakoneta Fisher

Cemetery

Town Line-Lima

Weimert School

10

11

12

Brown

Saint
Johns
Cem.

Old Saint
Johns Cem.

Pusheta

Wapak-Freyburg

15

14

13

Main

Walnut

Saint Johns Cem.

Schemel
Sidney

Fryburg

Van Buren

Freyburg

Freyburg East

22

23

24

Rupert

Rupert Cem.

Santa Fe-New Knoxville

Schuman

Shelby Freyburg

Winemiller

27

26

25

Auglaize County

Shelby County

34

35

36

Copyright 2006 Boyd IT, Inc. All Rights Reserved

Helpful Hints

1. This road map has a number of uses, but primarily it is to help you: a) find the present location of land owned by your ancestors (at least the general area), b) find cemeteries and city-centers, and c) estimate the route/roads used by Census-takers & tax-assessors.

2. If you plan to travel to Auglaize County to locate cemeteries or land parcels, please pick up a modern travel map for the area before you do. Mapping old land parcels on modern maps is not as exact a science as you might think. Just the slightest variations in public land survey coordinates, estimates of parcel boundaries, or road-map deviations can greatly alter a map's representation of how a road either does or doesn't cross a particular parcel of land.

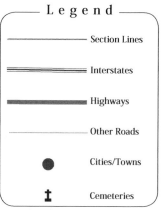

L e g e n d

———— Section Lines

══════ Interstates

━━━━━ Highways

———— Other Roads

● Cities/Towns

✝ Cemeteries

Scale: Section = 1 mile X 1 mile
(generally, with some exceptions)

Historical Map

T6-S R6-E
1st PM Meridian

Map Group 11

Cities & Towns
Fryburg

Cemeteries
Haruff Cemetery
Keller Cemetery
Old Saint Johns Cemetery
Rupert Cemetery
Saint Johns Cemetery
Saint Johns Cemetery
Schemmel Cemetery
Scott Cemetery

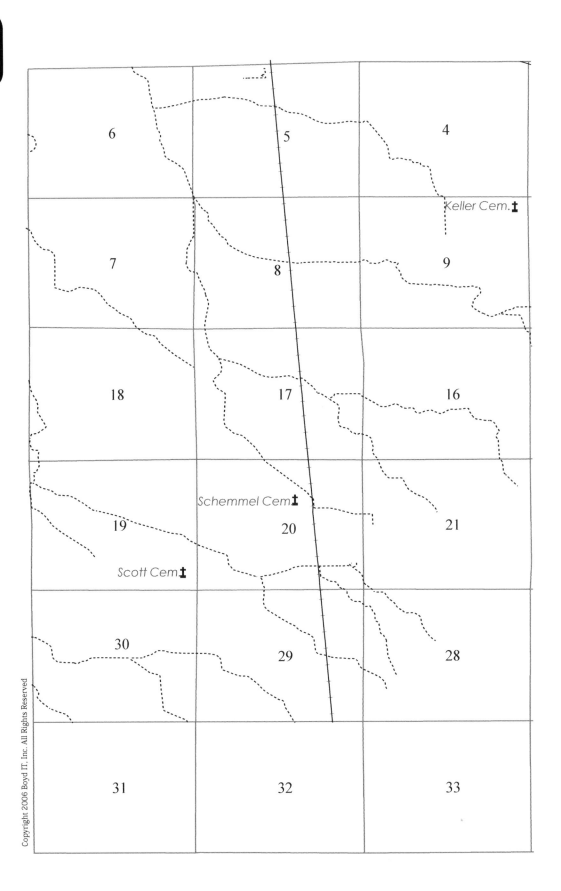

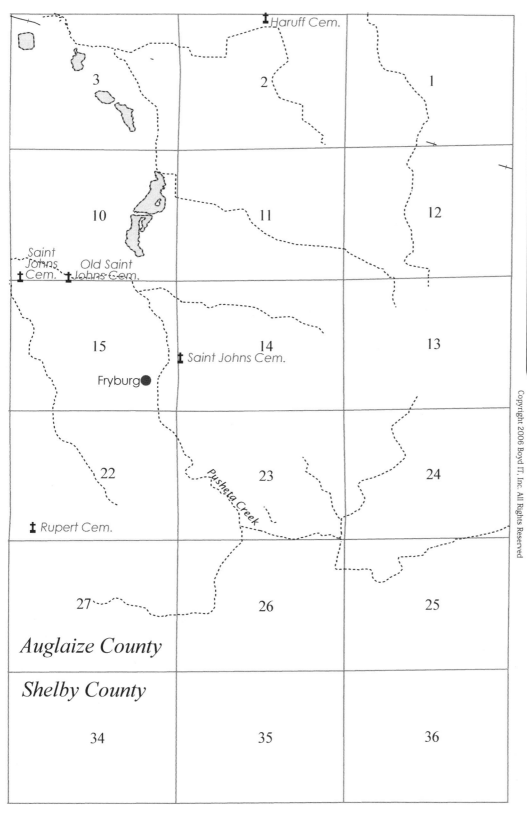

3

2

1 Haruff Cem.

10

11

12

Saint Johns Cem.

Old Saint Johns Cem.

15 14 13

Saint Johns Cem.

Fryburg

22 23 24

Pusheta Creek

Rupert Cem.

27 26 25

Auglaize County

Shelby County

34 35 36

Helpful Hints

1. This Map takes a different look at the same Congressional Township displayed in the preceding two maps. It presents features that can help you better envision the historical development of the area: a) Water-bodies (lakes & ponds), b) Water-courses (rivers, streams, etc.), c) Railroads, d) City/town center-points (where they were oftentimes located when first settled), and e) Cemeteries.

2. Using this "Historical" map in tandem with this Township's Patent Map and Road Map, may lead you to some interesting discoveries. You will often find roads, towns, cemeteries, and waterways are named after nearby landowners: sometimes those names will be the ones you are researching. See how many of these research gems you can find here in Auglaize County.

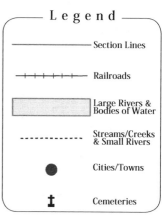

Legend

———————— Section Lines

+++++++++ Railroads

Large Rivers & Bodies of Water

- - - - - - Streams/Creeks & Small Rivers

● Cities/Towns

✝ Cemeteries

Scale: Section = 1 mile X 1 mile
(there are some exceptions)

Map Group 12: Index to Land Patents

Township 6-South Range 7-East (1st PM)

After you locate an individual in this Index, take note of the Section and Section Part then proceed to the Land Patent map on the pages immediately following. You should have no difficulty locating the corresponding parcel of land.

The "For More Info" Column will lead you to more information about the underlying Patents. See the Legend at right, and the "How to Use this Book" chapter, for more information.

```
                        LEGEND
              "For More Info . . . " column
A = Authority (Legislative Act, See Appendix "A")
B = Block or Lot (location in Section unknown)
C = Cancelled Patent
F = Fractional Section
G = Group  (Multi-Patentee Patent, see Appendix "C")
V = Overlaps another Parcel
R = Re-Issued (Parcel patented more than once)

(A & G items require you to look in the Appendixes referred
to above. All other Letter-designations followed by a number
require you to locate line-items in this index that possess
the ID number found after the letter).
```

ID	Individual in Patent	Sec.	Sec. Part	Date Issued	Other Counties	For More Info . . .
1914	APPLE, Daniel	7	NWSE	1836-02-15		A1
1915	" "	7	SWNE	1836-02-15		A1
1888	ARTHUR, Amos	23	NWNW	1837-03-16		A1
2011	BABCOCK, Joel	18	SWSE	1837-03-18		A1
2012	"	19	NE	1837-03-18		A1 F
2015	BAILEY, John	11	E½SE	1837-03-18		A1
2016	BAILY, John	11	E½SW	1837-03-18		A1
2017	" "	11	W½SE	1837-03-18		A1
2099	BAILY, Richard	11	NWSW	1837-03-15		A1
2100	" "	11	SWNW	1837-03-15		A1
2112	BALL, Stephen	25	SENE	1840-10-10		A1 F
1933	BARBER, David W	15	E½NW	1838-10-15		A1 F
1934	" "	17	S½SW	1840-10-10		A1
1970	BAUGHMAN, Henry	3	SWSW	1837-03-18		A1 F
1971	" "	4	E½NW	1837-03-18		A1
1972	" "	4	W½NE	1837-03-18		A1 F
1969	" "	3	NWSW	1837-03-20		A1 F
2013	BAYLIFF, Joel	7	SENE	1835-09-15		A1
2014	" "	8	SWNW	1835-09-15		A1
2078	BAYLIFF, Margaret	7	NESE	1837-03-15		A1
2104	BECHDOLETT, Samuel	7	SW	1835-10-07		A1
2092	BECHDOLT, Peter	7	S½NW	1839-07-02		A1
1996	BEER, James	7	SESE	1837-08-21		A1
2114	BEER, Thomas	9	SENW	1838-09-04		A1
1916	BEERY, Daniel	15	E½SW	1837-03-18		A1 F
1917	" "	15	NWSW	1837-03-18		A1 F
1922	BIER, David	7	SWSE	1837-03-15		A1
2110	BIGGS, Simeon	1	NW	1837-03-16		A1
2096	BILGA, Rebecca	26	E½NW	1840-10-10		A1 F
2097	" "	26	S½NW	1840-10-10		A1 F
1882	BILLGER, Abraham	20	NESE	1837-03-15		A1 F
1883	" "	20	NWSW	1837-03-15		A1 F
1884	" "	20	SESW	1837-03-15		A1 F
1885	" "	20	SWSW	1837-03-15		A1 F R1964
2124	BILTER, William	4	SWNW	1835-09-15		A1
1947	BISHOP, George	4	E½NE	1835-10-07		A1
1919	BITLER, Daniel	6	NWNE	1835-10-09		A1 G15 F
1918	" "	6	NENW	1835-10-16		A1
2105	BITLER, Samuel	9	NWNE	1856-04-15		A1
1907	BODENBENDER, Casper	8	NWSW	1837-11-21		A1
2101	BODKIN, Richard	14	E½NE	1838-09-04		A1 G18
2126	BRACKNEY, William	6	NWNW	1837-03-16		A1 F
2125	"	3	NWNW	1838-09-04		A1
1920	BRITLER, Daniel	4	NWNW	1838-09-04		A1 F
2087	BRODERICK, Nehemiah F	8	SENW	1835-10-07		A1
2088	" "	8	SWNE	1835-10-07		A1

ID	Individual in Patent	Sec.	Sec. Part	Date Issued	Other Counties	For More Info . . .
2079	BUCKHART, Mathias	17	W½SE	1837-11-21		A1
2054	BUSH, Joseph	18	E½SW	1835-10-07		A1
2055	" "	18	SWNE	1835-10-07		A1
1923	CALDWELL, David	12	E½NE	1844-09-10		A1
2128	CALLISON, William	26	NWNW	1844-08-01		A1 G23 C F
2127	CAMPBELL, William C	9	SWNE	1848-07-01		A1
2047	CAREY, John W	5	E½NW	1842-02-26		A1 G25
2108	CASPER, Scott	7	NENW	1835-10-09		A1
2109	" "	7	NWNE	1835-10-09		A1
1987	CHAMBERS, Jacob	22	E½NW	1837-03-16		A1 F
1988	" "	22	W½NW	1837-03-16		A1 F
1941	CLEVERSTEIN, Elizabeth	8	NENE	1845-06-01		A1 R1944
1973	COLEMAN, Henry	10	E½NE	1837-03-20		A1
1999	COLEMAN, James H	6	S½NW	1835-10-09		A1
2000	" "	6	SW	1835-10-09		A1
2001	" "	6	SWNE	1835-10-09		A1
2002	" "	6	W½SE	1835-10-09		A1
1921	COLGAN, Daniel	17	SWSE	1834-01-30		A1 G28 F
2018	COLLIER, John	27	NESW	1837-03-15		A1 F
2019	" "	27	NWSW	1837-03-15		A1 F
2020	" "	27	SESW	1837-03-15		A1
2021	" "	28	SESE	1837-03-15		A1 F
2129	COLLISTER, William	26	S½NE	1844-04-19		A1 F
1997	CONNER, James	27	SWNE	1837-03-20		A1 F
1881	COPELAND, Abner	11	N½NW	1844-08-01		A1
1891	COPELAND, Amos	3	SWNE	1840-10-10		A1 F
1890	" "	3	NWNE	1844-08-01		A1 F
1889	" "	3	E½NE	1845-06-01		A1 F
2023	COPELAND, John	5	SW	1834-01-30		A1
2022	" "	5	NWSE	1837-03-16		A1
2057	COPELAND, Joseph	13	NE	1844-08-01		A1
2074	COPELAND, Madison	13	E½SE	1844-08-01		A1
2075	" "	13	NWSE	1844-08-01		A1
2076	" "	13	SWNW	1844-08-01		A1
2077	" "	13	SWSE	1845-06-01		A1
2130	COPELAND, William	3	E½NW	1837-03-16		A1 F
2131	" "	3	NWSE	1838-09-04		A1
2026	CORDER, John	10	NWSE	1837-03-15		A1
2027	" "	10	SENW	1837-03-15		A1
2028	" "	10	SWNE	1837-03-15		A1
2024	" "	10	NENW	1837-03-16		A1 F
2025	" "	10	NWNW	1837-03-16		A1 F
2132	COUNSELLOR, William	10	NESE	1840-10-10		A1
1985	COY, Isaac	8	NESW	1837-03-16		A1
1974	CRAWEL, Henry	24	SENW	1845-06-01		A1
1975	CROWEL, Henry	28	SWSE	1844-08-01		A1
2029	CUNNINGHAM, John	17	W½NW	1840-10-10		A1
1968	DAVISON, Hamilton	9	NENW	1844-08-01		A1
1965	" "	10	SWSW	1844-09-10		A1 F
1966	" "	15	SWSW	1844-09-10		A1 F
1967	" "	3	SWNW	1844-09-10		A1 F
2009	DUNLAP, Jeptha	24	NWSW	1844-08-01		A1 G34
2106	DUNLAP, Samuel	25	SWSW	1844-08-01		A1
1998	ELLISON, James	27	SENE	1837-03-18		A1 F
1897	ELROD, Bartlet	27	NWSE	1837-03-16		A1 F
1948	ELSAS, George	20	N½SW	1835-09-15		A1 F
1949	" "	20	NW	1835-10-07		A1 F
1924	EVERSOLE, David	10	NWSW	1837-03-18		A1 F
1925	" "	10	SWNW	1837-03-18		A1 F
1927	" "	4	SE	1837-03-18		A1
1926	" "	15	N½NW	1840-10-10		A1 F
1977	EVERSOLE, Henry	22	S½NE	1836-02-15		A1
1976	" "	22	N½NE	1836-02-25		A1
1900	FALER, Benjamin	14	NW	1837-03-18		A1
2095	FETTERS, Philip	23	S½	1837-03-18		A1
2120	FLEGAL, Valentine	17	NESE	1837-03-16		A1
2121	FLEGEL, Valentine	17	E½NE	1837-11-21		A1
2031	FOREMAN, John	27	S½NW	1837-03-15		A1 F
2032	" "	28	E½NW	1837-03-16		A1 F
2098	FRANKS, Rezin	12	NW	1837-03-20		A1
2010	FURROW, Jeremiah	3	SWSE	1845-06-01		A1
1950	GEIER, George	21	NENW	1837-03-20		A1 F
1951	" "	21	NWNW	1837-03-20		A1 F

ID	Individual in Patent	Sec.	Sec. Part	Date Issued	Other Counties	For More Info . . .
1952	GEYER, George	26	NWNE	1883-09-15		A1 F
2059	GIBESON, Joseph	1	SESW	1844-09-10		A1
2080	GLASER, Mathias	28	W½NE	1837-03-15		A1 F
2047	GORDAN, James	5	E½NW	1842-02-26		A1 G25
2060	GRAHAM, Joseph	21	E½NE	1837-03-18		A1 F
2101	GRAY, John	14	E½NE	1838-09-04		A1 G18
2083	GROSS, Michael	16	E½SE	1844-09-10		A1
2090	GROSS, Nicholas	21	W½	1837-03-18		A1
2091	" "	21	W½SE	1837-03-18		A1 F
2089	" "	16	W½NW	1844-09-10		A1
1953	GUYER, George	16	SWSE	1845-06-01		A1
1911	HAHN, Christopher F	17	NENW	1845-06-01		A1
1946	HAHN, Frederick	29	W½SW	1835-10-07		A1
1921	HALLER, William	17	SWSE	1834-01-30		A1 G28 F
2003	HAMILTON, James	23	E½NW	1837-11-21		A1
2004	" "	23	SWNW	1837-11-21		A1
2111	HARROD, Sinthey	1	NE	1837-03-16		A1
1879	HARTLEY, Aaron	15	NE	1837-03-18		A1
1880	" "	22	E½SE	1837-03-18		A1
1940	HATHAWAY, Eleazar	8	NENW	1837-03-15		A1
1908	HAUKINSON, Charles	18	N½SE	1835-10-07		A1
2122	HAYS, Warren	25	NESW	1837-03-20		A1
2070	HELINLINGER, Lewis	20	NESE	1835-09-15		A1 F
2071	HELMINGES, Lewis	28	W½NW	1836-02-15		A1
2072	HELMLENGER, Lewis	20	NE	1835-10-07		A1 F
2073	" "	20	NWSE	1835-10-07		A1 F
1928	HENRY, David	6	E½SE	1834-01-30		A1
1929	" "	8	NWNW	1835-10-16		A1
2102	HENRY, Richard	7	NENE	1835-10-16		A1
1893	HERBST, Andrew	17	NWNE	1837-11-21		A1
1894	" "	8	SWSE	1837-11-21		A1
1945	HODGES, Evander T	5	NESE	1836-02-25		A1
2133	HOWELL, William	8	SESE	1837-03-16		A1
1892	HUNTER, Amos	24	W½NW	1837-08-21		A1
2123	HURLEY, William B	2	SWSE	1844-08-01		A1
1978	JEFFRIES, Henry	24	E½SW	1837-03-20		A1
1979	" "	24	SE	1837-03-20		A1 F
1980	" "	24	SWSW	1837-03-20		A1
2061	KING, Joseph	29	E½SE	1837-03-15		A1
1912	KRANER, Christopher	17	NWSW	1845-06-01		A1
1913	" "	18	SENE	1845-06-01		A1
2081	LANE, Micajah	2	SWSW	1844-09-10		A1
2082	" "	3	SESE	1844-09-10		A1
2084	LEATHERMAN, Michael	16	S½NE	1844-09-10		A1
2085	" "	16	SENW	1844-09-10		A1
1954	LINDER, George	18	W½SW	1835-10-07		A1
2034	LOCKART, John	4	SW	1837-08-21		A1
2058	LUSK, Joseph G	2	SESE	1852-06-01		A1
2006	MANNING, James	4	E½SW	1837-03-15		A1 F
2005	" "	10	S½SE	1837-08-21		A1
2007	" "	9	E½NE	1837-08-21		A1
1909	MARTIN, Charles	18	S½NW	1835-10-07		A1
1955	MARTIN, George M	2	S½NW	1844-08-01		A1
1930	MCKNIGHT, David	26	SE	1836-02-25		A1
1936	MCMILLIN, Doctor	9	W½NW	1837-03-15		A1
2035	MCNABB, John	10	NWNE	1845-06-01		A1
2030	MEFFERD, John D	15	SWNW	1837-03-18		A1 F
1989	MICHAEL, Jacob	27	E½SE	1837-03-18		A1 F
1990	" "	27	SWSE	1837-03-18		A1
1942	MILLER, Elizabeth	17	SESE	1837-11-21		A1
2134	MILLER, William	13	NWNW	1844-09-10		A1
2135	" "	13	W½SW	1845-06-01		A1
2136	" "	24	E½NE	1845-06-01		A1
1956	MINK, George	8	S½SW	1837-11-21		A1
2118	MIX, Uri	1	SWSW	1837-11-21		A1
2119	MIX, Uriah	1	NESW	1838-09-04		A1
1898	MOORE, Barzillai F	24	NENW	1844-09-10		A1
1899	" "	24	SWNE	1844-09-10		A1 F
2039	MOORE, John P	24	NWNE	1853-06-01		A1 F
2115	MOORE, Thomas	27	N½NW	1837-03-16		A1 F
2116	" "	27	NWNE	1837-03-16		A1 F
1995	MORRIS, James A	1	NWSW	1837-08-21		A1
2128	MORRIS, John K	26	NWNW	1844-08-01		A1 G23 C F

ID	Individual in Patent	Sec.	Sec. Part	Date Issued	Other Counties	For More Info . . .
1957	NEWMAN, George	18	SESE	1835-10-07		A1
2036	NIPGEN, John	25	W½W½N½	1838-09-04		A1 F
2037	" "	26	NENE	1838-09-04		A1 F
2086	NIPGEN, Michael	19	NW	1837-03-16		A1 F
2038	NOROT, John	16	SW	1844-09-10		A1
2117	OAKLEY, Thomas	11	SWSW	1845-06-01		A1
1943	OXLY, Enos S	5	SESE	1837-03-16		A1
1944	" "	8	NENE	1837-03-16		A1 R1941
2093	PHENEGAR, Peter	25	SESW	1836-02-15		A1
1887	PURCELL, Alfred	25	E½SE	1835-10-16		A1
2107	RASH, Samuel	2	NESW	1852-06-01		A1
1910	REED, Charles	25	SWNE	1837-03-20		A1 F
1932	REED, David	22	W½SW	1837-03-16		A1
1931	" "	21	E½SE	1837-11-21		A1
2103	REED, Robert	28	N½SE	1837-11-21		A1 F
1905	RICHARDSON, Byrd	5	NENE	1835-10-09		A1
1906	" "	5	SENE	1835-10-09		A1
1919	RICHARDSON, William	6	NWNE	1835-10-09		A1 G15 F
1983	RINEHART, Hugh T	2	N½SE	1837-08-21		A1
1984	" "	2	NE	1837-08-21		A1 F
2066	RINEHART, Julina	11	SENW	1837-08-21		A1
2067	" "	11	SWNE	1837-08-21		A1
1896	ROCK, Barbara	17	SWNE	1838-09-04		A1
1991	ROCK, Jacob	17	NESW	1838-09-04		A1
1992	" "	17	SENW	1838-09-04		A1
2009	ROCK, William	24	NWSW	1844-08-01		A1 G34
2040	ROGERS, John	5	SWSE	1837-03-18		A1
1937	ROSTORFER, Dors	16	NWSE	1845-06-01		A1
2094	ROTT, Peter	16	NENE	1844-09-10		A1
1958	RUNKLE, George	14	SE	1837-03-18		A1
1959	" "	14	W½NE	1837-03-18		A1
2137	RUNYAN, William	13	E½SW	1837-08-21		A1
2062	SCHLICHTIG, Joseph	28	SENE	1837-03-15		A1 F
1904	SEITER, Blazy	29	W½SE	1837-03-15		A1
1964	SEITER, Gervasy	20	SWSW	1837-08-21		A1 F R1885
2041	SHELBY, John	5	W½NE	1835-10-09		A1
2065	SHEPHERD, Julian	25	W½SE	1836-02-25		A1
1886	SKILLMAN, Abraham	9	S½	1835-10-09		A1
2042	SMITH, John	22	E½SW	1837-03-16		A1
2043	" "	22	W½SE	1837-03-16		A1
1993	SNIDER, Jacob	8	NWNE	1837-03-16		A1
1901	STILES, Benjamin	26	SW	1837-03-18		A1
1981	STODDARD, Henry	5	W½NW	1834-03-28		A1
1982	" "	6	E½NE	1834-03-28		A1
1902	STRAWSBURG, Benjamin	25	NWSW	1844-08-01		A1
1903	" "	25	S½NW	1844-08-01		A1 F
2044	STRICKLER, John	8	SENE	1840-10-10		A1
1960	SWICKARD, George	2	NWSW	1837-11-21		A1
1961	" "	3	NESE	1837-11-21		A1
2053	SWICKARD, Jonathan	2	N½NW	1837-11-21		A1
1963	THERSTICKER, Gerhart	23	NE	1837-11-21		A1
2045	TOBIAS, John	7	NWNW	1835-10-07		A1
2046	TONG, John	27	SWSW	1837-03-15		A1
1962	TRESHER, George	26	W½N½NW	1838-09-04		A1
1935	TRUMBO, Davis	3	E½SW	1837-03-18		A1 F
1895	WALCK, Andrew	28	NENE	1837-03-15		A1 F
2113	WARLING, Stephen	29	E½SW	1837-03-20		A1
2048	WATT, John	16	NENW	1844-09-10		A1
2049	" "	16	NWNE	1844-09-10		A1
2050	WEIMART, John	25	E½W½N½	1838-09-04		A1 F
2068	WERST, Leonard	18	N½NW	1837-08-21		A1
2069	" "	18	NWNE	1837-08-21		A1
1994	WETSTONE, Jacob	13	E½NW	1838-09-04		A1
2008	WHETSTONE, James	12	E½SE	1850-07-01		A1 F
1939	WILLIAMS, Edward	8	NWSE	1837-03-16		A1
1938	" "	8	NESE	1837-03-18		A1
1986	WILLIAMS, Isaac P	1	E½SE	1837-03-16		A1
2056	WILSON, Joseph C	21	NWNE	1837-03-16		A1 F
2051	WISS, John	28	E½SW	1837-03-20		A1 F
2052	" "	28	W½SW	1837-03-20		A1 F
2063	WRIGHT, Joseph	14	SW	1837-03-15		A1
2064	" "	15	SE	1837-03-15		A1
2033	YOSTING, John H	27	NENE	1844-09-10		A1 F

Patent Map

T6-S R7-E
1st PM Meridian

Map Group 12

Township Statistics

Parcels Mapped	:	259
Number of Patents	:	225
Number of Individuals	:	182
Patentees Identified	:	177
Number of Surnames	:	151
Multi-Patentee Parcels	:	6
Oldest Patent Date	:	1/30/1834
Most Recent Patent	:	9/15/1883
Block/Lot Parcels	:	3
Parcels Re - Issued	:	2
Parcels that Overlap	:	0
Cities and Towns	:	5
Cemeteries	:	3

Section 6

BRACKNEY William 1837
BITLER Daniel 1835
BITLER [15] Daniel 1835
STODDARD Henry 1834
COLEMAN James H 1835
COLEMAN James H 1835
COLEMAN James H 1835
COLEMAN James H 1835
COLEMAN James H 1835

Section 5

STODDARD Henry 1834
SHELBY John 1835
RICHARDSON Byrd 1835
CAREY [25] John W 1842
RICHARDSON Byrd 1835
COPELAND John 1837
HODGES Evander T 1836
COPELAND John 1834
ROGERS John 1837
OXLY Enos S 1837

Section 4

BRITLER Daniel 1838
BAUGHMAN Henry 1837
BAUGHMAN Henry 1837
BITLER William 1835
BISHOP George 1835
LOCKART John 1837
MANNING James 1837
EVERSOLE David 1837

Section 7

TOBIAS John 1835
CASPER Scott 1835
CASPER Scott 1835
BECHDOLT Peter 1839
APPLE Daniel 1836
BAYLIFF Joel 1835
APPLE Daniel 1836
BAYLIFF Margaret 1837
BECHDOLETT Samuel 1835
BIER David 1837
BEER James 1837

Section 8

HENRY Richard 1835
HENRY David 1835
HATHAWAY Eleazar 1837
SNIDER Jacob 1837
BAYLIFF Joel 1835
BRODERICK Nehemiah F 1835
BRODERICK Nehemiah F 1835
STRICKLER John 1840
BODENBENDER Casper 1837
COY Isaac 1837
WILLIAMS Edward 1837
WILLIAMS Edward 1837
MINK George 1837
HERBST Andrew 1837
HOWELL William 1837

Section 9

CLEVERSTEIN Elizabeth OXLY 1845
OXLY Enos S 1837
MCMILLIN Doctor 1837
DAVISON Hamilton 1844
BITLER Samuel 1856
BEER Thomas 1838
CAMPBELL William C 1848
MANNING James 1837
SKILLMAN Abraham 1835

Section 18

WERST Leonard 1837
WERST Leonard 1837
MARTIN Charles 1835
BUSH Joseph 1835
KRANER Christopher 1845
LINDER George 1835
18
HAUKINSON Charles 1835
BUSH Joseph 1835
BABCOCK Joel 1837
NEWMAN George 1835

Section 17

CUNNINGHAM John 1840
HAHN Christopher F 1845
HERBST Andrew 1837
ROCK Jacob 1838
17
ROCK Barbara 1838
FLEGEL Valentine 1837
KRANER Christopher 1845
ROCK Jacob 1838
BUCKHART Mathias 1837
FLEGAL Valentine 1837
BARBER David W 1840
COLGAN [28] Daniel 1834
MILLER Elizabeth 1837

Section 16

GROSS Nicholas 1844
WATT John 1844
WATT John 1844
ROTT Peter 1844
LEATHERMAN Michael 1844
LEATHERMAN Michael 1844
16
NOROT John 1844
ROSTORFER Dors 1845
GUYER George 1845
GROSS Michael 1844

Section 19

NIPGEN Michael 1837
BABCOCK Joel 1837
19

Section 20

ELSAS George 1835
HELMLENGER Lewis 1835
20
BILLGER Abraham 1837
ELSAS George 1835
BILLGER Abraham 1837
HELMLENGER Lewis 1835
HELINLINGER Lewis 1835
BILLGER Abraham 1837
SEITER Gervasy 1837
BILLGER Abraham 1837

Section 21

GEIER George 1837
GEIER George 1837
WILSON Joseph C 1837
GRAHAM Joseph 1837
GROSS Nicholas 1837
21
GROSS Nicholas 1837
REED David 1837

Section 30

30

Section 29

29
HAHN Frederick 1835
SEITER Blazy 1837
WARLING Stephen 1837
KING Joseph 1837

Section 28

HELMINGES Lewis 1836
GLASER Mathias 1837
WALCK Andrew 1837
FOREMAN John 1837
28
SCHLICHTIG Joseph 1837
WISS John 1837
REED Robert 1837
WISS John 1837
CROWEL Henry 1844
COLLIER John 1837

Section 31

31

Section 32

32

Section 33

33

BRACKNEY William 1838	COPELAND William 1837	COPELAND Amos 1844	COPELAND Amos 1845	SWICKARD Jonathan 1837	RINEHART Hugh T 1837

BRACKNEY William 1838

DAVISON Hamilton 1844

COPELAND William 1837

COPELAND Amos 1844

COPELAND Amos 1845

SWICKARD Jonathan 1837

MARTIN George M 1844

RINEHART Hugh T 1837

2

BIGGS Simeon 1837

1

HARROD Sinthey 1837

BAUGHMAN Henry 1837

3

COPELAND William 1838

SWICKARD George 1837

SWICKARD George 1837

RASH Samuel 1852

RINEHART Hugh T 1837

MORRIS James A 1837

MIX Uriah 1838

BAUGHMAN Henry 1837

TRUMBO Davis 1837

FURROW Jeremiah 1845

LANE Micajah 1844

LANE Micajah 1844

HURLEY William B 1844

LUSK Joseph G 1852

MIX Uri 1837

GIBESON Joseph 1844

WILLIAMS Isaac P 1837

CORDER John 1837

CORDER John 1837

MCNABB John 1845

COPELAND Abner 1844

FRANKS Rezin 1837

CALDWELL David 1844

EVERSOLE David 1837

CORDER John 1837

CORDER John 1837

COLEMAN Henry 1837

BAILY Richard 1837

RINEHART Julina 1837

RINEHART Julina 1837

EVERSOLE David 1837

10

COUNSELLOR William 1840

CORDER John 1837

BAILY Richard 1837

11

BAILY John 1837

12

WHETSTONE James 1850

DAVISON Hamilton 1844

MANNING James 1837

OAKLEY Thomas 1845

BAILY John 1837

BAILEY John 1837

EVERSOLE David 1840

HARTLEY Aaron 1837

FALER Benjamin 1837

RUNKLE George 1837

BODKIN [18] Richard 1838

MILLER William 1844

WETSTONE Jacob 1838

COPELAND Joseph 1844

MEFFERD John D 1837

BARBER David W 1838

14

COPELAND Madison 1844

BEERY Daniel 1837

15

WRIGHT Joseph 1837

WRIGHT Joseph 1837

RUNKLE George 1837

MILLER William 1845

13

COPELAND Madison 1844

COPELAND Madison 1844

DAVISON Hamilton 1844

BEERY Daniel 1837

RUNYAN William 1837

COPELAND Madison 1845

COPELAND Madison 1844

CHAMBERS Jacob 1837

EVERSOLE Henry 1836

ARTHUR Amos 1837

THERSTICKER Gerhart 1837

HUNTER Amos 1837

MOORE Barzillai F 1844

MOORE John P 1853

CHAMBERS Jacob 1837

EVERSOLE Henry 1836

HAMILTON James 1837

HAMILTON James 1837

CRAWEL Henry 1845

MOORE Barzillai F 1844

MILLER William 1845

REED David 1837

22

SMITH John 1837

23

FETTERS Philip 1837

DUNLAP [34] Jeptha 1844

24

JEFFRIES Henry 1837

SMITH John 1837

HARTLEY Aaron 1837

JEFFRIES Henry 1837

JEFFRIES Henry 1837

MOORE Thomas 1837

MOORE Thomas 1837

YOSTING John H 1844

CALLISON [23] William 1844

TRESHER George 1838

BILGA Rebecca 1840

GEYER George 1883

NIPGEN John 1838

FOREMAN John 1837

27

CONNER James 1837

ELLISON James 1837

BILGA Rebecca 1840

26

COLLISTER William 1844

NIPGEN John 1838

WEIMART John 1838

REED Charles 1837

25

STRAWSBURG Benjamin 1844

BALL Stephen 1840

COLLIER John 1837

COLLIER John 1837

ELROD Bartlet 1837

STILES Benjamin 1837

MCKNIGHT David 1836

STRAWSBURG Benjamin 1844

HAYS Warren 1837

SHEPHERD Julian 1836

TONG John 1837

COLLIER John 1837

MICHAEL Jacob 1837

MICHAEL Jacob 1837

DUNLAP Samuel 1844

PHENEGAR Peter 1836

PURCELL Alfred 1835

Auglaize County

Shelby County

34

35

36

Copyright 2006 Boyd IT, Inc. All Rights Reserved

Helpful Hints

1. This Map's INDEX can be found on the preceding pages.

2. Refer to Map "C" to see where this Township lies within Auglaize County, Ohio.

3. Numbers within square brackets [ ] denote a multi-patentee land parcel (multi-owner). Refer to Appendix "C" for a full list of members in this group.

4. Areas that look to be crowded with Patentees usually indicate multiple sales of the same parcel (Re-issues) or Overlapping parcels. See this Township's Index for an explanation of these and other circumstances that might explain "odd" groupings of Patentees on this map.

L e g e n d

—————— Patent Boundary

━━━━━━ Section Boundary

No Patents Found (or Outside County)

1., 2., 3., ... Lot Numbers (when beside a name)

[ ] Group Number (see Appendix "C")

Scale: Section = 1 mile X 1 mile (generally, with some exceptions)

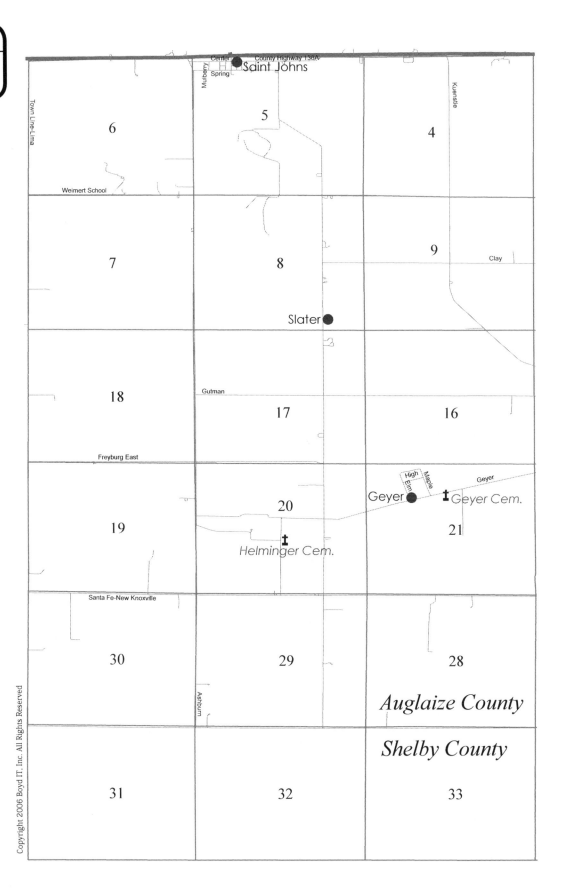

Road Map

T6-S R7-E
1st PM Meridian

Map Group 12

Cities & Towns

Geyer
Gutman
Saint Johns
Santa Fe
Slater

Cemeteries

Geyer Cemetery
Helminger Cemetery
Mount Tabor Cemetery

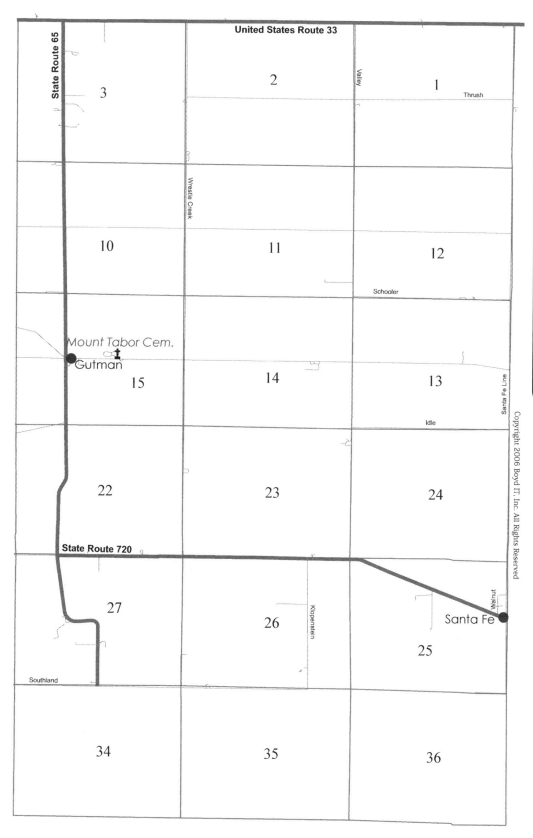

State Route 65

United States Route 33

Valley

3

2

1

Thrush

Wrestle Creek

10

11

12

Schooler

Mount Tabor Cem.

Gutman

15

14

13

Santa Fe Line

Idle

22

23

24

State Route 720

27

26

Klopenstein

Santa Fe

Walnut

25

Southland

34

35

36

Helpful Hints

1. This road map has a number of uses, but primarily it is to help you: a) find the present location of land owned by your ancestors (at least the general area), b) find cemeteries and city-centers, and c) estimate the route/roads used by Census-takers & tax-assessors.

2. If you plan to travel to Auglaize County to locate cemeteries or land parcels, please pick up a modern travel map for the area before you do. Mapping old land parcels on modern maps is not as exact a science as you might think. Just the slightest variations in public land survey coordinates, estimates of parcel boundaries, or road-map deviations can greatly alter a map's representation of how a road either does or doesn't cross a particular parcel of land.

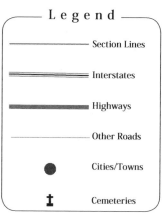

Legend

——————— Section Lines

═══════════ Interstates

━━━━━━━━━ Highways

·············· Other Roads

● Cities/Towns

✝ Cemeteries

Scale: Section = 1 mile X 1 mile
(generally, with some exceptions)

159

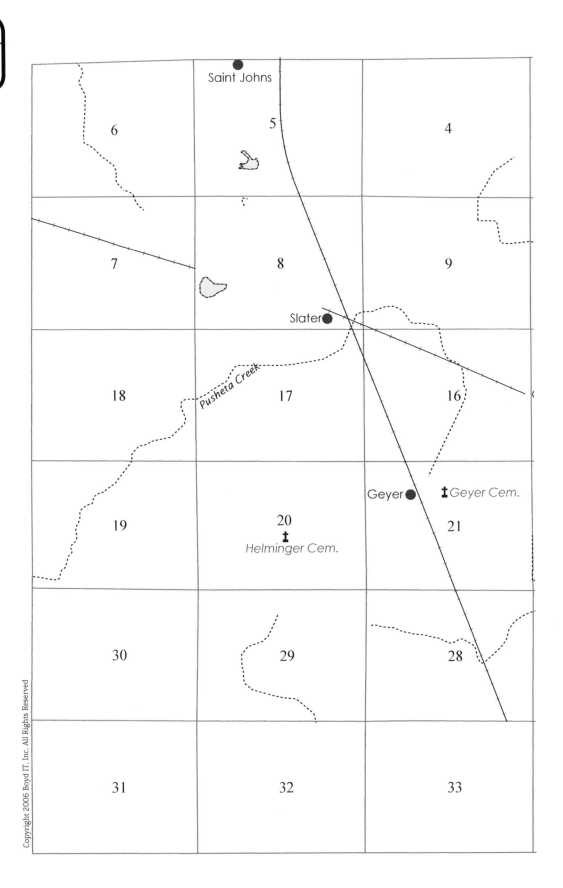

Historical Map

T6-S R7-E
1st PM Meridian

Map Group 12

<u>Cities & Towns</u>
Geyer
Gutman
Saint Johns
Santa Fe
Slater

<u>Cemeteries</u>
Geyer Cemetery
Helminger Cemetery
Mount Tabor Cemetery

Saint Johns

6   5   4

7   8   9

Slater

18   17   16

Pusheta Creek

Geyer   ✝ Geyer Cem.

19   20   21

✝
Helminger Cem.

30   29   28

31   32   33

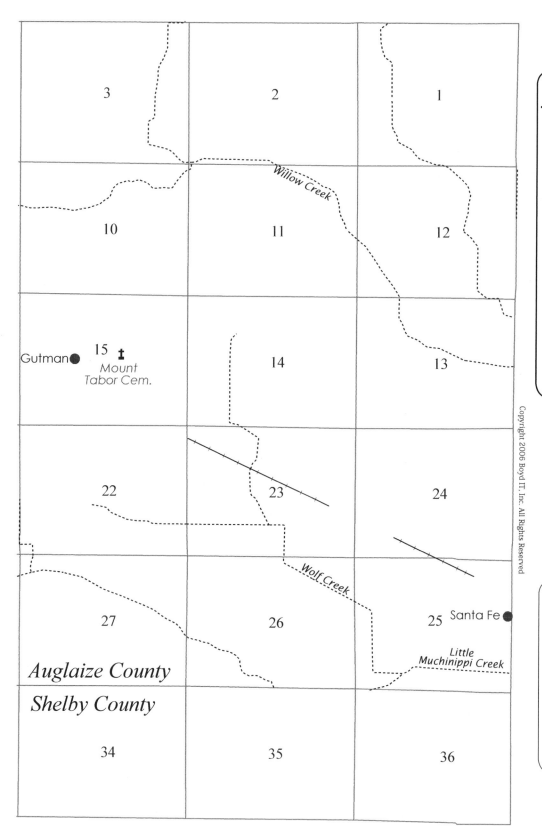

3

2

1

Willow Creek

10

11

12

Gutman● 15 ✝
*Mount
Tabor Cem.*

14

13

22

23

24

Wolf Creek

27

26

25 Santa Fe●

*Little
Muchinippi Creek*

Auglaize County

Shelby County

34

35

36

Helpful Hints

1. This Map takes a different look at the same Congressional Township displayed in the preceding two maps. It presents features that can help you better envision the historical development of the area: a) Water-bodies (lakes & ponds), b) Water-courses (rivers, streams, etc.), c) Railroads, d) City/town center-points (where they were oftentimes located when first settled), and e) Cemeteries.

2. Using this "Historical" map in tandem with this Township's Patent Map and Road Map, may lead you to some interesting discoveries. You will often find roads, towns, cemeteries, and waterways are named after nearby landowners: sometimes those names will be the ones you are researching. See how many of these research gems you can find here in Auglaize County.

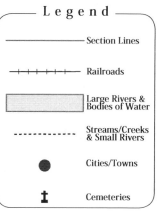

L e g e n d

————	Section Lines
+++++++	Railroads
▭	Large Rivers & Bodies of Water
- - - - -	Streams/Creeks & Small Rivers
●	Cities/Towns
✝	Cemeteries

Scale: Section = 1 mile X 1 mile
(there are some exceptions)

Map Group 13: Index to Land Patents

Township 6-South Range 8-East (1st PM)

After you locate an individual in this Index, take note of the Section and Section Part then proceed to the Land Patent map on the pages immediately following. You should have no difficulty locating the corresponding parcel of land.

The "For More Info" Column will lead you to more information about the underlying Patents. See the Legend at right, and the "How to Use this Book" chapter, for more information.

ID	Individual in Patent	Sec.	Sec. Part	Date Issued	Other Counties	For More Info . . .
2182	ADAIR, Robert	9	W½SE	1837-03-16	Logan	A1
2143	BOGGESS, Benjamin	7	NESE	1836-02-15	Logan	A1
2144	" "	7	SENE	1836-02-15	Logan	A1
2187	BUFENBARGER, Sampson	4	E½SW	1837-03-16		A1
2189	BUFENBARGER, Samuel	5	NE	1835-10-08		A1
2185	BUFFENBARGER, Salmon	7	NW	1836-02-15	Logan	A1
2186	" "	7	NWNE	1836-02-15	Logan	A1
2188	BUFFENBARGER, Sampson	4	NENW	1835-10-16		A1
2190	BUFFENBARGER, Samuel	5	N½SE	1835-10-09		A1
2202	BUFFINBARGER, Simonton	4	NENE	1836-02-15		A1 C
2153	CALDWELL, Ephraim	6	NESW	1840-11-10		A1
2175	CLINE, Joseph	4	W½NW	1835-09-15		A1
2212	CODDINGTON, William	5	S½SE	1835-09-15		A1
2166	CONNELLY, John	3	SWSE	1844-08-01		A1
2151	CORSON, Eli E	4	SENE	1837-03-16		A1
2152	" "	4	SWNE	1837-03-16		A1
2165	DENTON, James	3	W½NW	1835-10-08		A1
2167	DOUNAN, John	5	S½NW	1837-08-21		A1
2138	EARL, Alanson	8	SWNE	1835-10-09	Logan	A1
2179	FRANKS, Rezin	10	E½SE	1837-03-20	Logan	A1
2180	" "	10	NWSE	1837-03-20	Logan	A1
2150	GHORMLEY, David	11	SESW	1848-06-01	Logan	A1 F
2139	GRAY, Asa	6	E½NW	1837-03-18		A1
2140	" "	6	NWNW	1837-03-18		A1
2141	" "	6	SESE	1840-10-10		A1
2142	" "	6	SWNW	1840-10-10		A1
2203	HANKS, Solomon	4	W½SW	1836-02-15		A1
2204	" "	8	NENE	1836-02-15	Logan	A1
2148	HULL, Daniel	11	N½SW	1837-03-16	Logan	A1 F
2149	" "	11	SWSW	1837-03-16	Logan	A1
2159	HURLEY, Gilbert	10	SENE	1844-08-01	Logan	A1
2213	JETT, William	3	NWSW	1837-03-16		A1
2169	KINDLE, John	9	W½NW	1837-03-20	Logan	A1
2168	" "	9	NWSW	1840-10-10	Logan	A1
2160	KING, Henry	10	SENW	1844-08-01	Logan	A1
2161	" "	3	SESE	1844-08-01		A1
2176	KLINE, Joseph	5	N½NW	1837-03-16		A1
2214	MARQUIS, William	10	SWNE	1844-08-01	Logan	A1
2215	" "	11	NW	1844-08-01	Logan	A1 F
2178	MARZ, Nicholas	2		1844-08-01		A1 F
2170	MCCLEAN, John	6	N½SE	1837-08-21		A1
2171	" "	6	NE	1837-08-21		A1
2183	MCKNIGHT, Robert	10	W½SW	1836-02-25	Logan	A1
2184	" "	9	E½SE	1836-02-25	Logan	A1
2216	MCLAUGHLIN, William	6	SESW	1836-02-15		A1
2217	" "	6	SWSE	1836-02-15		A1

ID	Individual in Patent	Sec.	Sec. Part	Date Issued	Other Counties	For More Info . . .
2191	MOORCRAFT, Samuel	3	SENW	1835-10-16		A1
2181	MOORE, Richard G	10	NENW	1837-08-21	Logan	A1
2192	MOORE, Samuel	9	E½SW	1837-03-16	Logan	A1
2193	" "	9	SWSW	1840-10-10	Logan	A1
2196	MORECRAFT, Samuel	3	NWNE	1834-01-30		A1
2194	" "	3	NENE	1836-02-15		A1 F
2195	" "	3	NENW	1837-03-16		A1
2154	MURRAY, George	7	SESE	1836-02-15	Logan	A1
2155	" "	7	SW	1836-02-15	Logan	A1
2156	" "	7	W½SE	1836-02-15	Logan	A1
2157	" "	8	S½	1836-02-15	Logan	A1
2205	PATTERSON, Thomas	4	SENW	1837-03-16		A1
2206	" "	5	SW	1837-03-16		A1
2207	" "	8	E½NW	1837-03-16	Logan	A1
2208	" "	8	NWNE	1837-03-16	Logan	A1
2209	" "	8	NWNW	1837-03-16	Logan	A1
2210	REAMES, Vincent	3	NESW	1837-03-16		A1
2211	" "	3	NWSE	1837-03-16		A1
2177	SHAUL, Lemuel	10	NESW	1840-10-10	Logan	A1
2200	SHAUL, Saul	10	SESW	1837-03-16	Logan	A1
2201	" "	10	SWSE	1837-03-16	Logan	A1
2145	SKILLINGS, Charles	3	NESE	1835-12-24		A1
2146	" "	3	S½NE	1835-12-24		A1
2147	SMITH, Christian	9	E½NW	1840-10-10	Logan	A1
2199	SMITH, Sarah	10	W½NW	1840-10-10	Logan	A1
2172	STARRET, John	3	SESW	1840-10-10		A1
2173	STARRETT, John	3	SWSW	1840-10-10		A1 C R2174
2174	" "	3	SWSW	1902-01-15		A1 R2173
2164	TRINT, James D	4	SE	1837-03-16		A1
2197	WATSON, Samuel	8	SENE	1838-09-04	Logan	A1
2163	WEAVER, Jacob	4	NWNE	1835-10-08		A1
2158	WILLIAMS, George P	6	W½SW	1837-03-16		A1
2162	WILLIAMS, Isaac P	7	NENE	1837-03-16	Logan	A1
2198	WILLIAMS, Samuel	8	SWNW	1836-02-15	Logan	A1

Patent Map

T6-S R8-E
1st PM Meridian

Map Group 13

Township Statistics

Parcels Mapped	:	80
Number of Patents	:	67
Number of Individuals	:	51
Patentees Identified	:	51
Number of Surnames	:	43
Multi-Patentee Parcels	:	0
Oldest Patent Date	:	1/30/1834
Most Recent Patent	:	1/15/1902
Block/Lot Parcels	:	0
Parcels Re - Issued	:	1
Parcels that Overlap	:	0
Cities and Towns	:	1
Cemeteries	:	0

Note: the area contained in this map amounts to far less than a full Township. Therefore, its contents are completely on this single page (instead of a "normal" 2-page spread).

Legend

— Patent Boundary

— Section Boundary

No Patents Found
(or Outside County)

1., 2., 3., ... Lot Numbers
(when beside a name)

[ ] Group Number
(see Appendix "C")

Scale: Section = 1 mile X 1 mile
(generally, with some exceptions)

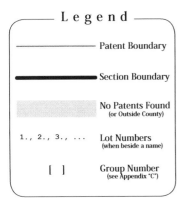

GRAY
Asa
1837

WILLIAMS
George P
1837

GRAY
Asa
1840

GRAY
Asa
1837

BUFFENBARGER
Salmon
1836

MURRAY
George
1836

McLAUGHLIN
Ephraim
1840

CALDWELL
William
1838

MCLEAN

7

18

McLAUGHLIN
John
1837

MCCLEAN
John
1837

6

MURRAY
George
1836

BUFFENBARGER
Salmon
1836

WILLIAMS
Isaac P
1837

McLAUGHLIN
William
1838

GRAY
Asa
1840

MCCLEAN
John
1837

MURRAY
George
1836

BOGGESS
Benjamin
1836

BOGGESS
Benjamin
1836

WILLIAMS
Samuel
1836

PATTERSON
Thomas
1837

PATTERSON
Thomas
1837

DOUNAN
John
1837

KLINE
Joseph
1837

17

MURRAY
George
1836

8

PATTERSON
Thomas
1837

PATTERSON
Thomas
1837

5

EARL
Alanson
1835

CODDINGTON
William
1835

BUFFENBARGER
Samuel
1835

BUFFENBARGER
1835

WATSON
Samuel
1836

HANKS
Solomon
1836

MOORE
Samuel
1840

KINDLE
John
1840

KINDLE
John
1837

HANKS
Solomon
1836

CLINE
Joseph
1835

16

MOORE
Samuel
1837

SMITH
Christian
1840

9

BUFFENBARGER
Sampson
1837

4

PATTERSON
Thomas
1837

BUFFENBARGER
Sampson
1835

CORSON
Eli E
1837

WEAVER
Jacob
1835

BUFFENBARGER
Simon
1836

ADAIR
Robert
1837

TRINT
James D
1837

CORSON
Eli E
1837

Logan County

Auglaize County

MCKNIGHT
Robert
1836

MCKNIGHT
Robert
1836

SMITH
Sarah
1840

MOORE
Richard G
1837

STARRETT
John
1902

STARRETT
John
1840

JETT
William
1837

REAMES
Vincent
1837

DENTON
James
1835

MORECRAFT
Samuel
1837

15

SHAUL
1837

SHAUL
Lemuel
1840

KING
Henry
1844

10

STARRETT
John
1840

REAMES
Vincent
1837

MOORECRAFT
Samuel
1835

MORECRAFT
Samuel
1834

SHAUL
Saul
1837

FRANKS
1837

MARQUIS
William
1844

CONNELLY
John
1844

SKILLINGS
Charles
1835

MORECRAFT
Samuel
1835

3

FRANKS
Rezin
1837

HURLEY
Gilbert
1844

KING
Henry
1844

SKILLINGS
Charles
1835

HULL
Daniel
1837

MARZ
Nicholas
1844

2

HULL
Daniel
1837

MARQUIS
William
1844

11

14

GHORMLEY
David
1848

N

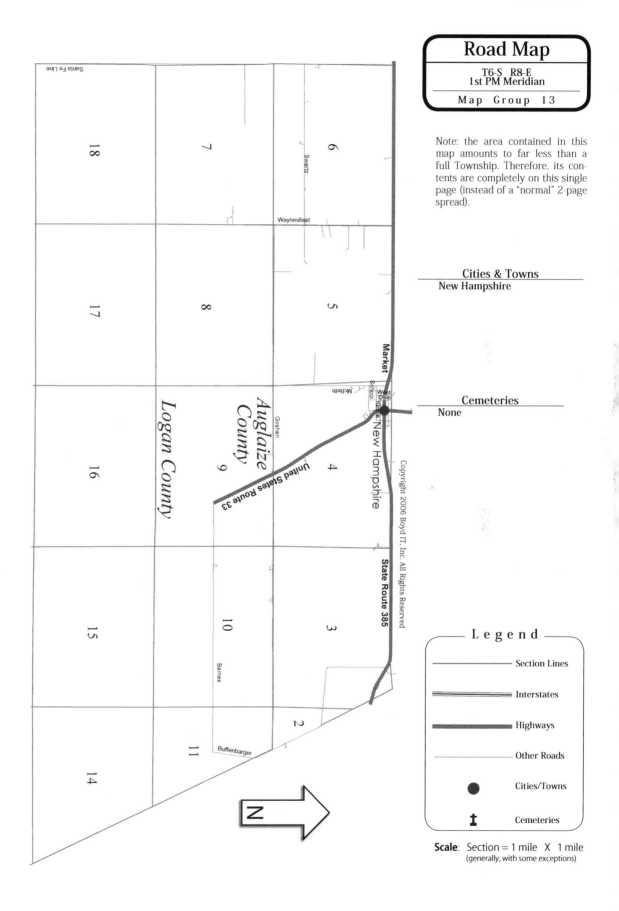

Note: the area contained in this map amounts to far less than a full Township. Therefore, its contents are completely on this single page (instead of a "normal" 2-page spread).

Cities & Towns
New Hampshire

Cemeteries
None

Legend
— Section Lines
═ Interstates
━ Highways
— Other Roads
● Cities/Towns
⊥ Cemeteries

Scale: Section = 1 mile X 1 mile
(generally, with some exceptions)

Historical Map

T6-S R8-E
1st PM Meridian

Map Group 13

Note: the area contained in this map amounts to far less than a full Township. Therefore, its contents are completely on this single page (instead of a "normal" 2-page spread).

Cities & Towns
New Hampshire

Cemeteries
None

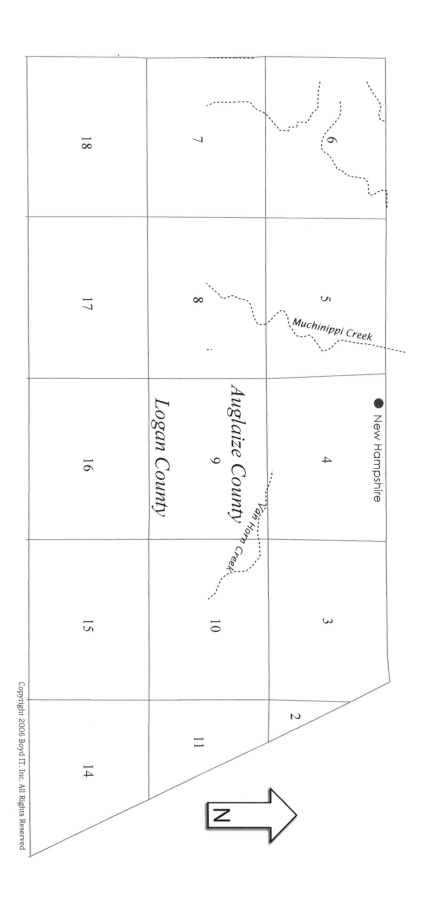

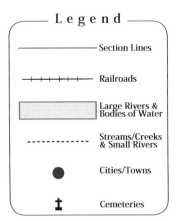

Legend

———— Section Lines

+ + + + + + Railroads

Large Rivers & Bodies of Water

– – – – – Streams/Creeks & Small Rivers

● Cities/Towns

⚡ Cemeteries

Scale: Section = 1 mile X 1 mile
(there are some exceptions)

Map Group 14: Index to Land Patents

Township 7-South Range 4-East (1st PM)

After you locate an individual in this Index, take note of the Section and Section Part then proceed to the Land Patent map on the pages immediately following. You should have no difficulty locating the corresponding parcel of land.

The "For More Info" Column will lead you to more information about the underlying Patents. See the Legend at right, and the "How to Use this Book" chapter, for more information.

ID	Individual in Patent	Sec.	Sec. Part	Date Issued	Other Counties	For More Info . . .
2249	ADELMEYER, Bernd H	23	NESE	1835-10-09		A1
2250	" "	23	W½SE	1835-10-09		A1
2383	ALBAS, John B	29	SWNE	1835-10-09		A1
2382	" "	29	NWNE	1848-06-01		A1
2466	ALLEN, Mundy	15	E½NE	1827-05-22		A1
2384	ARIMAN, John B	17	N½NE	1835-10-09		A1
2248	ARNS, Bernd	33	SESE	1835-10-09		A1
2292	AUBELIN, Frederick	11	SWSE	1835-10-08		A1
2294	AUBELIN, Frederick H	11	SESE	1835-10-09		A1
2408	BAKEMAN, John H	23	S½SW	1833-11-27		A1
2251	BARGMANN, Bernd H	25	SW	1835-10-09		A1
2409	BARHORST, John H	21	SESE	1835-10-16		A1 R2352
2488	BARNAR, William	22	S½NW	1833-11-27		A1
2489	" "	22	SW	1833-11-27		A1
2490	BECKEMAN, William	8	NWSE	1835-10-07		A1 G13
2331	BECKMAN, Henry	26	E½NE	1835-10-09		A1 G14
2275	BEDINGHOUSE, Detrick	21	W½SE	1835-10-09		A1
2258	BENHERT, Charles	33	E½NW	1835-10-09		A1
2259	BENNER, Christian	21	NESE	1835-10-09		A1
2491	BERNER, William	15	NESW	1834-10-30		A1
2492	"	15	NWSW	1835-10-16		A1
2236	BLAKKA, Bernard	30	E½SW	1835-10-16		A1 G17
2226	BOOCKER, Anton	29	SESW	1835-10-16		A1
2293	BORT, Frederick	5	SWSW	1846-11-05		A1
2399	BOSCHE, John F	17	SWNE	1846-10-01		A1
2400	" "	17	W½NW	1846-10-01		A1
2401	" "	9	NENW	1846-10-01		A1
2393	BOWEN, John	22	E½SE	1827-04-15		A1
2410	BRAMMELAGE, John H	33	NESE	1834-01-30		A1
2394	BREWSTER, John	5	E½SE	1826-05-10		A1
2411	BRUGGEMAN, John H	5	E½NE	1848-06-01		A1
2412	" "	5	NWNE	1848-06-01		A1
2238	BRUNE, Bernard	7	NESE	1846-11-05		A1 G20
2237	" "	7	SESE	1846-11-05		A1
2395	BRUNS, John	19	SENW	1848-06-01		A1 F
2227	BULMAHNN, Anton F	23	N½SW	1835-10-07		A1
2228	BULMAHUN, Anton F	23	S½NW	1833-11-27		A1
2240	BUSSE, Bernard H	27	SENW	1833-11-27		A1
2340	BYENBROOK, Henry G	8	E½SE	1835-10-09		A1
2341	" "	8	SWSE	1835-10-09		A1
2396	CAMMON, John C	21	SENE	1835-10-09		A1
2247	COOPER, Bernd A	36	E½SE	1835-10-16		A1
2465	CORNELL, Moses	22	W½SE	1827-04-15		A1
2271	COTTERLIN, David	2	E½SW	1825-09-03		A1
2413	DARLINGHAUS, John H	31	NWSW	1848-07-01		A1 F
2332	DARSTON, Henry	28	W½SW	1835-10-09		A1

ID	Individual in Patent	Sec.	Sec. Part	Date Issued	Other Counties	For More Info . . .
2478	DAVIS, Samuel	24	N½SE	1835-10-16		A1
2479	" "	24	S½SE	1835-10-16		A1
2295	DICKMAN, Frederick H	9	E½SE	1833-11-27		A1
2361	DOHMANN, Herman H	31	SENW	1848-07-01		A1 F
2333	DONNEBERG, Henry	4	E½SE	1835-10-09		A1
2334	DOSTON, Henry	29	NESE	1835-10-16		A1 G31
2464	DREES, Michael	25	SE	1835-10-09		A1
2487	DREES, Tobias	36	SWNE	1835-10-09		A1
2336	DURSTEN, Henry	19	SESE	1848-06-01		A1
2335	"	19	NESE	1848-08-01		A1
2311	EBERD, George	36	SWSW	1835-10-08		A1
2414	ELLEMAN, John H	7	SENW	1846-11-05		A1 F
2318	ELLERMAN, Gerhard H	17	NWSW	1846-11-05		A1
2319	" "	17	SWSW	1848-08-01		A1
2322	ELLERMAN, Gerhard W	7	NENW	1846-11-05		A1 F
2323	"	7	SENE	1848-06-01		A1
2441	ELLERMAN, John W	7	NESE	1846-11-05		A1 F
2260	ELLERMANN, Christian F	7	W½NE	1846-10-01		A1
2320	ELLERMANN, Gerhard H	17	NESW	1846-10-01		A1
2324	ELLERMANN, Gerhard W	7	NENE	1846-10-01		A1
2442	ELLERMANN, John W	7	NWSE	1846-10-01		A1
2338	ENNEKING, Henry	28	E½SE	1835-10-08		A1 G36
2337	" "	24	SWNW	1835-10-09		A1
2338	ENNEKING, Joseph	28	E½SE	1835-10-08		A1 G36
2452	" "	23	NENE	1835-10-09		A1
2453	" "	24	NWNW	1835-10-09		A1
2415	FAIK, John H	5	SWNE	1848-06-01		A1 F
2386	FELDMAN, John B	26	S½NW	1833-11-27		A1 G38
2385	" "	34	E½SE	1833-11-27		A1
2416	FELDMANN, John H	35	SWNE	1833-11-27		A1
2417	" "	35	W½SE	1833-11-27		A1
2493	FERREL, William	27	N½NE	1833-11-27		A1
2277	FIELD, Dudley	18	NWSW	1835-10-08		A1
2316	FLOHR, George N	17	SESW	1848-06-01		A1
2404	FONKMAN, John	35	SESE	1835-10-09		A1
2362	FORNHOLT, Herman H	4	W½SE	1835-10-09		A1
2387	FREDERICKS, John B	24	N½NE	1835-10-09		A1
2418	FRELING, John H	24	NENW	1835-10-09		A1
2469	FULLENKAMP, Nicholas	19	W½SW	1846-11-05		A1 F
2373	FURNOW, James G	34	W½SE	1832-11-05		A1
2221	GARBERRY, Andreas	9	NWNW	1835-10-16		A1
2222	GAST, Andrew	27	SWNW	1834-01-30		A1
2223	" "	28	SENE	1834-01-30		A1
2255	GAUSEPOHL, Carl	23	SENE	1835-10-09		A1
2256	" "	23	W½NE	1835-10-09		A1
2419	GEHVERS, John H	35	SW	1833-11-27		A1 G41
2262	GREBER, Christoff	9	E½NE	1833-11-27		A1
2263	" "	9	NWNE	1833-11-27		A1
2342	GREESHOPF, Henry	32	NWNW	1835-10-09		A1
2360	GRINKEMEYER, Herman	7	SESW	1848-06-01		A1 F
2369	HALL, Isabella	1	W½NW	1832-11-05		A1
2370	" "	2	E½NE	1832-11-05		A1
2266	HANSFELD, Clemes	19	E½NE	1848-06-01		A1
2267	" "	19	NWNE	1848-06-01		A1
2470	HARDENBROOK, Peter	14	SE	1833-11-27		A1
2480	HATFIELD, Samuel	15	SE	1827-04-15		A1
2494	HEATH, William	10	W½NW	1824-08-09		A1
2476	HEBENSTREIT, Phillip	9	SWSE	1833-11-27		A1
2236	HELMSING, Henry	30	E½SW	1835-10-16		A1 G17
2434	HERGENROTHER, John	33	W½SW	1835-10-09		A1
2282	HILLMANN, Francis	24	SWSW	1835-10-16		A1
2274	HINDERS, Dedrick	30	W½SW	1835-10-16		A1
2435	HITEMAN, John	32	NWSW	1835-10-09		A1
2238	HOHNE, Detrich	7	NESE	1846-11-05		A1 G20
2363	HOLLA, Herman H	14	NENW	1835-10-09		A1
2330	HOLTFOCHT, Harman H	29	E½NW	1835-10-16		A1
2334	HOLTFOCHT, Henry	29	NESE	1835-10-16		A1 G31
2376	HOUSE, Joel	13	W½NW	1833-11-27		A1
2377	"	14	NE	1833-11-27		A1
2276	HUGEMAN, Diederich	21	NESW	1848-06-01		A1
2233	HUKRIDE, Bals H	1	NENW	1848-06-01		A1 F
2371	HURTLE, Jacob	27	S½NE	1833-11-27		A1
2224	JACKSON, Andrew	2	S½SE	1835-10-09		A1 V2468

ID	Individual in Patent	Sec.	Sec. Part	Date Issued	Other Counties	For More Info . . .
2272	JORDAN, David J	10	E½SW	1833-11-27		A1
2397	JORDAN, John C	7	NWNW	1848-06-01		A1 F
2343	KELLER, Henry	9	NESW	1835-10-08		A1
2344	" "	9	NWSE	1835-10-08		A1
2325	KISER, Gerhart	21	SESR	1848-06-01		A1
2420	KLATTA, John H	3	E½SW	1833-11-27		A1
2241	KLOAS, Bernard	20	NENE	1835-10-09		A1 G50
2359	KLUIS, Herman B	23	SESE	1835-10-09		A1
2345	KNUPKE, Henry	30	NE	1835-10-16		A1
2388	KOKENGE, John B	26	NESE	1835-10-09		A1
2331	KRAMER, John B	26	E½NE	1835-10-09		A1 G14
2421	KUNNING, John H	11	SW	1833-11-27		A1
2235	KUPER, Bernard A	27	NENW	1833-11-27		A1
2269	LAMB, Daniel G	20	E½SW	1835-10-08		A1
2270	" "	20	W½SE	1835-10-08		A1
2290	LAUGER, Francis	24	NWSW	1835-10-16		A1
2378	LEMKOHL, John A	9	SENW	1835-10-08		A1
2379	" "	9	SWNE	1835-10-08		A1
2302	LENNENEVER, Frederick	3	N½NW	1833-11-27		A1
2457	LEPPERT, Laurence	29	W½SE	1835-10-09		A1
2278	LIGHTFOOT, Edward B	2	W½SW	1827-08-10		A1
2389	LINING, John B	32	NENW	1835-10-09		A1
2390	" "	32	S½NW	1835-10-09		A1
2454	LOCKET, Joseph	8	E½NE	1828-01-03		A1
2230	LUERS, Arend H	28	NWSE	1835-10-09		A1
2231	LURES, Arend H	28	E½SW	1835-10-09		A1
2436	MACER, John J	32	E½SW	1835-10-09		A1
2437	" "	32	SWSW	1835-10-09		A1
2495	MAJOR, William	15	W½NE	1824-08-09		A1
2326	MAJORS, Hamilton	4	W½SW	1826-05-10		A1
2374	MAJORS, James	22	NE	1825-09-03		A1
2346	MALCOS, Henry	20	SENE	1835-10-16		A1
2468	MEAD, Nathaniel	2	W½SE	1833-11-27		A1 V2224
2347	MELCHER, Henry	21	SWNW	1846-11-05		A1
2391	MESLOH, John B	11	N½NW	1833-11-27		A1
2438	METSKER, John	21	NENE	1835-10-09		A1
2242	MEYER, Bernard	36	E½NE	1835-10-09		A1
2243	" "	36	NWNE	1835-10-09		A1
2265	MIDDLEBECKE, Clemens A	28	SWNW	1835-10-09		A1
2257	MILLER, Ceviller	18	NW	1835-10-09		A1
2303	MILLER, Frederick	11	NESE	1835-10-09		A1
2366	MILLER, Isaac	35	E½NE	1833-11-27		A1
2367	" "	36	N½NW	1833-11-27		A1
2467	MILLER, Nancy	35	NESE	1833-11-27		A1
2304	MIRING, Frederick	9	SWNW	1835-10-08		A1
2273	MITTENDORF, Dedrick B	9	W½SW	1835-10-09		A1
2310	MOEKER, Garet W	11	NWSE	1834-01-30		A1
2241	MOHR, John	20	NENE	1835-10-09		A1 G50
2439	" "	29	E½NE	1835-10-09		A1
2440	" "	33	NE	1835-10-09		A1
2314	MOJER, George H	23	N½NW	1833-11-27		A1
2229	MOKKARHIDER, Anton	3	S½NW	1833-11-27		A1
2364	MOORMAN, Herman H	26	NENW	1835-10-09		A1
2348	MOORMANN, Henry	26	NWNW	1833-11-27		A1
2315	MORTON, George	12	NW	1833-11-27		A1
2372	MOURER, Jacob	1	S½	1835-10-09		A1
2328	MURKER, Harman F	3	NE	1833-11-27		A1
2482	NAGLE, Sebastian	5	SESW	1846-10-01		A1
2483	" "	5	W½SE	1846-10-01		A1
2261	NEITER, Christian F	17	SENE	1835-10-09		A1
2455	NIEMAN, Joseph	30	W½SE	1835-10-09		A1
2484	NOKEL, Sebastian	17	NENW	1835-10-16		A1
2234	NOLAN, Benjamin	24	NESW	1835-10-16		A1
2422	OLMAN, John	4	NWNE	1835-10-09		A1
2472	OPDYCKE, Peter	5	W½NW	1822-04-08		A1
2471	" "	5	E½NW	1835-10-08		A1
2473	OPDYKE, Peter	4	W½NW	1826-05-10		A1
2244	ORTMAN, Bernard	21	E½NW	1835-10-16		A1
2380	OSTERLOH, John A	31	SENE	1846-11-05		A1
2381	" "	31	SWNE	1848-07-01		A1
2423	OSTERLOH, John H	31	E½SE	1835-10-09		A1
2424	" "	31	NWSE	1835-10-09		A1
2218	PAUL, Adam	1	SENE	1848-06-01		A1

ID	Individual in Patent	Sec.	Sec. Part	Date Issued	Other Counties	For More Info . . .
2253	PENING, Bernd	24	SESW	1835-10-16		A1
2496	PITMAN, William	2	W½NE	1833-11-27		A1
2301	POLMANN, Frederick L	4	E½NE	1835-10-08		A1
2365	QURTMAN, Herman H	29	NESW	1835-10-09		A1
2485	RAMSEY, Susan	12	NESW	1834-01-30		A1
2463	REKEL, Mekel	17	SENW	1835-10-16		A1
2349	RODEKORTH, Henry	11	S½NW	1833-11-27		A1
2350	ROFLES, Henry	29	SWSW	1835-10-09		A1
2351	" "	30	SESE	1835-10-09		A1
2402	ROHENKOHL, John F	27	SW	1833-11-27		A1
2443	ROOF, John W	32	NENE	1835-10-08		A1
2445	" "	33	NWNW	1835-10-08		A1
2444	" "	32	SENE	1835-10-09		A1
2446	" "	33	SWNW	1835-10-09		A1
2481	ROOTS, Samuel	27	NWNW	1833-11-27		A1
2220	SACKETT, Alexander	8	W½NE	1832-11-05		A1
2486	SCHAMMEL, Theodore	21	W½SW	1835-10-09		A1
2425	SCHARDELMANN, John H	3	SE	1833-11-27		A1
2352	SCHOULTE, Henry	21	SESE	1835-10-16		A1 R2409
2296	SCHROEDER, Frederick H	10	E½NW	1833-11-27		A1
2297	" "	10	N½SE	1833-11-27		A1
2298	" "	10	NE	1833-11-27		A1
2300	" "	15	NW	1834-01-30		A1
2299	" "	10	W½SW	1835-10-09		A1
2245	SCHULZE, Bernard	36	E½SW	1835-10-09		A1
2225	SCHWEINEFUSZ, Anthony	19	NENW	1848-06-01		A1 F
2305	SEAMAR, Frederick	15	SWSW	1833-11-27		A1
2306	" "	22	N½NW	1833-11-27		A1
2477	SERGES, Rudolph	4	SESW	1835-10-09		A1
2307	SHELMITTER, Frederick	31	E½SW	1835-10-16		A1 G62
2308	" "	31	SWSE	1835-10-16		A1 G62
2307	SHELMITTER, John G	31	E½SW	1835-10-16		A1 G62
2308	" "	31	SWSE	1835-10-16		A1 G62
2252	SHEPPER, Bernd H	33	W½SE	1835-10-09		A1 G63
2252	SHEPPER, Francis H	33	W½SE	1835-10-09		A1 G63
2309	SHULENBARG, Frederick	15	SESW	1833-11-27		A1
2246	SMITH, Bernard	19	W½SE	1848-08-01		A1
2321	SOLLMAN, Gerhard H	17	NWSE	1846-11-05		A1
2403	SOLLMAN, John F	17	SWSE	1846-11-05		A1
2447	SOLLMAN, John W	7	SWSE	1846-11-05		A1
2353	SOLMON, Henry	17	E½SE	1835-10-16		A1
2426	SOURMANN, John H	30	NESE	1835-10-09		A1
2427	"	31	NENE	1835-10-09		A1
2280	SPREHEE, Francis H	28	N½NW	1835-10-09		A1
2386	STALLO, Francis J	26	S½NW	1833-11-27		A1 G38
2283	" "	26	SW	1833-11-27		A1
2284	" "	26	SWSE	1833-11-27		A1
2285	" "	27	SE	1833-11-27		A1
2286	" "	34	NE	1833-11-27		A1
2287	" "	34	NW	1833-11-27		A1
2288	" "	35	NW	1833-11-27		A1
2289	" "	35	NWNE	1833-11-27		A1
2419	" "	35	SW	1833-11-27		A1 G41
2368	STATLER, Isaac	20	W½SW	1834-01-30		A1
2375	STATLER, Jane	29	W½NW	1835-10-08		A1
2428	STEINEMANN, John H	31	NENW	1835-10-09		A1
2429	STEINMANN, John H	9	SESW	1846-10-01		A1
2458	STELTZER, Leon	19	W½NW	1846-11-05		A1 F
2459	STELTZER, Leopold	19	E½SW	1846-11-05		A1 F
2317	STINE, George P	12	SE	1835-10-09		A1
2474	STORCK, Peter	7	SWNW	1848-06-01		A1 F
2475	" "	7	W½SW	1848-06-01		A1 F
2291	STUBBE, Frederick A	36	W½SE	1835-10-09		A1
2497	SUNDERLAND, William	25	N½NW	1833-11-27		A1
2498	" "	25	NE	1833-11-27		A1
2430	SURMANN, John H	34	SW	1833-11-27		A1
2254	TABA, Bernd	36	SENW	1835-10-09		A1
2239	TANGEMANN, Bernard F	31	SWSW	1848-07-01		A1 F
2405	TAUBEN, John G	26	NWSE	1833-11-27		A1
2406	" "	26	W½NE	1833-11-27		A1
2312	THIMANN, George F	1	SENW	1846-11-05		A1 F
2313	" "	1	SWNE	1846-11-05		A1 F
2281	TOMAN, Francis H	21	NWNW	1835-10-16		A1

ID	Individual in Patent	Sec.	Sec. Part	Date Issued	Other Counties	For More Info . . .
2398	TOMON, John C	25	S½NW	1835-10-16		A1
2407	TONGAMAN, John G	2	E½NW	1835-10-08		A1
2460	TUCKER, Manning R	13	S½	1833-11-27		A1
2339	TUNEMANN, Henry F	21	W½NE	1835-10-09		A1
2356	TUPP, Henry	1	N½NE	1849-02-01		A1
2268	VEHORN, Clemment	19	SWNE	1848-08-01		A1
2456	VINTER, Joseph	29	NWSW	1835-10-09		A1
2354	VOORHIS, Henry T	13	E½NW	1833-11-27		A1
2355	"	"	13	NE	1833-11-27		A1
2392	WALKE, John B	26	SESE	1835-10-08		A1
2450	WALLACE, John	11	NE	1833-11-27		A1
2499	WELDEHR, William	28	SENW	1835-10-09		A1
2500	"	"	28	W½NE	1835-10-09		A1
2448	WELDELN, John W	28	NENE	1835-10-09		A1
2431	WELLMAN, John H	14	NWNW	1833-11-27		A1
2432	"	"	14	S½NW	1833-11-27		A1
2433	WELLMANN, John H	14	SW	1833-11-27		A1
2327	WESJOHN, Harm H	31	NWNE	1835-10-09		A1
2279	WETTERER, Ferdinand	29	SESE	1835-10-09		A1
2232	WICHER, Arnst H	3	W½SW	1833-11-27		A1
2461	WICHMANN, Martin	36	NWSW	1835-10-08		A1
2462	WICKMAN, Martin	36	SWNW	1835-10-09		A1
2449	WIEMEYER, John W	5	N½SW	1848-06-01		A1
2219	WIENNER, Adam	33	E½SW	1835-10-09		A1
2329	WINDELER, Harman F	10	S½SE	1833-11-27		A1
2490	WINTHORT, Francis	8	NWSE	1835-10-07		A1 G13
2357	WORMANN, Henry	31	NWNW	1846-11-05		A1 F
2358	"	"	31	SWNW	1848-07-01		A1 F
2264	WUPPENHARST, Christoff	2	W½NW	1833-11-27		A1
2451	YOUNKER, John	32	W½NE	1835-10-09		A1

Patent Map

T7-S R4-E
1st PM Meridian

Map Group 14

Township Statistics

Parcels Mapped	:	283
Number of Patents	:	269
Number of Individuals	:	230
Patentees Identified	:	226
Number of Surnames	:	209
Multi-Patentee Parcels	:	12
Oldest Patent Date	:	4/8/1822
Most Recent Patent	:	2/1/1849
Block/Lot Parcels	:	0
Parcels Re-Issued	:	1
Parcels that Overlap	:	2
Cities and Towns	:	4
Cemeteries	:	5

Section 6

Section 5
OPDYCKE Peter 1822
OPDYCKE Peter 1835
BRUGGEMAN John H 1848
BRUGGEMAN John H 1848
FAIK John H 1848
WIEMEYER John W 1848
NAGLE Sebastian 1846
BREWSTER John 1826
BORT Frederick 1846
NAGLE Sebastian 1846

Section 4
OPDYKE Peter 1826
OLMAN John H 1835
POLMANN Frederick L 1835
MAJORS Hamilton 1826
FORNHOLT Herman H 1835
DONNEBERG Henry 1835
SERGES Rudolph 1835

Section 7
JORDAN John C 1848
ELLERMAN Gerhard W 1846
ELLERMANN Christian F 1846
ELLERMANN Gerhard W 1846
STORCK Peter 1848
ELLEMAN John H 1846
ELLERMAN Gerhard W 1848
STORCK Peter 1848
ELLERMAN John W 1846
ELLERMANN John W 1846
BRUNE [20] Bernard 1846
GRINKEMEYER Herman 1848
SOLLMAN John W 1846
BRUNE Bernard 1846

Section 8
SACKETT Alexander 1832
LOCKET Joseph 1828
BECKEMAN [13] William 1835
BYENBROOK Henry G 1835
BYENBROOK Henry G 1835

Section 9
GARBERRY Andreas 1835
BOSCHE John F 1846
GREBER Christoff 1833
MIRING Frederick 1835
LEMKOHL John A 1835
LEMKOHL John A 1835
GREBER Christoff 1833
KELLER Henry 1835
KELLER Henry 1835
DICKMAN Frederick H 1833
MITTENDORF Dedrick B 1835
STEINMANN John H 1846
HEBENSTREIT Phillip 1833

Section 18
MILLER Ceviller 1835
FIELD Dudley 1835

Section 17
BOSCHE John F 1846
NOKEL Sebastian 1835
ARIMAN John B 1835
REKEL Mekel 1835
BOSCHE John F 1846
NEITER Christian F 1835
ELLERMAN Gerhard H 1846
ELLERMANN Gerhard H 1846
SOLLMAN Gerhard H 1846
ELLERMAN Gerhard H 1848
FLOHR George N 1848
SOLLMAN John F 1846
SOLMON Henry 1835

Section 16

Section 19
STELTZER Leon 1846
SCHWEINEFUSZ Anthony 1848
HANSFELD Clemes 1848
BRUNS John 1848
VEHORN Clemment 1848
HANSFELD Clemes 1848
FULLENKAMP Nicholas 1846
SMITH Bernard 1848
DURSTEN Henry 1848
STELTZER Leopold 1846
DURSTEN Henry 1848

Section 20
KLOAS [50] Bernard 1835
MALCOS Henry 1835
STATLER Isaac 1834
LAMB Daniel G 1835
LAMB Daniel G 1835

Section 21
TOMAN Francis H 1835
TUNEMANN Henry F 1835
METSKER John 1835
MELCHER Henry 1846
ORTMAN Bernard 1835
CAMMON John C 1835
SCHAMMEL Theodore 1835
HUGEMAN Diederich 1848
BEDINGHOUSE Detrick 1835
BENNER Christian 1835
KISER Gerhart 1848
BARHORST John H 1835
SCHOULTE Henry 1835

Section 30

Section 29
STATLER Jane 1835
HOLTFOCHT Harman H 1835
ALBAS John B 1848
KNUPKE Henry 1835
ALBAS John B 1835
MOHR John 1835

Section 28
SPREHEE Francis H 1835
WELDEHR William 1835
WELDELN John W 1835
MIDDLEBECKE Clemens A 1835
WELDEHR William 1835
GAST Andrew 1834

HINDERS Dedrick 1835
NIEMAN Joseph 1835
SOURMANN John H 1835
VINTER Joseph 1835
QURTMAN Herman H 1835
LEPPERT Laurence 1835
DOSTON [31] Henry 1835
DARSTON Henry 1835
LUERS Arend H 1835
ENNEKING [36] Henry 1835
BLAKKA [17] Bernard 1835
ROFLES Henry 1835
ROFLES Henry 1835
BOOCKER Anton 1835
WETTERER Ferdinand 1835
LURES Arend H 1835

Section 31
WORMANN Henry 1846
STEINEMANN John H 1835
WESJOHN Harm H 1835
SOURMANN John H 1835
WORMANN Henry 1848
DOHMANN Herman H 1848
OSTERLOH John A 1848
OSTERLOH John A 1846
DARLINGHAUS John H 1848
OSTERLOH John H 1835
TANGEMANN Bernard F 1848
SHELMITTER [62] Frederick 1835
SHELMITTER [62] Frederick 1835
OSTERLOH John H 1835

Section 32
GREESHOPF Henry 1835
LINING John B 1835
YOUNKER John 1835
ROOF John W 1835
LINING John B 1835
HITEMAN John 1835
MACER John J 1835
MACER John J 1835

Section 33
ROOF John W 1835
ROOF John W 1835
MOHR John 1835
BENHERT Charles 1835
HERGENROTHER John 1835
SHEPPER [63] Bernd H 1835
BRAMMELAGE John H 1834
WIENNER Adam 1835
ARNS Bernd 1835

		WUPPENHARST Christoff 1833	PITMAN William 1833		HALL Isabella 1832	HUKRIDE Bals H 1848	TUPP Henry 1849	
LENNENEVER Frederick 1833	MURKER Harman F 1833	TONGAMAN John G 1835	HALL Isabella 1832	THIMANN George F 1846	THIMANN George F 1846	PAUL Adam 1848		
MOKKARHIDER Anton 1833								
WICHER Arnst H 1833	**3** SCHARDELMANN John H 1833	LIGHTFOOT Edward B 1827	**2** COTTERLIN David 1825	MEAD Nathaniel 1833		**1** MOURER Jacob 1835		
KLATTA John H 1833					JACKSON Andrew 1835			

HEATH William 1824	SCHROEDER Frederick H 1833	SCHROEDER Frederick H 1833	MESLOH John B 1833	WALLACE John 1833		MORTON George 1833	**12**	
			RODEKORTH Henry 1833					
SCHROEDER Frederick H 1835	**10**	SCHROEDER Frederick H 1833	**11** KUNNING John H 1833	MOEKER Garet W 1834	MILLER Frederick 1835	RAMSEY Susan 1834	STINE George P 1835	
JORDAN David J 1833		WINDELER Harman F 1833		AUBELIN Frederick 1835	AUBELIN Frederick H 1835			

SCHROEDER Frederick H 1834	**15**	MAJOR William 1824	ALLEN Mundy 1827	WELLMAN John H 1833	HOLLA Herman H 1835	HOUSE Joel 1833		VOORHIS Henry T 1833
				WELLMAN John H 1833		HOUSE Joel 1833	VOORHIS Henry T 1833	
BERNER William 1835	BERNER William 1834	HATFIELD Samuel 1827	**14** WELLMANN John H 1833	HARDENBROOK Peter 1833		**13** TUCKER Manning R 1833		
SEAMAR Frederick 1833	SHULENBARG Frederick 1833							

SEAMAR Frederick 1833	MAJORS James 1825	MOJER George H 1833	GAUSEPOHL Carl 1835	ENNEKING Joseph 1835	ENNEKING Joseph 1835	FRELING John H 1835	FREDERICKS John B 1835	
BARNAR William 1833		BULMAHUN Anton F 1833	**23** GAUSEPOHL Carl 1835	ENNEKING Henry 1835	**24**			
22 BARNAR William 1833	CORNELL Moses 1827	BULMAHNN Anton F 1835	ADELMEYER Bernd H 1835	LAUGER Francis 1835	NOLAN Benjamin 1835	DAVIS Samuel 1835		
	BOWEN John 1827	BAKEMAN John H 1833	ADELMEYER Bernd H 1835	KLUIS Herman B 1835	HILLMANN Francis 1835	PENING Bernd 1835	DAVIS Samuel 1835	

ROOTS Samuel 1833	KUPER Bernard A 1833	FERREL William 1833	MOORMANN Henry 1833	MOORMAN Herman H 1835	TAUBEN John G 1833	SUNDERLAND William 1833		SUNDERLAND William 1833
GAST Andrew 1834	BUSSE Bernard H 1833	HURTLE Jacob 1833	FELDMAN [38] John H 1833	**26**	BECKMAN [14] Henry 1835	TOMON John C 1835		
27 ROHENKOHL John F 1833	STALLO Francis J 1833	STALLO Francis J 1833	TAUBEN John G 1833	KOKENGE John B 1835	**25** BARGMANN Bernd H 1835	DREES Michael 1835		
			STALLO Francis J 1833	WALKE John B 1835				

STALLO Francis J 1833	STALLO Francis J 1833	STALLO Francis J 1833	STALLO Francis J 1833		MILLER Isaac 1833		MEYER Bernard 1835	
34		**35**	FELDMANN John H 1833	MILLER Isaac 1833	WICKMAN Martin 1835	TABA Bernd 1835	DREES Tobias 1835	MEYER Bernard 1835
SURMANN John H 1833	FURNOW James G 1832	GEHVERS [41] John H 1833	FELDMANN John H 1833	MILLER Nancy 1833	WICHMANN Martin 1835	**36** STUBBE Frederick A 1835		COOPER Bernd A 1835
	FELDMAN John B 1833			FONKMAN John 1835	EBERD George 1835	SCHULZE Bernard 1835		

Helpful Hints

1. This Map's INDEX can be found on the preceding pages.

2. Refer to Map "C" to see where this Township lies within Auglaize County, Ohio.

3. Numbers within square brackets [ ] denote a multi-patentee land parcel (multi-owner). Refer to Appendix "C" for a full list of members in this group.

4. Areas that look to be crowded with Patentees usually indicate multiple sales of the same parcel (Re-issues) or Overlapping parcels. See this Township's Index for an explanation of these and other circumstances that might explain "odd" groupings of Patentees on this map.

Legend

————	Patent Boundary
▬▬▬▬	Section Boundary
▨	No Patents Found (or Outside County)
1., 2., 3., ...	Lot Numbers (when beside a name)
[ ]	Group Number (see Appendix "C")

Scale: Section = 1 mile X 1 mile (generally, with some exceptions)

Road Map

T7-S R4-E
1st PM Meridian

Map Group 14

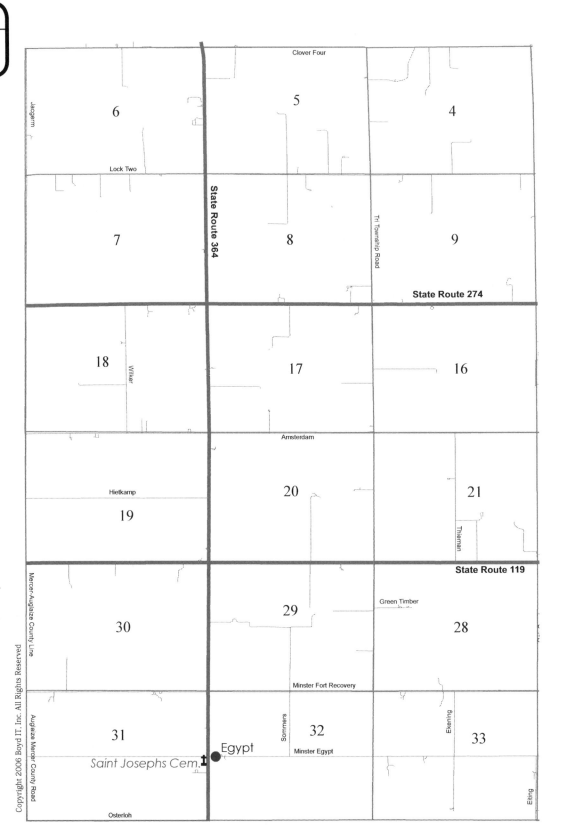

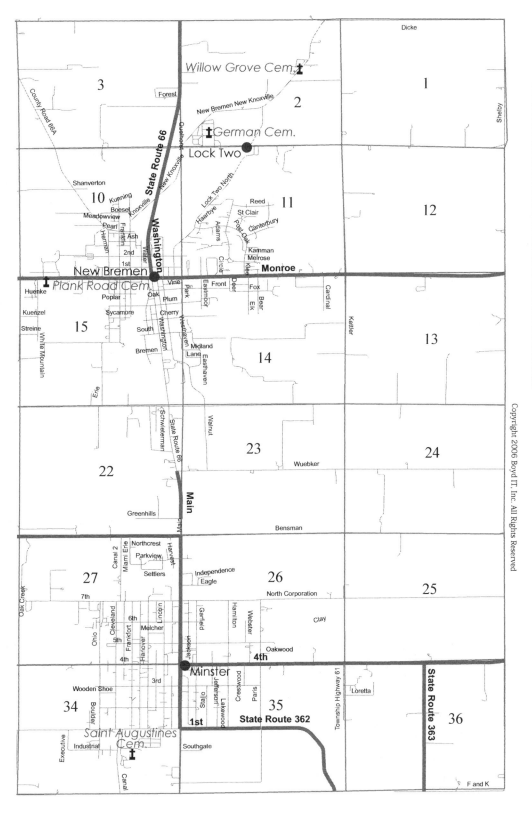

Dicke

Willow Grove Cem. †

3

1

Forest

New Bremen New Knoxville

2

Shelby

German Cem. †

Lock Two

Shanverton

10

Kunning

Boesel

Meadowview

11

Reed

St Clair

Canterbury

12

Pearl

Ash

Haarbye

Adams

Post Oak

Herman

Franklin

2nd

1st

Water

Kamman

Melrose

Circle

Kieл

Monroe

New Bremen

† **Plank Road Cem.**

Vine

Oak

Front

Fox

Deer

Cardinal

Huenke

Poplar

Plum

Park

Eastmor

Elk

Bear

Kuenzel

Sycamore

Cherry

South

Washington

Midland

Ketler

13

Streine

15

Westhaven

Bremen

Lane

14

White Mountain

Erie

Easthaven

Schwieterman

Walnut

23

24

State Route 66

Wuebker

22

Greenhills

Main

Bensman

Canal 2

Miami Erie

Northcrest

Parkview

Harvest

27

Settlers

Independence

Eagle

26

25

Oak Creek

7th

North Corporation

Cleveland

Frankfort

Ohio

6th

Melcher

5th

Garfield

Hamilton

Webster

Clay

Lincoln

Hanover

Jackson

4th

Oakwood

4th

Minster

3rd

Wooden Shoe

Boulder

Otis

Jefferson

Lakewood

Crestwood

Paris

Township High Highway 19

Loretta

34

35

State Route 362

State Route 363

36

1st

Saint Augustines Cem. †

Executive

Industrial

Southgate

Canal

F and K

Helpful Hints

1. This road map has a number of uses, but primarily it is to help you: a) find the present location of land owned by your ancestors (at least the general area), b) find cemeteries and city-centers, and c) estimate the route/roads used by Census-takers & tax-assessors.

2. If you plan to travel to Auglaize County to locate cemeteries or land parcels, please pick up a modern travel map for the area before you do. Mapping old land parcels on modern maps is not as exact a science as you might think. Just the slightest variations in public land survey coordinates, estimates of parcel boundaries, or road-map deviations can greatly alter a map's representation of how a road either does or doesn't cross a particular parcel of land.

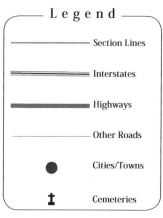

Legend

———————	Section Lines
══════════	Interstates
━━━━━━━━━	Highways
··········	Other Roads
●	Cities/Towns
†	Cemeteries

Scale: Section = 1 mile X 1 mile
(generally, with some exceptions)

Historical Map

T7-S R4-E
1st PM Meridian

Map Group 14

Cities & Towns
Egypt
Lock Two
Minster
New Bremen

Cemeteries
German Cemetery
Plank Road Cemetery
Saint Augustines Cemetery
Saint Josephs Cemetery
Willow Grove Cemetery

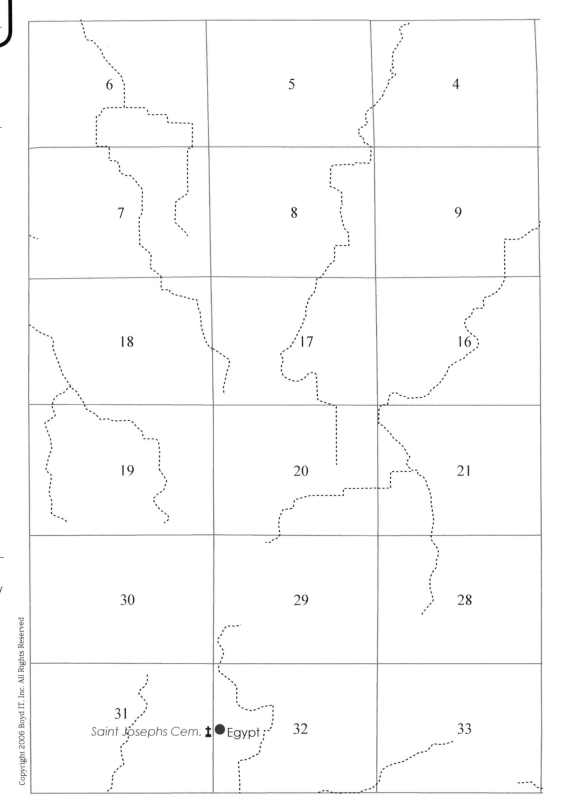

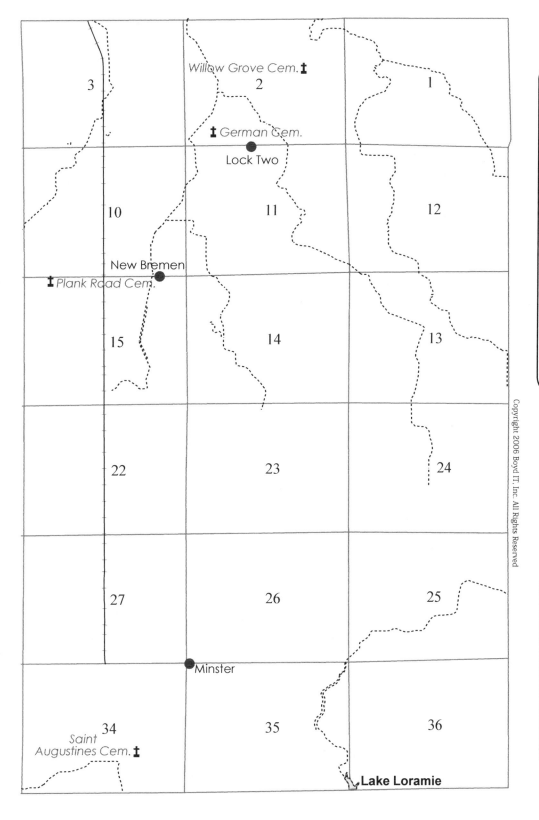

3

Willow Grove Cem. ‡

2

1

‡ *German Cem.*

Lock Two

10

11

12

New Bremen

‡ *Plank Road Cem.*

15

14

13

22

23

24

27

26

25

Minster

34

35

36

Saint Augustines Cem. ‡

Lake Loramie

Helpful Hints

1. This Map takes a different look at the same Congressional Township displayed in the preceding two maps. It presents features that can help you better envision the historical development of the area: a) Water-bodies (lakes & ponds), b) Water-courses (rivers, streams, etc.), c) Railroads, d) City/town center-points (where they were oftentimes located when first settled), and e) Cemeteries.

2. Using this "Historical" map in tandem with this Township's Patent Map and Road Map, may lead you to some interesting discoveries. You will often find roads, towns, cemeteries, and waterways are named after nearby landowners: sometimes those names will be the ones you are researching. See how many of these research gems you can find here in Auglaize County.

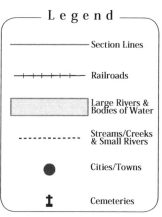

Legend

———— Section Lines

┼┼┼┼┼┼ Railroads

▭ Large Rivers & Bodies of Water

------ Streams/Creeks & Small Rivers

● Cities/Towns

‡ Cemeteries

Scale: Section = 1 mile X 1 mile
(there are some exceptions)

Map Group 15: Index to Land Patents

Township 8-South Range 4-East (1st PM)

After you locate an individual in this Index, take note of the Section and Section Part then proceed to the Land Patent map on the pages immediately following. You should have no difficulty locating the corresponding parcel of land.

The "For More Info" Column will lead you to more information about the underlying Patents. See the Legend at right, and the "How to Use this Book" chapter, for more information.

ID	Individual in Patent	Sec.	Sec. Part	Date Issued	Other Counties	For More Info . . .
2503	COLEMAN, John B	6	E½NE	1835-10-16		A1
2504	DREESE, John H	7	E½	1848-06-01		A1 G32 F
2504	DREESE, John R	7	E½	1848-06-01		A1 G32 F
2502	ROLFES, Henry	7	W½E½	1852-06-01		A1 F
2501	" "	7	E½W½	1853-06-01		A1 F
2505	STEINEMAN, John H	7	W½W½	1853-06-01		A1 F

Patent Map

T8-S R4-E
1st PM Meridian

Map Group 15

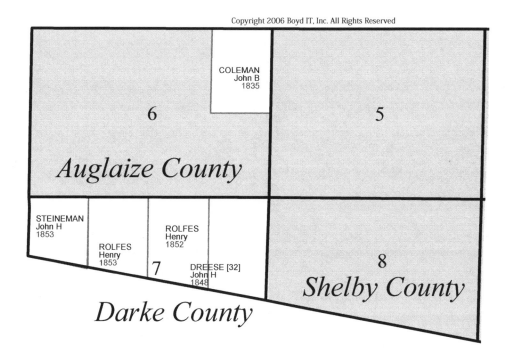

COLEMAN
John B
1835

6

5

Auglaize County

STEINEMAN
John H
1853

ROLFES
Henry
1852

ROLFES
Henry
1853

7

DREESE [32]
John H
1848

8

Shelby County

Darke County

Township Statistics

Parcels Mapped	:	5
Number of Patents	:	5
Number of Individuals	:	5
Patentees Identified	:	4
Number of Surnames	:	4
Multi-Patentee Parcels	:	1
Oldest Patent Date	:	10/16/1835
Most Recent Patent	:	6/1/1853
Block/Lot Parcels	:	0
Parcels Re - Issued	:	0
Parcels that Overlap	:	0
Cities and Towns	:	0
Cemeteries	:	0

Note: the area contained in this map amounts to far less than a full Township. Therefore, its contents are completely on this single page (instead of a "normal" 2-page spread).

L e g e n d

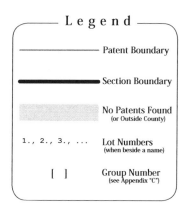

———— Patent Boundary

━━━━ Section Boundary

No Patents Found
(or Outside County)

1., 2., 3., ...   Lot Numbers
(when beside a name)

[ ]   Group Number
(see Appendix "C")

Scale: Section = 1 mile X 1 mile
(generally, with some exceptions)

181

Road Map

T8-S R4-E
1st PM Meridian

M a p   G r o u p   1 5

Note: the area contained in this map amounts to far less than a full Township. Therefore, its contents are completely on this single page (instead of a "normal" 2-page spread).

Cities & Towns
None

Cemeteries
None

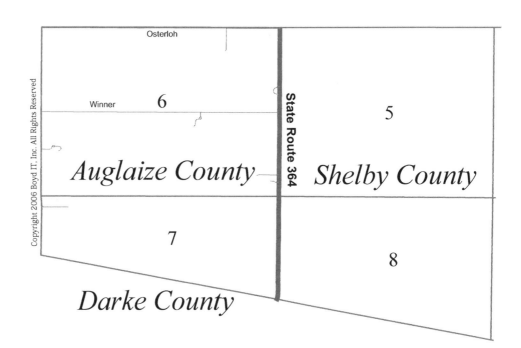

Osterloh

Winner   6

State Route 364

5

Auglaize County   *Shelby County*

7

8

Darke County

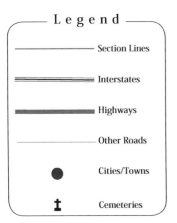

L e g e n d

———————— Section Lines

════════ Interstates

▬▬▬▬▬▬ Highways

·············· Other Roads

● Cities/Towns

† Cemeteries

Scale: Section = 1 mile X 1 mile
(generally, with some exceptions)

Historical Map

T8-S R4-E
1st PM Meridian

Map Group 15

Note: the area contained in this map amounts to far less than a full Township. Therefore, its contents are completely on this single page (instead of a "normal" 2-page spread).

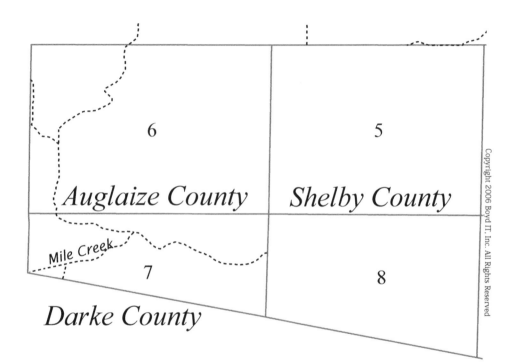

Cities & Towns
None

Cemeteries
None

L e g e n d

―――――― Section Lines

+―+―+―+―+ Railroads

Large Rivers & Bodies of Water

- - - - - - - Streams/Creeks & Small Rivers

● Cities/Towns

⚑ Cemeteries

Scale: Section = 1 mile X 1 mile
(there are some exceptions)

Appendices

Appendix A - Acts of Congress Authorizing the Patents Contained in this Book

The following Acts of Congress are referred to throughout the Indexes in this book. The text of the Federal Statutes referred to below can usually be found on the web. For more information on such laws, check out the publishers's web-site at www.arphax.com, go to the "Research" page, and click on the "Land-Law" link.

Ref. No.	Date and Act of Congress	Number of Parcels of Land
1	April 24, 1820: Sale-Cash Entry (3 Stat. 566)	2501
2	May 20, 1862: Homestead EntryOriginal (12 Stat. 392)	4

Appendix B - Section Parts (Aliquot Parts)

The following represent the various abbreviations we have found thus far in describing the parts of a Public Land Section. Some of these are very obscure and rarely used, but we wanted to list them for just that reason. A full section is 1 square mile or 640 acres.

Section Part	Description	Acres
<none>	Full Acre (if no Section Part is listed, presumed a full Section)	640
<1-??>	A number represents a Lot Number and can be of various sizes	?
E½	East Half-Section	320
E½E½	East Half of East Half-Section	160
E½E½SE	East Half of East Half of Southeast Quarter-Section	40
E½N½	East Half of North Half-Section	160
E½NE	East Half of Northeast Quarter-Section	80
E½NENE	East Half of Northeast Quarter of Northeast Quarter-Section	20
E½NENW	East Half of Northeast Quarter of Northwest Quarter-Section	20
E½NESE	East Half of Northeast Quarter of Southeast Quarter-Section	20
E½NESW	East Half of Northeast Quarter of Southwest Quarter-Section	20
E½NW	East Half of Northwest Quarter-Section	80
E½NWNE	East Half of Northwest Quarter of Northeast Quarter-Section	20
E½NWNW	East Half of Northwest Quarter of Northwest Quarter-Section	20
E½NWSE	East Half of Northwest Quarter of Southeast Quarter-Section	20
E½NWSW	East Half of Northwest Quarter of Southwest Quarter-Section	20
E½S½	East Half of South Half-Section	160
E½SE	East Half of Southeast Quarter-Section	80
E½SENE	East Half of Southeast Quarter of Northeast Quarter-Section	20
E½SENW	East Half of Southeast Quarter of Northwest Quarter-Section	20
E½SESE	East Half of Southeast Quarter of Southeast Quarter-Section	20
E½SESW	East Half of Southeast Quarter of Southwest Quarter-Section	20
E½SW	East Half of Southwest Quarter-Section	80
E½SWNE	East Half of Southwest Quarter of Northeast Quarter-Section	20
E½SWNW	East Half of Southwest Quarter of Northwest Quarter-Section	20
E½SWSE	East Half of Southwest Quarter of Southeast Quarter-Section	20
E½SWSW	East Half of Southwest Quarter of Southwest Quarter-Section	20
E½W½	East Half of West Half-Section	160
N½	North Half-Section	320
N½E½NE	North Half of East Half of Northeast Quarter-Section	40
N½E½NW	North Half of East Half of Northwest Quarter-Section	40
N½E½SE	North Half of East Half of Southeast Quarter-Section	40
N½E½SW	North Half of East Half of Southwest Quarter-Section	40
N½N½	North Half of North Half-Section	160
N½NE	North Half of Northeast Quarter-Section	80
N½NENE	North Half of Northeast Quarter of Northeast Quarter-Section	20
N½NENW	North Half of Northeast Quarter of Northwest Quarter-Section	20
N½NESE	North Half of Northeast Quarter of Southeast Quarter-Section	20
N½NESW	North Half of Northeast Quarter of Southwest Quarter-Section	20
N½NW	North Half of Northwest Quarter-Section	80
N½NWNE	North Half of Northwest Quarter of Northeast Quarter-Section	20
N½NWNW	North Half of Northwest Quarter of Northwest Quarter-Section	20
N½NWSE	North Half of Northwest Quarter of Southeast Quarter-Section	20
N½NWSW	North Half of Northwest Quarter of Southwest Quarter-Section	20
N½S½	North Half of South Half-Section	160
N½SE	North Half of Southeast Quarter-Section	80
N½SENE	North Half of Southeast Quarter of Northeast Quarter-Section	20
N½SENW	North Half of Southeast Quarter of Northwest Quarter-Section	20
N½SESE	North Half of Southeast Quarter of Southeast Quarter-Section	20

Section Part	Description	Acres
N½SESW	North Half of Southeast Quarter of Southwest Quarter-Section	20
N½SESW	North Half of Southeast Quarter of Southwest Quarter-Section	20
N½SW	North Half of Southwest Quarter-Section	80
N½SWNE	North Half of Southwest Quarter of Northeast Quarter-Section	20
N½SWNW	North Half of Southwest Quarter of Northwest Quarter-Section	20
N½SWSE	North Half of Southwest Quarter of Southeast Quarter-Section	20
N½SWSE	North Half of Southwest Quarter of Southeast Quarter-Section	20
N½SWSW	North Half of Southwest Quarter of Southwest Quarter-Section	20
N½W½NW	North Half of West Half of Northwest Quarter-Section	40
N½W½SE	North Half of West Half of Southeast Quarter-Section	40
N½W½SW	North Half of West Half of Southwest Quarter-Section	40
NE	Northeast Quarter-Section	160
NEN½	Northeast Quarter of North Half-Section	80
NENE	Northeast Quarter of Northeast Quarter-Section	40
NENENE	Northeast Quarter of Northeast Quarter of Northeast Quarter	10
NENENW	Northeast Quarter of Northeast Quarter of Northwest Quarter	10
NENESE	Northeast Quarter of Northeast Quarter of Southeast Quarter	10
NENESW	Northeast Quarter of Northeast Quarter of Southwest Quarter	10
NENW	Northeast Quarter of Northwest Quarter-Section	40
NENWNE	Northeast Quarter of Northwest Quarter of Northeast Quarter	10
NENWNW	Northeast Quarter of Northwest Quarter of Northwest Quarter	10
NENWSE	Northeast Quarter of Northwest Quarter of Southeast Quarter	10
NENWSW	Northeast Quarter of Northwest Quarter of Southwest Quarter	10
NESE	Northeast Quarter of Southeast Quarter-Section	40
NESENE	Northeast Quarter of Southeast Quarter of Northeast Quarter	10
NESENW	Northeast Quarter of Southeast Quarter of Northwest Quarter	10
NESESE	Northeast Quarter of Southeast Quarter of Southeast Quarter	10
NESESW	Northeast Quarter of Southeast Quarter of Southwest Quarter	10
NESW	Northeast Quarter of Southwest Quarter-Section	40
NESWNE	Northeast Quarter of Southwest Quarter of Northeast Quarter	10
NESWNW	Northeast Quarter of Southwest Quarter of Northwest Quarter	10
NESWSE	Northeast Quarter of Southwest Quarter of Southeast Quarter	10
NESWSW	Northeast Quarter of Southwest Quarter of Southwest Quarter	10
NW	Northwest Quarter-Section	160
NWE½	Northwest Quarter of Eastern Half-Section	80
NWN½	Northwest Quarter of North Half-Section	80
NWNE	Northwest Quarter of Northeast Quarter-Section	40
NWNENE	Northwest Quarter of Northeast Quarter of Northeast Quarter	10
NWNENW	Northwest Quarter of Northeast Quarter of Northwest Quarter	10
NWNESE	Northwest Quarter of Northeast Quarter of Southeast Quarter	10
NWNESW	Northwest Quarter of Northeast Quarter of Southwest Quarter	10
NWNW	Northwest Quarter of Northwest Quarter-Section	40
NWNWNE	Northwest Quarter of Northwest Quarter of Northeast Quarter	10
NWNWNW	Northwest Quarter of Northwest Quarter of Northwest Quarter	10
NWNWSE	Northwest Quarter of Northwest Quarter of Southeast Quarter	10
NWNWSW	Northwest Quarter of Northwest Quarter of Southwest Quarter	10
NWSE	Northwest Quarter of Southeast Quarter-Section	40
NWSENE	Northwest Quarter of Southeast Quarter of Northeast Quarter	10
NWSENW	Northwest Quarter of Southeast Quarter of Northwest Quarter	10
NWSESE	Northwest Quarter of Southeast Quarter of Southeast Quarter	10
NWSESW	Northwest Quarter of Southeast Quarter of Southwest Quarter	10
NWSW	Northwest Quarter of Southwest Quarter-Section	40
NWSWNE	Northwest Quarter of Southwest Quarter of Northeast Quarter	10
NWSWNW	Northwest Quarter of Southwest Quarter of Northwest Quarter	10
NWSWSE	Northwest Quarter of Southwest Quarter of Southeast Quarter	10
NWSWSW	Northwest Quarter of Southwest Quarter of Southwest Quarter	10
S½	South Half-Section	320
S½E½NE	South Half of East Half of Northeast Quarter-Section	40
S½E½NW	South Half of East Half of Northwest Quarter-Section	40
S½E½SE	South Half of East Half of Southeast Quarter-Section	40

Section Part	Description	Acres
S½E½SW	South Half of East Half of Southwest Quarter-Section	40
S½N½	South Half of North Half-Section	160
S½NE	South Half of Northeast Quarter-Section	80
S½NENE	South Half of Northeast Quarter of Northeast Quarter-Section	20
S½NENW	South Half of Northeast Quarter of Northwest Quarter-Section	20
S½NESE	South Half of Northeast Quarter of Southeast Quarter-Section	20
S½NESW	South Half of Northeast Quarter of Southwest Quarter-Section	20
S½NW	South Half of Northwest Quarter-Section	80
S½NWNE	South Half of Northwest Quarter of Northeast Quarter-Section	20
S½NWNW	South Half of Northwest Quarter of Northwest Quarter-Section	20
S½NWSE	South Half of Northwest Quarter of Southeast Quarter-Section	20
S½NWSW	South Half of Northwest Quarter of Southwest Quarter-Section	20
S½S½	South Half of South Half-Section	160
S½SE	South Half of Southeast Quarter-Section	80
S½SENE	South Half of Southeast Quarter of Northeast Quarter-Section	20
S½SENW	South Half of Southeast Quarter of Northwest Quarter-Section	20
S½SESE	South Half of Southeast Quarter of Southeast Quarter-Section	20
S½SESW	South Half of Southeast Quarter of Southwest Quarter-Section	20
S½SESW	South Half of Southeast Quarter of Southwest Quarter-Section	20
S½SW	South Half of Southwest Quarter-Section	80
S½SWNE	South Half of Southwest Quarter of Northeast Quarter-Section	20
S½SWNW	South Half of Southwest Quarter of Northwest Quarter-Section	20
S½SWSE	South Half of Southwest Quarter of Southeast Quarter-Section	20
S½SWSE	South Half of Southwest Quarter of Southeast Quarter-Section	20
S½SWSW	South Half of Southwest Quarter of Southwest Quarter-Section	20
S½W½NE	South Half of West Half of Northeast Quarter-Section	40
S½W½NW	South Half of West Half of Northwest Quarter-Section	40
S½W½SE	South Half of West Half of Southeast Quarter-Section	40
S½W½SW	South Half of West Half of Southwest Quarter-Section	40
SE	Southeast Quarter Section	160
SEN½	Southeast Quarter of North Half-Section	80
SENE	Southeast Quarter of Northeast Quarter-Section	40
SENENE	Southeast Quarter of Northeast Quarter of Northeast Quarter	10
SENENW	Southeast Quarter of Northeast Quarter of Northwest Quarter	10
SENESE	Southeast Quarter of Northeast Quarter of Southeast Quarter	10
SENESW	Southeast Quarter of Northeast Quarter of Southwest Quarter	10
SENW	Southeast Quarter of Northwest Quarter-Section	40
SENWNE	Southeast Quarter of Northwest Quarter of Northeast Quarter	10
SENWNW	Southeast Quarter of Northwest Quarter of Northwest Quarter	10
SENWSE	Souteast Quarter of Northwest Quarter of Southeast Quarter	10
SENWSW	Southeast Quarter of Northwest Quarter of Southwest Quarter	10
SESE	Southeast Quarter of Southeast Quarter-Section	40
SESENE	SoutheastQuarter of Southeast Quarter of Northeast Quarter	10
SESENW	Southeast Quarter of Southeast Quarter of Northwest Quarter	10
SESESE	Southeast Quarter of Southeast Quarter of Southeast Quarter	10
SESESW	Southeast Quarter of Southeast Quarter of Southwest Quarter	10
SESW	Southeast Quarter of Southwest Quarter-Section	40
SESWNE	Southeast Quarter of Southwest Quarter of Northeast Quarter	10
SESWNW	Southeast Quarter of Southwest Quarter of Northwest Quarter	10
SESWSE	Southeast Quarter of Southwest Quarter of Southeast Quarter	10
SESWSW	Southeast Quarter of Southwest Quarter of Southwest Quarter	10
SW	Southwest Quarter-Section	160
SWNE	Southwest Quarter of Northeast Quarter-Section	40
SWNENE	Southwest Quarter of Northeast Quarter of Northeast Quarter	10
SWNENW	Southwest Quarter of Northeast Quarter of Northwest Quarter	10
SWNESE	Southwest Quarter of Northeast Quarter of Southeast Quarter	10
SWNESW	Southwest Quarter of Northeast Quarter of Southwest Quarter	10
SWNW	Southwest Quarter of Northwest Quarter-Section	40
SWNWNE	Southwest Quarter of Northwest Quarter of Northeast Quarter	10
SWNWNW	Southwest Quarter of Northwest Quarter of Northwest Quarter	10

Section Part	Description	Acres
SWNWSE	Southwest Quarter of Northwest Quarter of Southeast Quarter	10
SWNWSW	Southwest Quarter of Northwest Quarter of Southwest Quarter	10
SWSE	Southwest Quarter of Southeast Quarter-Section	40
SWSENE	Southwest Quarter of Southeast Quarter of Northeast Quarter	10
SWSENW	Southwest Quarter of Southeast Quarter of Northwest Quarter	10
SWSESE	Southwest Quarter of Southeast Quarter of Southeast Quarter	10
SWSESW	Southwest Quarter of Southeast Quarter of Southwest Quarter	10
SWSW	Southwest Quarter of Southwest Quarter-Section	40
SWSWNE	Southwest Quarter of Southwest Quarter of Northeast Quarter	10
SWSWNW	Southwest Quarter of Southwest Quarter of Northwest Quarter	10
SWSWSE	Southwest Quarter of Southwest Quarter of Southeast Quarter	10
SWSWSW	Southwest Quarter of Southwest Quarter of Southwest Quarter	10
W½	West Half-Section	320
W½E½	West Half of East Half-Section	160
W½N½	West Half of North Half-Section (same as NW)	160
W½NE	West Half of Northeast Quarter	80
W½NENE	West Half of Northeast Quarter of Northeast Quarter-Section	20
W½NENW	West Half of Northeast Quarter of Northwest Quarter-Section	20
W½NESE	West Half of Northeast Quarter of Southeast Quarter-Section	20
W½NESW	West Half of Northeast Quarter of Southwest Quarter-Section	20
W½NW	West Half of Northwest Quarter-Section	80
W½NWNE	West Half of Northwest Quarter of Northeast Quarter-Section	20
W½NWNW	West Half of Northwest Quarter of Northwest Quarter-Section	20
W½NWSE	West Half of Northwest Quarter of Southeast Quarter-Section	20
W½NWSW	West Half of Northwest Quarter of Southwest Quarter-Section	20
W½S½	West Half of South Half-Section	160
W½SE	West Half of Southeast Quarter-Section	80
W½SENE	West Half of Southeast Quarter of Northeast Quarter-Section	20
W½SENW	West Half of Southeast Quarter of Northwest Quarter-Section	20
W½SESE	West Half of Southeast Quarter of Southeast Quarter-Section	20
W½SESW	West Half of Southeast Quarter of Southwest Quarter-Section	20
W½SW	West Half of Southwest Quarter-Section	80
W½SWNE	West Half of Southwest Quarter of Northeast Quarter-Section	20
W½SWNW	West Half of Southwest Quarter of Northwest Quarter-Section	20
W½SWSE	West Half of Southwest Quarter of Southeast Quarter-Section	20
W½SWSW	West Half of Southwest Quarter of Southwest Quarter-Section	20
W½W½	West Half of West Half-Section	160

Appendix C - Multi-Patentee Groups

The following index presents groups of people who jointly received patents in Auglaize County, Ohio. The Group Numbers are used in the Patent Maps and their Indexes so that you may then turn to this Appendix in order to identify all the members of the each buying group.

Group Number 1
AFFOLTIR, John; HAGY, Samuel

Group Number 2
ALBR, Henry; HORTAS, Conrad

Group Number 3
AUGHENBAUGH, Peter; BARNETT, Joseph; WILDS, Jonathan K

Group Number 4
AUGHENBOUGH, Peter; BARNETT, Joseph; WILDS, Jonathan K

Group Number 5
AUGKINBAUGH, Peter; BARNETT, Joseph

Group Number 6
AYERS, Grover; KIESEKAMP, Henry

Group Number 7
AYERS, Jeremiah; KIESEKAMP, Henry

Group Number 8
AYRES, Jeremiah; RICHARDSON, William

Group Number 9
AYRES, Jeremiah; TAM, John

Group Number 10
BACH, Adam; KOCH, John; SNYDER, Adam

Group Number 11
BARNETT, Joseph; WILDS, Jonathan K

Group Number 12
BATES, Timothy G; HELFENSTEIN, William L

Group Number 13
BECKEMAN, William; WINTHORT, Francis

Group Number 14
BECKMAN, Henry; KRAMER, John B

Group Number 15
BITLER, Daniel; RICHARDSON, William

Group Number 16
BLACK, William; PETTY, George

Group Number 17
BLAKKA, Bernard; HELMSING, Henry

Group Number 18
BODKIN, Richard; GRAY, John

Group Number 19
BROWNELL, L R; YOUNG, Robert

Group Number 20
BRUNE, Bernard; HOHNE, Detrich

Group Number 21
BUCHANNAN, John; FRAZIER, John

Group Number 22
BURK, George; BURK, William T

Group Number 23
CALLISON, William; MORRIS, John K

Group Number 24
CAREY, John W; DEEMS, John

Group Number 25
CAREY, John W; GORDAN, James

Group Number 26
CAREY, Thomas M; CUMMINGS, Joseph

Group Number 27
CARY, John W; GORDON, James

Group Number 28
COLGAN, Daniel; HALLER, William

Group Number 29
DAVISSON, Amaziah; DAVISSON, Arthur C; DAVISSON, David

Group Number 30
DICK, Peter; RISBARGER, Michael

Group Number 31
DOSTON, Henry; HOLTFOCHT, Henry

Group Number 32
DREESE, John H; DREESE, John R

Group Number 33
DUMBROFF, Eva; HERZING, Phillip

Group Number 34
DUNLAP, Jeptha; ROCK, William

Group Number 35
ELLIOTT, James; VAN HORNE, THOMAS B

Group Number 36
ENNEKING, Henry; ENNEKING, Joseph

Group Number 37
FARIS, Michael; HAMER, Joseph

Group Number 38
FELDMAN, John B; STALLO, Francis J

Group Number 39
FRANKLIN, George F; HOLDRIDGE, Hiram H

Group Number 40
FREAS, John; MILLER, John

Group Number 41
GEHVERS, John H; STALLO, Francis J

Group Number 42
GRIZER, Jacob; HORSIMER, Henry

Group Number 43
HAMMELL, Peter; HOWELL, Samuel

Group Number 44
HARMEL, Lewis; KLIPFEL, Francis; MATHER, Andrew

Group Number 45
HATCHER, John L; NICHOLS, Isaac

Group Number 46
HOUSTON, William A; MURRY, Charles

Group Number 47
KEENER, Adam; KERR, Nicholas; ROLLINS, Mihew

Group Number 48
KEEVER, Adam; NERR, Nicholas

Group Number 49
KIRKBRIDE, Abel; VANFLEET, Phelix W

Group Number 50
KLOAS, Bernard; MOHR, John

Group Number 51
KLOPF, Martin; MONTER, Andreas

Group Number 52
LAUER, Phillip; SPURRIER, Beal

Group Number 53
LINTCH, David; LINTCH, Joseph

Group Number 54
LYONS, Joseph; SWEARINGEN, William

Group Number 55
MACKLIN, Juliann; SAUM, Solomon

Group Number 56
MCMILLIN, Bushrod T; SHULL, Henry

Group Number 57
MILLER, John; WILKINS, James

Group Number 58
OSBORNE, Eliza; OSBORNE, Michael; OSBORNE, Penelope; OSBORNE, William; WILCOX, Phineas B

Group Number 59
POOL, Guy W; WILDS, Jonathan K

Group Number 60
RONEY, Charles; RONEY, Thomas

Group Number 61
SEITER, Gerwasy; SEITER, Michael

Group Number 62
SHELMITTER, Frederick; SHELMITTER, John G

Group Number 63
SHEPPER, Bernd H; SHEPPER, Francis H

Group Number 64
SKINNER, Robert J; THORN, Henry B

Group Number 65
SKINNER, Robert J; VAN HORNE, WILLIAM A

Group Number 66
STROH, Conrad; STROH, John; WELLMAN, Henry

Group Number 67
VAN BLARICOM, HENRY; VAN HORNE, THOMAS B

Group Number 68
WEST, Jonathan; WEST, Thomas J

Group Number 69
WHETSTONE, Adonijah; WHETSTONE, Elizabeth; WHETSTONE, John; WHETSTONE, Mary J

Group Number 70
WILHELM, Catherine; WILHELM, George; WILHELM, Roliburn

Group Number 71
WILKINS, Billitha; WILKINS, Reuben

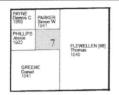

Extra! Extra! (about our Indexes)

We purposefully do not have an all-name index in the back of this volume so that our readers do not miss one of the best uses of this book: finding misspelled names among more specialized indexes.

Without repeating the text of our "How-to" chapter, we have nonetheless tried to assist our more anxious researchers by delivering a short-cut to the two county-wide Surname Indexes, the second of which will lead you to all-name indexes for each Congressional Township mapped in this volume :

For your convenience, the "How To Use this Book" Chart on page 2 is repeated on the reverse of this page.

We should be releasing new titles every week for the foreseeable future. We urge you to write, fax, call, or email us any time for a current list of titles. Of course, our web-page will always have the most current information about current and upcoming books.

Arphax Publishing Co.
2210 Research Park Blvd.
Norman, Oklahoma 73069
(800) 681-5298 toll-free
(405) 366-6181 local
(405) 366-8184 fax
info@arphax.com

www.arphax.com

How to Use This Book - A Graphical Summary

Part I
"The Big Picture"

Map A ▸ *Counties in the State*

Map B ▸ *Surrounding Counties*

Map C ▸ *Congressional Townships (Map Groups) in the County*

Map D ▸ *Cities & Towns in the County*

Map E ▸ *Cemeteries in the County*

Surnames in the County ▸ *Number of Land-Parcels for Each Surname*

Surname/Township Index ▸ Directs you to Township Map Groups in Part II

The Surname/Township Index can direct you to any number of **Township Map Groups**

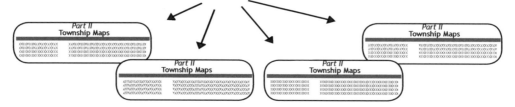

Part II
Township Map Groups
(1 for each Township in the County)

Each Township Map Group contains all four of of the following tools . . .

Land Patent Index ▸ *Every-name Index of Patents Mapped in this Township*

Land Patent Map ▸ *Map of Patents as listed in above Index*

Road Map ▸ *Map of Roads, City-centers, and Cemeteries in the Township*

Historical Map ▸ *Map of Railroads, Lakes, Rivers, Creeks, City-Centers, and Cemeteries*

Appendices

Appendix A ▸ *Congressional Authority enabling Patents within our Maps*

Appendix B ▸ *Section-Parts / Aliquot Parts (a comprehensive list)*

Appendix C ▸ *Multi-patentee Groups (Individuals within Buying Groups)*

Made in the USA
Lexington, KY
18 October 2015